Violence in Contemporary Canadian Society

The John Howard Society
of Canada

Published by
The John Howard Society of Canada 1987
55 Parkdale Avenue, Ottawa, Ontario, Canada K1Y 1E5

ISBN 0-9693196-0-6

Publication Design:
Digital Design Desktop Publishing Services
Nepean, Ontario, Canada K2G 1V3

Printed in Canada

Table of Contents

INTRODUCTION

On June 8, 1986, a four day conference opened in Ottawa entitled "Violence in Contemporary Canadian Society". It was unique, because it marked the first time the topic of violence was discussed from an entirely Canadian perspective, and because of the scope of perspectives it sought to expose.

The conference was the inspiration of the John Howard Society of Canada which is the largest community based voluntary criminal justice agency in the country. The Society has been active for over half a century in prison aftercare programs and in providing services of all kinds throughout the criminal justice field.

It was the view of the John Howard Society that the fear of violence in Canada was generating increased attention to the phenomenon of violence which, in turn, was causing even more fear. This "cycle of fear" ultimately affects the types of policies, programs and legislation which our governments develop. It is the view of the Society that effective social policy should be based upon the best knowledge available and upon rational planning. There are consequences to ill thought out programs (and legislation) which are brought about through popular notions, and contemporary "wisdom". Social policy in general has suffered (with monotonous regularity) from the effects of fads in the guise of solutions to profound social problems. One of the best examples of this is the cyclical call for capital punishment, and while Canada has put that issue to rest most recently on June 30, 1987, there is a general assumption among those in the field that in due course, the issue will surface again. The call for action (even ill conceived action) by a population is a cry for help. And the capital punishment issue was clearly a statement that many Canadians were concerned about violence in a way they never were before. It was this, then, that led the Society to decide to focus attention on the phenomenon of violence.

Violence, however, is much more complex than is at first evident. It operates as much in our minds, through our perception of it, as it does in fact.

In addition, it was quickly realized that the topic was not restricted to criminal justice matters alone. To think of violence, one must by necessity also consider its role in such fields as religion, culture, politics, and even economics. In other words, there are elements of violence which are integral to many of our social institutions. The challenge was to find some way to grasp this interrelatedness so that we might begin to understand.

Violence also affects all of us as individuals. It touches each of us in different ways and can have a devastating impact upon our lives. For this reason, we cannot ignore it. We must "deal" with it in some way. The question is how?

One of the ways the John Howard Society envisioned was to gather together a large group of Canadian practitioners with special experience in the various aspects of violence in Canada to present and to share their findings, to discuss their views, fears and hopes, and to address the question of violence directly. Another was to make this information available to the Canadian public, and to all those groups and individuals who, in one way or another, contribute to the "management" of violence in this country.

Early in 1985, the John Howard Society approached the Law Reform Commission of Canada, the Ministry of the Solicitor General, and the Department of Justice to seek support for the conference. The supportive response was quick and positive - in itself an indication of the timeliness and necessity for an event of this nature.

The mechanics of organizing an event of this magnitude were then put into motion which was no small task. It meant many long hours of contacting, arranging, scheduling, planning, coordinating and hard work to bring together the most notable "experts" on crime and violence in Canada. There were three major types of experts who were approached - academic and theoretical; legislators and policy developers; and direct service workers. It finally all came together with gratifying and stimulating results. Over 200 participants gathered from across North America.

The John Howard Society looked beyond the physical staging of the conference to the responsibility of recording and studying the information presented by the participants and eventually of sharing this valuable body of knowledge. With this purpose in mind the Society established the following objectives for the conference on "Violence in Contemporary Canadian Society":

- compile data from many perspectives on the extent and nature of violence in Canadian society;
- discuss the implications of the data presented;
- suggest plans of action, helping all Canadians to understand the nature of violence and dangerousness;
- suggest plans of action that will help us to cope, as a society, with the phenomenon of violence and dangerous behavior;
- publish the proceedings as a benchmark for future study and action, and as a base for public policy development.

As is clear from the objectives, the conference was only the starting point. The John Howard Society must now make sure that the discussion that took place during those four days in June, 1986 continues.

In November 1986 the Society prepared a "Preliminary Report" on the conference and distributed it to government and to those individuals and organizations who were involved in the conference. That report brought comments and letters of encouragement for us to proceed with full publication.

The material presented herein has been transcribed from audio tape to word processor and from word processor through various edits to layout and to print. As is usually the case, if we were to do it again, there are a number of things we would do differently.

In a few instances, as a result of technical difficulties, we did not have a complete audio recording to transcribe and we were reluctantly forced to drop some of the presentations.

Another particular problem occurred because of the structure of the conference itself. We wished to experience a very broad spectrum of perceptions of violence embracing what the planning committee referred to as "macro" theory through to specific field programs and we did just that. In print, however, the presentations of workshop speakers are by necessity quite short, leaving (perhaps) the impression that these presentations were less important in some way. Nothing could be further from the truth, for it is at the direct service level that we learn so much about implications for treatment and about theory development. The simple fact is that workshop presenters were severely limited in the time given to them. That accounts for the brevity of some papers.

A few of our presenters are from the United States. They were asked to participate in the conference because the planning committee had determined that they had particularly relevant data or perceptions to share. We are pleased that they were willing and able to do so and we are satisfied that their contributions do indeed provide useful insights into our analysis.

The stated purpose of this document is to "publish the proceedings as a benchmark for future study and action, and as a base for public policy development."We hope that this will stimulate continued study of the whole question of violence. We have edited for the purpose of communication. Our desire is to inform ourselves about the nature of violence in the Canadian context. We encourage follow up, and for readers particularly interested in the technicalities of the research methodologies behind some of these papers to contact the presenters directly.

In our opinion the value of this publication comes not so much from the perspective of a unified theoretical analysis of our topic as it does through a look at its parts, much the same as the art of the French Impressionists. It should be a bench mark, a starting point in the quest for anyone wishing to study or to understand this particular issue.

We recognize that programs and legislation designed to address violence or any other social deviancy does not simply "wait" for research. But there is no reason why we must proceed into the future as if nothing has gone on before. We should always have some notion of the relationship of our particular piece of the puzzle to the larger picture.

Where our efforts will take us is not entirely clear, but this much is certain; we must seek knowledge of the nature of violence persistently because to fail to do so, will lead us to increased irrational fear followed by needless suppression of rights (which we now take for granted) and programs which bear no relationship to real problems.

There are many people to whom we owe a debt of gratitude. Some have been recognized elsewhere in another form. Special thanks for this particular phase of the project however, are owed to Donna Goldman who did a difficult first edit under severe time restrictions; to Vera Hyndman who dutifully and cheerfully typed and retyped the manuscripts; and to Marny McCook who solved problems, gave advice and support and generally expedited the project. Many thanks.

James M. MacLatchie,
Executive Director/Editor.

PART I

INVITED SPEAKERS

OPENING ADDRESS

Perrin Beatty
Solicitor General of Canada

The John Howard Society Conference on Violence In Contemporary Canadian Society is important because it is the first time that a national conference has been devoted solely to the theme of violence in our society. About a decade ago, my Ministry participated with the Centre of Criminology of the University of Toronto in holding a small workshop on Violence in Canadian Society. Never before, however, has a conference on violence been held on this scale giving us as Canadians a significant opportunity to bring our knowledge and experience and our attitudes and personal concerns to a discussion of this issue. I am confident that the exchange of ideas that can flourish in this type of forum will help us to find more effective approaches for containing and preventing violence.

The conference is special for another reason. It illustrates what can be achieved when the voluntary and public sectors in criminal justice work closely together as partners.

Planning for this conference has been truly a collaborative effort. The John Howard Society of Canada has been working closely with my Ministry, the Department of Justice, the Law Reform Commission, National Health and Welfare and the University of Ottawa. It has been a collaboration which has certainly borne fruit and has shown that we can indeed work together effectively in criminal justice, encouraging and stimulating each other in meeting the problems of crime and violence directly. The John Howard Society must be commended for conceiving and organizing the conference.

We are fortunate in this country to have a long tradition of active and committed voluntary agencies in criminal justice. The John Howard Societies across Canada are exemplary. Their extensive programs in 10 provinces and 55 communities make them part of the very fabric of our criminal justice system. The fact that such a network of agencies exists, each operating under the direction of a volunteer board of directors closely tied and responsive to their communities, attests to the energy and commitment of Canadians to develop community approaches for dealing with crime and its consequences.

One of my aims as Solicitor General has been to enhance the vital and dynamic partnership between my Ministry and the voluntary and private sectors. I have sought to strengthen this partnership because I believe firmly that it is only through increased grass-roots involvement that we as Canadians can become more fully aware of the nature of crime and develop a long-term vision for dealing effectively with its social and economic costs. Anyone working with offenders knows how scarce the resources available for corrections are. It is difficult to work with violent offenders, and we can justifiably argue that too much is being asked of many of us in addressing the problem of violence in society.

Those working with victims and their families see daily how a violent act can affect other human beings. You witness the trauma, anger and confusion, and you can argue, justifiably, that not enough is being done to prevent violence. You may argue that offenders are dealt with too leniently, and the threat of more severe and certain punishment would deter the potentially violent.

The police have the responsibility to work with all who are involved in violence, to prevent it, to apprehend the offenders and to meet the immediate needs of victims. They encounter the violence in our society "in the raw" often risking their own safety in the process. The police may argue, justifiably, that society and each of us as individuals are not taking violence seriously enough.

Others involved in research and policy development enjoy the luxury of a more detached and analytic perspective. They are aware of the complexity of the issues, of the stereotypes and myths that persist and of the lack of knowledge and considerable disagreement over the causes of violence and approaches for dealing with it. They may argue, justifiably, that despite the demands for concrete action in a given area, it would be unwise to change social policy too drastically because not enough is known. Consequences that are unintended may be too difficult to anticipate. All of these perspectives are valid. In the end it is in the balance of concerns that the most reasonable course of action can be found. I ask that you consider this balance in your deliberations and that you temper your enthusiasm for any particular approach with the knowledge, in these times of limited resources, that any redoubling of efforts in one area will mean that we have less to direct to some other area.

Violence, and approaches for dealing with violent individuals, are gut-level issues to which we all react strongly. We are also prone to hold on to particular points of view with considerable conviction and zeal, sometimes in ways that hinder rational analysis.

Let me outline, therefore, what I see as major pitfalls that we must try to avoid in thinking about violence.

First, there is the predilection for simple solutions. All of us know that violence occurs for different reasons and in different circumstances, and that there is no quick fix. Nevertheless, the inclination towards a simple response to violence creeps up on us.

Second, there is the tendency to fall into dichotomous thinking. Offenders are either villains or victims, deeply disturbed or just self-centred and calculating. We should either punish or treat, only provide opportunities or actively assist. Perhaps, like each of us, offenders are motivated in different ways, and we should respond in kind sometimes by punishing, sometimes by providing vocational opportunities and sometimes by giving more directed assistance and specialized treatment.

Third, there is a perception, which I believe is clearly unfounded, that the criminal justice system cannot properly attend to the needs of both victims and offenders at the same time. There need not be any competition for resources or any conflict in objectives. The difficulty of the problems that offenders present cannot blind us to the real and deep suffering of victims. I believe that services and programs for victims can benefit both victims and offenders.

Finally, I would like to challenge the assumption that attending to the problems of violence in our society increases fear and promotes an unhealthy fortress mentality. If this occurs, we are not attending to the problems of violence appropriately. We cannot afford to hesitate in dealing with violence firmly and resolutely.

Let me emphasize that I do not believe that new directions are needed because violence in our society is so much on the increase or because our approaches to date have been so terribly unsuccessful. I believe that we are a relatively peaceful nation with a history of respect for law and order, proud of our freedom and intolerant of individual abuses of that freedom. It is precisely because we have a peaceful society with relatively little violence that I believe we have the social framework to reduce the level of violence even further.

Comparisons with our neighbors to the South are poignant. Some American cities experience more murders in one week than our major cities experience in an entire year. The number of firearm deaths in this country is a small fraction of those occurring in the United States. The overall rate of violent crime in Canada is about one-fifth that of the United States, and violent offenses constitute only about eight per cent of reported offenses against our Criminal Code.

Yet these encouraging contrasts should not make us complacent. It is also true that even a small amount of violence is too much. We must remain vigilant and consistently intolerant of violence.

I am concerned particularly about the varieties of hidden violence in our society which are increasingly coming to our attention and am acutely concerned about the security of those groups most vulnerable to the consequences of violent crime. These are women, the elderly, our young children, Native Canadians and other minority groups.

We know from the findings of our Canadian Urban Victimization Survey that more than half of all incidents of criminal victimization never reach the attention of the police. Even more striking, we know that nearly two-thirds of those incidents involving violence or the threat of violence are never reported. More than one-half of assault incidents involving weapons go unreported, and only about one-third of those incidents in which victims must stay in hospital overnight are reported to police. Sexual assault and domestic violence continue to be particularly well-hidden, and most women continue on their own to cope with the trauma of these victimizations.

Many of us are aware of recent findings suggesting that Canadians considerably overestimate the incidence of violent crime. Most Canadians believe crime is increasing in their cities even though only about one-third believe crime is increasing in their own neighborhood. There is a lingering and confining fear of violent crime, an insidious fear of danger lurking around that next corner. This concerns me deeply. The fear is concentrated most intensely among elderly people and women, but it has also gripped other segments of our society. It is expressed to a greater degree, for example, by the poor, the less well-educated and those living in high-density housing.

The human side of our criminal justice system demands that we be responsive to, and rely upon, the communities and neighborhoods we serve. I believe this is the key to reducing the level of fear in our society and the key to bringing the hidden violence out into the open so that we can better understand it, control it and manage its consequences.

Over the past several years, we have worked effectively in raising national awareness regarding the potential benefits of community approaches. National Crime Prevention Week and the Solicitor General's Awards Program have captured the attention of the media and the public. Requests for information and assistance have increased dramatically, and a network of active citizens and groups developing innovative programs in communities across the country has grown out of our efforts to work closely with provincial and territorial governments, local municipalities and community groups and the voluntary and private sectors.

I have been heartened by this response, and I am convinced that by pulling together the creativity and energy of concerned Canadians, we can have a significant impact in preventing crime even with a minimal infusion of resources. We have devoted a small fraction of federal government criminal justice expenditures to crime prevention efforts, but the payoffs to date have been concrete and far reaching.

Our work is not done. The challenge for the future as I see it is to increase grass-roots community involvement and leadership in tackling the basic causes of crime. Programs to reduce the opportunities for crime must be combined with programs to eliminate the reasons for crime. Improvements in the way criminal justice agencies react to crime must be combined with development of community infrastructures to prevent crime.

We know that there are social problems that can generate crime, youth unemployment, neighborhood degeneration and family instability. We also know from past experience that significant and durable impact in dealing with these problems will be elusive unless our neighborhoods and communities see themselves as the initiators and not just the recipients of assistance. Community crime prevention must be seen principally as community self-help. Our challenge is to encourage all communities and all neighborhoods to adopt this perspective.

To continue to be effective we will need new ideas and fresh approaches. Our research and development activities should be augmented, particularly those that relate to the most difficult and persistent problems. Examples of these are the victimization of women both in and outside the home and the victimization of native peoples for which we currently have few effective approaches.

Here I believe more emphasis should be placed on that particular brand of research combining the vast traditions of the academic and public service orientations, action research aimed towards developing not just a single program or service but an integrated process of changes in community and agency responses to a problem. We supported this kind of work in London, Ontario, for example, and the resulting model of coordinated police and agency responses to domestic violence is now being adopted in communities across the country. We are currently involved in a similar action-oriented project with police and social agencies in Metropolitan Toronto examining responses to sexual assault. More work of this type is needed to develop coordinated strategies for dealing with particular problems of violence.

A strong federal-provincial partnership is needed to ensure that those groups who are most vulnerable receive special assistance. The elderly, for example, are a growing segment of our Canadian population who are most fearful of crime and most likely to suffer severe loss or injury when victimized. They are also least likely to be aware of, or participate in, community crime prevention programs. This social withdrawal may compound their isolation and fear of crime. New approaches are required to elicit the involvement of elderly Canadians in developing programs that respond to their specific concerns.

In collaboration with the Justice Institute of British Columbia, we have sponsored a series of very successful public workshops for seniors focusing on ways they can protect and defend themselves in their homes, on the street and in the marketplace. More concerted efforts should be made along these lines to reach our elderly citizens.

We are becoming increasingly sensitive to the problem of child abduction and the sexual and other violent abuse of children. Broader and better coordinated prevention programs are crucially needed to mobilize community involvement and to focus the efforts of organizations in the social service, health and education fields in heading off this growing problem.

I have already announced a series of initiatives in response to the problem of abductions and runaways. My Ministry held a national conference on missing children in April, and we are now working towards developing many of the programs and research proposals that were suggested. We will soon have a functioning central registry on missing children that can be used by police forces across the country to improve our efforts to locate these children.

We know that the largest group of children who are missing are runaways who are caught in a dismal cycle of violence, abused and exploited on the street frequently after being neglected and abused at home. We need to know more about the kinds of family situations that may precipitate such dreadful events and gain the knowledge to intervene effectively at an early point in the cycle.

I believe that finding ways to intervene early in the cycle of violence is a key to preventing violence. Early intervention is something I would like to emphasize in the area of domestic violence, Natives and young children. As we begin to gain greater understanding of how violence escalates and the factors that can mitigate or exacerbate it, we may be able to make significant headway with early intervention efforts.

The possibility of developing effective programs for early intervention with high risk pre-delinquents is especially exciting. We know that there are precursors of serious delinquency and high rate adult offending that can be reliably identified as early as age seven or eight. Young children of lower socio-economic backgrounds with anti-social or criminal family members who have experienced parental separations, who are exposed to cold, rejecting and inconsistent discipline and who begin to display behavioral problems and poor achievement in school are particularly at risk to become serious delinquents and chronic adult offenders. Although relatively few in number, these individuals as adults seem to be very persistent in their criminal behavior accounting for a disproportionately large amount of violent offenses, particularly the most serious assaults and homicides.

We must find ways to work together in promoting prevention programs for youth and children who are having serious problems at home and at school. The Waterloo-Wellington Attendance Centre in Kitchener, Ontario is a fine example. The John Howard Society established the centre with funding assistance from my Ministry to target youth at risk of coming into conflict with the law. The program involves an intensive eight to 10 weeks of counselling from professional and volunteer staff. In its first two years of operation, only one child in 84 was subsequently charged with a criminal offence. This kind of documented success is impressive and encouraging.

But there are many good things happening in our correctional systems including dedicated staff working under demanding conditions attempting to effect some positive change with our most violent and recalcitrant offenders. We all benefit from these efforts, and it is sad that the few tragic incidents overshadow the level of accomplishment of our correctional system.

Canadians seem to believe that most offenders released on parole or under MS from our penitentiaries offend again within a short time. In reality, two-thirds of these individuals complete their period of community supervision successfully. Moreover, of those who fail either during or after their period of community supervision, only one in six is returned for offences more serious than those for which they were originally incarcerated.

Canadians also believe that ex-offenders account for a large proportion of the violent crime in our society. In reality, in a given year, offenders on parole or MS are responsible for fewer than one-half of one per cent of the violent offences reported to police.

I would suggest that our correctional system is not a wasteland in need of massive reform. It is working well although we perhaps do less than we could to promote and support it.

I believe we must be reasonable in the demands we make of our correctional system. For it to continue to function effectively, we must be cautious that it is not taxed beyond its capabilities.

Violence knows no boundaries or jurisdictions. We are becoming increasingly aware that as nations on our own, we are limited in our ability to contain violence. It is in this context of the need for international cooperation that Canada played a leading role in the Seventh United Nations Congress on the prevention of Crime and the Treatment of Offenders. We assisted in drafting Guiding Principles and a Plan of Action for crime prevention both of which were adopted by the General Assembly of the United Nations. These documents call on each member state to undertake research on the social and economic causes and correlates of crime, to attack the root problems underlying crime, to increase awareness of crime prevention in social and economic planning and to share information internationally.

I see these as fundamental goals for my Ministry, and I am confident that we can move resolutely towards developing an effective and long-term crime prevention strategy for our country.

In our eagerness to take on new initiatives, we should not ignore or neglect our correctional system. It is an essential component of our efforts to contain and prevent violent crime.

Corrections and correctional staff are unfortunately much maligned. An offender who commits a heinous crime while on parole or mandatory supervision is taken as evidence of the inadequacies of the entire system. There is rarely good news coming from corrections, or at least good news which is regarded as newsworthy.

Crowding in our institutions has lead to increased unrest and violence and a scattering of efforts to provide services for offenders. For the first time in the history of our correctional system, we are faced with the situation where new prison construction will not keep pace with our growing prison population.

I have asked my officials to respond swiftly to this situation, to assess realistic options for managing some of our lower-risk offenders and to encourage the development of a broader spectrum of community-based alternatives.

The aims of denunciation and incapacitation need not be achieved solely through confinement in a prison cell. In some cases where offenders are likely to pose a minimal risk for physical violence, these aims may be achieved through appropriately tough alternatives with provisions for intensive supervision and surveillance and with requirements for substantial restitution to victims and to the community. Mentally disordered offenders are also increasingly being confined in our penitentiaries, and I believe that more humane, secure alternatives can be found for these individuals.

The Correctional Service of Canada has recently undertaken a major review of its case management procedures and a thorough examination of programs and support services offered to offenders. The aim is to seek better ways to identify the lowest-risk offenders and develop a process for managing offenders that will help concentrate resources on those individuals who are at highest risk and have the greatest needs.

We have made significant progress in our exchange of service agreements with the provinces thereby alleviating the pressures of overcrowding in some regions of the country. I propose to proceed even further in this area, particularly in terms of joint funding of specialized community programs and services for offenders.

I am sure you all would agree that the genesis of violent behavior, and of criminal behavior more generally, is exceedingly complex. In the face of this complexity, calls for a simple retributive response in the form of increased use of incarceration are shortsighted. In the end, overuse of incarceration may offer less protection to society as limited resources may be left to do anything other than contain individuals for a period of time.

Crime should not pay, and those who commit crimes should be punished. Justice demands it. Justice for victims demands it. Protection of society demands it. Punishment of offenders restores the rightful balance because it is the criminal who profits by crime and the law-abiding who suffer.

At the same time, the effectiveness of the criminal justice system demands that we retain some flexibility in how we punish. I believe that safety and security in our society can be most effectively achieved not by using incarceration indiscriminately for all offenders, but by meeting out appropriate punishment in different ways for different individuals.

INVITED SPEAKER

Edward L. Greenspan, Q.C.
Greenspan, Rosenberg Law Firm
Toronto, Ontario

When I looked at the brochure that sets out the purpose and the reasons for the conference, I was initially heartened by what I read. The conference was held because it is the view of the John Howard Society that the fear of violence in Canada is generating increased attention to the phenomenon of violence. This in turn is causing yet more fear. This cycle of fear as recognized by the John Howard Society has an effect upon the type of programs which develop and has had an effect upon legislation of recent years.

The conference asks a critical question in a critically questioning way, whether or not the fear of violence is something that is much greater and much worse than violence itself. I have no doubt the answer is an unequivocal yes. And yet, as I read the program, I was dismayed that the focus is on the causes of violence and prevention of violence. As a result, I asked myself whether or not the conference itself, because of the title of "Violence in Contemporary Canadian Society" and the emphasis of the program on the causes of violence and the prevention of violence, may in itself have a negative effect. In fact, I wonder whether the publicized fact of this conference may not by itself continue to cause Canadians to be concerned about the fear of violence. We should never forget the reasons for this conference and constantly remind ourselves that the fear of violence is indeed much greater than actual violence itself.

There is no doubt that crime is a major political issue and, judging by the uproar in the media, the middle class of this country at least is convinced that there is more and worse crime in the cities than ever before. If we move out into the cooler world of criminologists and historians, we discover a curious fact. Social scientists and historians are not at all sure that the rate of violent crime is increasing. Essays such as "The Myth of Crime Waves" teach us that over a period of maybe the last 100 years there is no evidence that the rate of crime is rising. The evidence goes the other way. Few people seem to recognize how inaccurate crime statistics are. If it is hard to prove a rising crime rate, why the great political turmoil over crime? Is it mere demagogy? The demagogue rarely invents his issue; he exploits one that is already there. There is no doubt that the kind of crime makes a difference. The young tough who rapes and murders an old woman in her living room evokes, and rightly so, far more outrage and fear than if one tough kills another in a bar brawl.

Some people think that the nature of violent crime has changed since 1870. They think that crime, apart from its prevalence, is simply more violent today. They feel that there is more senseless, oppressive violence, violence that cannot be anticipated and explained. It is no longer, if it ever was, a question of opting into a violent world (like a gunfighter or a mercenary) or out of it. People are particularly afraid of desperate crime, half-rational amateur crime, made more dangerous because the criminals are themselves cornered, clumsy and afraid. This is addict crime above all.

Even if the face of crime has changed, it may not entirely explain the public concern. In any event, what is really at issue is not the rate of crime but the rate of social tolerance of crime. This varies over time and space and by no means necessarily parallels the true rate of crime. The tolerance rate can rise or fall on its own, faster or slower than the crime rate. If it falls much faster, then we have something rather like a "revolution of rising expectations." Objectively, things are getting better, but people are less satisfied. That may be where we are today. Possibly in the area of violence, the tolerance for crime is dropping. But, the crime rate, if it drops at all, does not drop as fast. People demand more law and order, more crime control than the authorities are able or willing to give.

Tolerance levels are sensitive to social and economic change. In each period, each society has its own idea of crime, its own level of tolerance. The criminal justice system will act to enforce the status quo. But there is another, more subtle demand for protection, less economic than cultural, a demand that moral domination remain where it lies. The middle and upper classes have a moral code as well as economic power to uphold. People appear to feel great satisfaction when their values are the official values, when the country flies their flag, sings their tune, enforces their rules. Quite reasonable men can make demands that seem totally unreasonable out of an instinct to preserve their moral power. The middle class sees what it thinks while others see too much permissiveness. Liberals worry about poverty and the roots of crime. A few lawyers, judges and reformers try to bring more justice into criminal justice. Civil liberty groups always seem to take the prisoner's side.

Above all, there is a revolt of the underdogs, the poor, the sexual minorities. It is a struggle against stigmatization, a demand for equal justice under law, and these great earth movements may portend to the middle class that their monopoly is breaking down. This may make them as insecure in their neat suburban homes as the elderly poor in their urban rabbit warrens. Insecurity lowers their level of tolerance for crime while it exacerbates the demand for law and order.

Our political leaders do nothing to allay their fears. They do nothing other than accommodate people's perceived interests. After all, it is so much easier that way.

Consider the question of family violence. In the last few years, public outrage at physical and sexual abuse within the family unit has become considerable. It is a very hot topic, and the newest trendies on the scene, the abuse of the elderly proponents, are starting to make their mark. The media decries one after another sordid example of child abuse or spouse abuse. It is as if they have just discovered the topic.

The Minister of Justice announced to applause at the 49th Annual Conference of the Federal Canadian Municipalities that he proposes to introduce new legislation relating to child abuse. Yet no one has ever presented satisfactory empirical evidence that wife beating and child abuse are increasing. In fact, research studies conclude exactly the opposite. National surveys on this matter in the United States by Murray Strauss of the Family Research Laboratory at the University of New Hampshire, in an article entitled "Societal Change and Change in Family Violence from 1975 to 1985," compared the rate of physical abuse of children and spouses from a 1975 study with the rate from a 1985 replication. The major study concludes that the child abuse rate is way down, and the wife abuse rate is also way, way down.

What is clear is that the so-called statistics that are gathered by various interest groups are escalating. One of the reasons is that, without us realizing it, certain persons in our community are attempting to create new standards which are, in fact, evolving with respect to how much violence parents can use in child rearing. The definition of child abuse, for example, is being gradually enlarged to include acts which were never previously thought of as child abuse, and this by itself can create a misleading impression of an epidemic of child abuse. Spanking or slapping a child or even hitting a child with a stick or belt has not been thought of as abuse in past years according to either the legal or informal norms of Canadian society. Is it child abuse to throw something, push, grab, shove, slap, spank, kick, bite, hit with a fist? What is child abuse? Without understanding what its definition is, how can anyone possibly know whether it is on the increase or whether it is remaining constant?

It has been pointed out that most child abuse and wife abuse is associated with unemployment and economic stress, and if the economic climate improves within the country, then it will reduce child abuse and wife abuse. As well, new treatment programs and innovative attempts to prevent child abuse and wife abuse have proliferated during the last 20 years. This obviously has an impact too. The Minister of Justice could be well-advised to read this paper.

Let me deal with a different aspect of the issue of family violence. The solution everyone focuses on to deal with this "new" problem is the use of drastically increased sentences imposed through that faithful old stalwart, the criminal justice system. Yet anyone considering using the bluntest instrument of all, the criminal justice system, has to examine two questions. First, what is the purpose of the criminal law? Second, what is the impact of resorting to that system?

In my view the criminal law must be looked at as a complete system. It does not operate merely as a convenient device for protecting the law-abiding and punishing the guilty. It is a system put in place to detect crime, apprehend offenders, fairly try the alleged accused and impose appropriate sanctions upon persons found guilty. Once the criminal law is in motion, it has a momentum of its own. Even persons found to be innocent do not emerge unscathed from the system. In even the most trivial of cases, the system exacts a huge penalty on those caught up in it.

While the system also hopefully protects the law-abiding, the primary mechanism, deterrence, is cumbersome and unreliable. While putting a person in jail no doubt deters that person from further observable crime for the period he is incarcerated, it is a grand act of self-delusion to believe that such a person inevitably or even possibly comes out of jail a better, more law-abiding person. It is an even greater flight of fancy to believe that his conviction and imprisonment will deter other like-minded individuals from engaging in similar conduct. I say this bearing in mind the problems of family violence. It must be self-evident that in the dynamics of the family, particularly a family in trouble and under stress, the concept of modifying behavior through deterrence is somewhat illusory. Deterrence is a thin reed upon which to treat the protection of family members. This is not to say that charges involving violence among family members should never be laid, or if laid, not prosecuted. Violence is violence. Assault, the intentional infliction of harm on another without consent, is a crime. If revealed, it should be prosecuted like any other criminal offence, no better, but also no worse.

The authors of the recent government-sponsored Badgley Report observed that no clear-cut procedures have been established to determine when either provincial welfare legislation or the criminal justice system or both should be used to protect children. As a result, "instances occur that constitute grave negligence either because there is insufficient assessment of the child's needs or because there is inadequate follow-up to assure that the child is fully protected from the risk of further sexual abuse." It may be that in the whole area of family violence, a similar statement could be made. Children, spouses, even whole families in need of protection fall through the cracks in the system. The answer does not lie in increased reliance on the criminal justice system.

The safeguards which are an inherent and necessary part of the system unfortunately make the criminal law an inefficient means of coping with problems of the individual victim or family. This is particularly the case with domestic violence. Unlike property or similar offenses where the parties are strangers, the crimes take place in public and there are clear victims and criminals, studies have consistently shown that abuse of family members is "concealed in the recesses of the family unit which is normally inaccessible to outside intervention." (Bailey and McCable, "Reforming the Law of Incest", 1979 Crim. C.R. 749 at 755) The unfortunate reality is that a reliance on the criminal law to protect family members means that help comes too late; the damage is done to the accused, to the victim, to the family. Imprisoning the rapist father, the criminally negligent mother, the brutal husband perhaps temporarily relieves the problem, but I have grave doubts that it can prevent the damage or permanently solve the problem.

What then of the aspect of the role of the criminal justice system, its impact? While the purpose of the criminal law cuts across all types of crime, criminals and victims, the impact of the criminal law is not so egalitarian. First of all, it impacts heavily on the poor, the mentally ill, the intellectually impaired and generally on those members of society least able to defend themselves. But it saves its special impact for the family. It is the rare family that emerges unscarred and intact after the conviction of one of its members. More often, the family members are confused, embittered, disillusioned. Once the criminal justice system is engaged, there is a real likelihood that the family will be destroyed. Until the amendments to the Divorce Act last year, it was a specific ground for divorce in the Divorce Act that one of the spouses has been imprisoned for two years.

My message then is a simple one. The criminal justice system must be viewed as a means of last resort, to deal only with that conduct for which other means of social control are inadequate or inappropriate and then only to the minimum extent necessary. Put another way, I do not see the laying of criminal charges as another item in the social workers' bag of tricks to be brought out and tried and discarded if something else comes along, or, as is more likely, it proves misguided or unsuccessful. Again, I do not suggest criminal charges should never be laid, that the full weight of the criminal justice system never be brought to bear, but it should be done in full recognition of the terrible costs and doubtful benefits.

Departing from the general principles about which I have been discussing, I will deal with the sentencing aspect of family violence cases. I have noted what I consider to be an increasingly disturbing escalation in sentences imposed in domestic violence cases. I have no quarrel with the imposition of an appropriate sentence, a sentence tailored to the crime and the offender. What is happening with increasing frequency is that the courts are turning away from this basic principle of fairness and imposing sentence on purely retributive grounds. Let me say at once that this is not done in the Old Testament rhetoric of "an eye for an eye" and a "tooth for a tooth." This is the 20th century. However, in response to some perceived unease in the body politic, retribution has nevertheless reared its ugly head dressed now in the civilized language of "societal denunciation." The courts now impose heavy and vengeful sentences to reflect "society's revulsion" at the particular crime. While such language is not restricted to crimes of domestic violence, it most often crops up in such cases.

In my view, this is not a fit role for the criminal law. People commit some terrible crimes, but even the worst child abuser has the right to an impartial hearing and the right to be sentenced by a judge untainted by the strong sentiments which the crime may evoke. This may not be a popular view, but I have no doubt that it is the right view. Moreover, this current, popular trend towards retribution is all the more surprising since the courts, relying on the best medical evidence available, can show refreshing sensitivity in certain cases as to the devastating consequences of imprisonment. The courts are capable of recognizing illness where others see only criminal conduct and of recognizing the value of treatment rather than imprisonment. Surely, where the expert evidence is available, it is correct and proper that expertise be brought to bear to alleviate as far as possible the destructive effects of the criminal justice system and, particularly in the case of domestic violence, repair some of the damage to the victim, the family and the offender.

It has been said that many of the problems of our modern society, increased lawlessness, disrespect for authority, drug abuse, sexual immorality and so on stem from the breakdown of the traditional family unit, not just the abandonment of the extended family but the disintegration of the nuclear family. It has almost become a cliche. Church leaders, journalists and politicians say it is so. I am not a psychiatrist or a psychologist or even a criminologist, but I have seen enough accused persons and read enough pre-sentence reports and psychiatric reports to testify as to the accuracy of such statements. It therefore seems self-defeating and indeed the height of foolishness to adopt techniques and to emphasize measures which, whether by design or result, are inevitably destructive of the family unit. Of course there are certain families which are not worth saving, where the parent-child or spousal relationship is merely a cover for the gravest abuse and indignity. Let us save the criminal law for those cases. We should be very careful not to employ means to further weaken and undermine the family's authority, privacy and uniqueness because the family, this unique, cellular basic entity, alone can make a healthy society. By encouraging people to take their family problems to the police, society makes a mistake. It is right for the police to be called in as a last resort. If the criminal justice system has a role in areas of domestic violence, it is as the tool of last resort when there is nothing to save, nothing to be worked out and imprisonment and destruction of the family are the proper and just result.

It is important that at this conference you look at the compiled data from many perspectives as to the extent and nature of violence in Canadian society and discuss the implications of the data received over the next three days. The question as to the causes of crime, in particular the causes of violent crime, has no easy answer.

When it comes to the causes of crime, there is no dearth of answers. The laws are too lenient. Penalties are not severe enough. The breakdown of the family, neighborhood and community as socializing units occurs. There is lack of parental guidance, poverty, joblessness, permissiveness in the home, school and society, racial, ethnic or class tensions, unequal opportunities, drugs and drug addiction, disrespect for authority and the law, irresponsibility, the breakdown of religion, alienation, glamorization of crime and violence in films, television and the press, overpopulation, moral decay, the welfare state, abnormal chromosomes, pornography, alcohol and alcoholism, hereditary genetic defects. This list is by no means complete.

Even though most of these explanations confuse cause, symptoms and pathology, they probably all contribute, to some extent, to crime. So the explanations a given spokesman pinpoints as the real causes of crime are more likely to reflect his policies, values and morals, not to mention his vested interests, than they are to express true understanding.

There are labelling theorists who look at the causes of crime in a non-political way. There are critical criminologists who look at the causes of crime in a political way. There are those who say part of what causes crime is criminal law itself. There are those like Durkheim who suggested that society needs crime. For what it is worth, and given what I do for a living, I could not agree more with Professor Durkheim. I know I need it.

Yes, the experts simply cannot agree because the fact is that we do not know what causes crime, particularly violent crime. All we have been able to do is to describe the conditions under which some people commit some kind of crime some time and some motives. We do not understand why that happens. We do not know why everyone exposed to the same deleterious influences does not become a violent criminal.

You will see in the upcoming issue of the American Journal of Psychiatry a recent study that was completed of 13 men and two women convicted of murder and awaiting execution in American prisons.

If this study of the 15 death row occupants examined is a representative study, the only conclusion that can be reached is that many condemned individuals probably suffer a multiplicity of hitherto unrecognized psychiatric and neurological disorders including seizures, blackouts and partial brain atrophy.

No sooner was this study revealed then Dr. Jerome Engel of the University of California in Los Angeles, a specialist in seeking the roots of violence, immediately noted the difficulty in assessing the relative roles of environmental factors and physical damage to the brain. He pointed out that individuals such as those examined in the study often grow up in a world in which they both witness violence and are subjected to it.

On the one hand, animal studies have shown that damage to certain areas of the brain can lead to violent behavior, but on the other hand it can easily be argued that humans are much more complex than a cat or a rat.

A subsequent study of 30 murderers including eight from the study I just mentioned found that the histories of 19 of the offenders displayed a special combination of factors that may have predisposed the individuals to unprovoked violence. Such impulsive violence seemed out of character with the normal behavior of the individual, severe repeated head injuries leading to neurological abnormalities, epileptic symptoms but without some of the usual signs of the disease, a history of brief episodic psychotic symptoms such as hallucinations, bizarre behavior and intense alteration of mood, a history of having been the victim of extraordinary physical or sexual abuse or of having witnessed extreme family violence.

Dr. Dorothy Lewis, Professor of Psychiatry at the New York University Medical School, who reported these studies, has concluded that while a history of having been the victim of extraordinary physical or sexual abuse or having witnessed extreme family violence appears to be associated with violence later in life, the researchers in that study believe that such a disposition is much stronger if the other four factors are also at work. Dr. Lewis went on to point out that many other studies have associated childhood abuse with later violence, but in only 20% of such cases. As a result, she concludes that abuse alone is not a satisfactory explanation.

Many believe that until we understand much more about how brain activity is reflected in behavior, we can never fully understand what causes individual violence. Anyone who stresses solely the role of the brain, the organ of behavior, truly denies the importance of social influences on people.

Likewise, anyone who looks solely to the importance of social influences on behavior truly denies the role of the brain in behavior.

The theories about violence which focus on human nature and its interactions with environment as well as our social attitudes towards criminal law and personal responsibility all seem to take for granted that every individual has a normally functioning, entirely healthy brain.

There are environmental conditions that can effect the resulting anatomical maldevelopment in the brain because, of course, when it occurs, it is irreversible even though environmental conditions may later be corrected and improved. For example, there was a study that showed that infant monkeys reared in an abnormal social environment, deprived of their mothers and any other living monkey substitute, grew to be incurably deviant. A hot water bottle, the sound of a ticking clock or ample nourishment provided mechanically simply did not offer enough significant environmental stimuli later to allow certain parts of their emotional brain to mature in a normal fashion.

Many studies indicate that when environmental conditions alter brain structure, the changes may affect behavior because they affect how the brain perceives, fails to perceive or misperceives incoming stimuli. For instance, a person whose violence is related to the presence of brain disease generally does not attack others without what he considers to be provocation. What happens is that the brain misperceives some incoming stimulus, a harmless gesture or a joking remark, as extremely threatening or enraging when it is in fact not so. If another driver cuts such a person's car off at a stop light, his brain interprets it as a deadly insult, and he reacts accordingly. Since his brain may also misinterpret information from his internal environment (that is, his own body, as in the case of depressed blood sugar level) or miscontrol the physical reactions such as the adrenalin level that accompanies emotion, he will also have great difficulty in governing his rage once it is aroused.

Others, and in particular, psychiatrist Rollo May, see a connection between crime and powerlessness. He says that "deeds of violence in our society are performed largely by those trying to establish their self-esteem, to defend their self image and to demonstrate that, they too, are significant."

When self-affirmation and self-assertion are denied an individual, his resulting impotence is often expressed as violence. If Dr. May's insights are correct, measures we take to control violent behavior will serve invariably to reinforce an offender's sense of impotence, worthlessness and powerlessness. In short, they should produce a result precisely opposite to that which we intend.

I have thought about the question of crime and the causes of crime throughout much of my life, and I am still satisfied that until we better understand human behavior we cannot hope to understand criminal behavior. In the meantime, the only useful generalization is that there are probably as many causes of crime as there are criminals.

As important as this conference is, do not think for one minute that anyone possesses the answers to all the questions and the solution to all the problems.

INVITED SPEAKER

Ken Keyes
Minister of Correctional Services and Solicitor General
Province of Ontario

I am no stranger to the role of the volunteer sector in corrections. As Minister of Correctional Services for Ontario, a post I have held for just under a year, I am well aware of the impact made by some 5,000 volunteers within my Ministry who work in our system. They have participated in counselling programs, visitations, have acted as volunteer probation officers, have helped the offenders' families and have provided countless other services in a spirit of generosity and caring.

I am a former mayor of the city of Kingston, Ontario, that heartland of the Thousand Islands. We have the record of having more federal penitentiaries in Kingston than any other city in Canada or in North America. We have no fewer than eight federal penitentiaries.

I have had an opportunity over a 37-year career as a school teacher/ principal to work with a great many groups and individuals providing volunteer services in the correctional community. As a private individual, I have personally worked as a volunteer on many occasions at the prison for women. I have also worked at the Collins Bay Penitentiary, in the Joyceville institution and at the Kingston Penitentiary, the oldest one in Canada.

Prison is not a pleasant place to be. Incarceration in itself is largely ineffective as a deterrent against crime. It is inappropriate as an environment to foster attitudinal and behavioral changes among those who offend against society's laws. We are skeptical about the likelihood of imparting a sense of responsibility among inmates by removing all opportunities for decision-making as is the case in any correctional institution. We are concerned with society's expectations that we rehabilitate all those who come into our care although they are with us often for periods as brief as a few days.

Thanks in large measure to the efforts of the volunteer sector, the focus of corrections has shifted throughout the past decade and a half from institutionalization to alternatives within the community. Today in Ontario, well over 85% of our offenders are serving their sentences in the community either on probation in lieu of a term of imprisonment, on parole after having served part of their sentence in custody or on temporary absence from a correctional institution in order to work or attend school.

The implementation of the Young Offenders Act in 1984 and 1985, with its emphasis on minimal intervention for youthful offenders, gave additional impetus to our search for meaningful, effective community corrections and programming. Jurisdictions across the country have been diligently working to put the necessary services and facilities in place to accommodate this particular group.

Other trends in modern correctional policy include explorations into the potential of house arrests. The potential of the measure of house arrests, attendant centres and intensive supervision gives a clear indication that alternatives to jail are on the rise. For those of us interested in the human aspects of corrections as well as the social economic aspects, this is encouraging news.

There is another trend in corrections today that we in Ontario are experiencing. It is perceived to be a negative trend and a reaction to the zeal with which the public sector has been pursuing community alternatives. In the town halls, community centres and homes across the province, citizens are banding together to share their apprehension and their fears about facing up to community responsibility for crime and justice and their role in treating the offender.

I spoke in Sudbury to a very agitated group of 300 people opposing the potential establishment of a psychiatric treatment facility for offenders of our northern part of this province. Again, it was that fear of the unknown, the fear of what happens if someone should happen to get out.

Such fears are always evident in the daily newspapers with such headlines as Youth Detention Centre Plan Troubles the Neighbors, Petition Opposes Offenders Home, Board Moves to Block Halfway House, Town Digging in Heels Against Young Offenders Home.

In a city just 50 miles from Ottawa, the municipal council has totally changed its zoning bylaw in order to prevent us from establishing an open custody facility for six young offenders. Then there is this headline Residents Fear Youth Centre Would Bring Crime.

In Sudbury they said, "Are you going to compensate us, Mr. Keyes, when you build that facility, and our $250,000 homes suddenly lose at least 20% of their value?" I said, "Of course I am not, but I could feel like guaranteeing you there will be no loss because I happen to come from Kingston. If you want to visit our most exclusive residential subdivision, come and I will take you and show you that it is directly against the walls of Kingston Penitentiary." The backyards of our most exclusive subdivision, are built against a wall of little more than the height of Kingston Penitentiary.

Nevertheless, the residents worry about their property values, the vandalism and the potential for theft. There is that anxiety about the possible influence of the residents of such a facility on their children and the teenagers on the street.

As one of my officials said in a CBC commentary, "These are all based on honestly held beliefs." It is now proving to be a liability in our efforts to re-integrate offenders into society. This stigma is supported by an endless collection of myth and half truths about crime and criminality in our society.

Most prevalent is the notion that violent crime is rampant and widespread. Those of us who work in the justice system know that this is simply not the case. Most of us like to reassure ourselves that we do not believe everything we read in the newspaper or see on television or hear on the radio. But there is no denying that the various and numerous media can and do influence our beliefs and attitudes.

Dr. Julian Roberts of the Department of Psychology at the University of Toronto linked the prevalence of stories about violent crime in the news media to public overestimation of the actual rates of violent crime. In one study, Dr.Roberts found that more than half the front page stories in Toronto newspapers dealing with crime concerned homicides. However, in 1984-85 fewer than .03% of those sentenced to terms of imprisonment in Ontario were involved in homicides. In fact, statistics of offenses indicate that the vast majority of offenders have no known propensity towards violence.

While it is important to put the incidence of murder and mayhem into a realistic perspective, I think we have to be careful not to gloss over some of the other, perhaps less visible but equally insidious, forms of violence in our society. We have found ourselves dealing with a new class of offender over the past decade. These are otherwise law-abiding citizens who, by and large, would never consider stealing, cheating or blowing up a building but who have no compunction about physically abusing their spouses and children. Family violence is not new, but public acknowledgement of it is.

Statistical findings revealing that most batterers had been abused at home as children or had been exposed to abusive role models helped to explain, but in no way excuse, the occurrence of physical abuse among family members.

The lowering of community tolerance of family violence has lead to the development by the Ministry of Correctional Services of a number of innovative programs focusing on the management of anger. Programs consisting of group discussions, anger control exercises and teaching of alternative outlets for violent impulses are now being sponsored at many of our institutions and probation parole offices across Ontario. We expect that such programs will become standard components of correctional programming throughout Ontario's correctional system in the future.

No less serious, but unfortunately all too frequent, is the violence administered by those who choose to operate motor vehicles under the influence of alcohol. We have taken the position in Ontario that accidents involving drunk drivers are not accidents. They are calculated as acts of violence directed indiscriminately at anyone. It is no less wanton and irresponsible than firing a loaded gun into a crowd blindfolded. We have moved on mandatory jail terms for multiple offenders. We have also moved on automatic license suspensions, and most importantly we have directed the establishment of driving-while-impaired programs meant to hammer home the stupidity of partaking in the unconscionable combination of drinking and driving. Such programs have become fixtures in every major community in the province and will continue to receive support from my Ministry as long as this particular form of violence exists.

I am pleased to report that the John Howard Society volunteers play a major role in the delivery of many of these programs. and we salute their efforts in this seemingly relentless pursuit.

Neither the problem of violence in our society nor the problems presented by other forms of illegal behavior can be addressed by any one response. The challenge is to provide a balanced correctional system capable of responding to the vast spectrum of unlawful behavior with sanctions appropriate to each case.

We have the greatest respect for those who advocate abolition of correctional institutions. In our most recent trend to open up a new facility for women in Toronto, a very outstanding volunteer group known as the Quakers were very critical of the fact that we were opening another jail. Nonetheless, we recognize that the protection of society demands that some individuals must be separated from the rest of the community. Let it be clear that my government is deeply committed to the need to reduce prison populations by offering meaningful alternatives to incarceration.

While we acknowledge that we have only just begun in our efforts to find alternatives, we are encouraged by the recent Nielson Task Force report which was highly supportive of the initiatives that we have taken in Ontario to date. This Ministry funded bail programs, community service order programs, victim offender reconciliation projects, employment counselling programs, awareness programs geared to those driving while impaired, community resource centre residences and other specialized correctional programming at a cost of more than $13.2 million in 1984-85. We provided more than $380,000 in grants to community organizations that support this Ministry's aims.

While no conclusive evidence is yet available on the effectiveness of community service orders reducing recidivism, preliminary indications support our belief that the $2.4 million funding for community service orders in the last fiscal year was well spent. We will be looking for a greater participation by the private sector in this area.

We are sharpening our focus on the employment needs of offenders and ex-offenders. Joblessness is an economic and a personal tragedy shared by countless thousands of Ontario residents, but nowhere is the sting of employment or unemployment felt so keenly as among this group of offenders. The real irony is that the needs of offenders and ex-offenders for self esteem, sense of personal accomplishment and an honest source of income must be met before we can even hope for a successful re-integration into society.

The ministry maintains a serious investment in the employment programs and job readiness training provided by probation parole offices and private agencies in many Ontario communities. I am particularly pleased to note the leadership being provided again by the John Howard Society in this important endeavor.

The development of community resource centres is an area that has enjoyed substantial progress throughout the past 10 years, and it is one from which we will be looking for even greater progress in the future. Thirty-one community resource centres are operated throughout Ontario by community correctional agencies under contract with our ministry, and the impact of these centres on the lives of their residents is substantial. Many centres deal with alcoholic offenders; others, with drug dependency problems. Two in the north specialize in some of the unique problems faced by our native offenders.

Community resource centres have proven themselves in the lives of offenders, but they also have a marked impact on society. Residents earn an income, pay room and board, support their families and honor other financial obligations. In short, they are not the drain on tax dollars that they would be as inmates in a correctional institution. While far from being self- supporting, community resource centres have proven to hold major cost-saving potential. Through our ongoing relationship with community correctional agencies which include those affiliated with the John Howard Society, the St. Leonard's Society, the Elizabeth Fry Society and the Salvation Army, this Ministry will continue to encourage and support the development of community resource centres.

These are just a few of the areas of exploration that have borne fruit in our efforts to establish a correctional presence in the different communities of this province.

There have also been some disappointments. Chief among them is the unwillingness of some neighbors and neighborhoods in Ontario to accept the importance of open custody residences for young offenders as directed by the Young Offenders Act of Canada. I mentioned Brockville, Ontario; Smith Falls, Ontario; Sudbury, Ontario; certain parts of Toronto, and the list goes on.

Such resistance is symptomatic of the disproportionate fear of violence that I described earlier. Addressing the myths and the misconceptions that give rise to this fear is one way where all of us can make significant gains towards sensitizing our communities to their vital role in the rehabilitation of offenders.

PART II

DEFINING AND UNDERSTANDING VIOLENCE

DEFINING AND UNDERSTANDING VIOLENCE

Desmond Ellis
York University

In my new book *The Wrong Stuff* I discuss the relationship between definitions and understanding vis-a-vis corporate violence and police violence. This includes the relationship between definitions and understanding when it comes to wife abuse as well as to vandalism. I show how adult and state authority interact and impose certain definitions on adolescents and how vandalism may be seen in that context.

The definition of violence I found most convenient for my purpose refers to non-violable behavior that is strongly associated with reactions intended to inhibit its future occurrence. This definition with subjectively oriented people in the study of deviance, such as Becker Erickson and Leonard Catusi who focus on reactions, becomes a label successfully attached to something. Violence is a label successfully attached to something too. We know this because violence has such a connection with legitimacy that things considered illegitimate are often called violence, and those that are believed to be legitimate are not. Similar behavior can have very different names attached to it. For the United States State Department, both the Contras and Sandanistas can blow up people, one group being called freedom fighters and the other group being called terrorists.

Naming is the end point of all their activity. When you end up calling someone a terrorist with explanation, it is a major achievement. It makes things clearer, and they do not need necessary statistics. If it makes sense to someone, that is sufficient. Naming definitions is the whole point of theorizing. My approach and this definition both deal with the sociology of deviance. Crime is deviant behavior committed against the State. The State feels it is wrong so we must correct these uncooperative, coercive people ourselves.

The different variables can be classified as antecedent, intervening, independent, dependent. It makes a great deal of difference how you conceive of the State. If it is antecedent, independent or intervening, we are drawing attention to the State and saying one way or another that it is not intended. This is not a bleak hypothesis about the State operations because there is room for the State to be benign as well as to malign, but we may be short circuiting any discussion we have about most things. If we divert attention to how the State is implicated in whatever we are doing, then in *The Wrong Stuff* I have to take the State into account when dealing with vandalism, wife abuse, corporate violence and police violence.

The first conclusion was to make a definition removed from massive, escalating syndromes of definition. The best predictor of the number of definitions is the number of people making them. The more people involved in the definitions business, the more they chop up homogeneous categories.

We look at this heterogeneity and say these are manifestations of just basic things. Elderly abuse has spiralled this way. But when you read Spitzer, you ask what it all means. He would categorize all the abused old people as social junk, the deviant, the dependent. Who is doing bad things to this so- called social junk? Is it the elderly or the social dynamite? Spitzer goes one step further. He shows how, if you relate it to the economy, the same economy that produces social junk produces social dynamite. It has to do with the relative ratios of the stagnant and floating elements among the unemployed. It is a very nice theory which associates elderly abuse with the dynamic, the movement of unemployment.

We do not do anything about particular individuals who bash each other. We have lost sight of them. We are looking at the economy and how it moves people to be unkind so that one of them ends up in an emergency ward. Then we want to categorize the kinds of people who do this. Spitzer is an example of how you take taxonomies containing various different types and simply collapse them into two general categories, social junk which includes the elderly, the retarded and those who cannot function properly and social dynamite who are provided by the economy. All we need is for someone to take seriously the possibility of relations between social junk and social dynamite and to devise a theory of elderly abuse unrelated to the particular individuals who are involved. At some point you have to deal with such classified individuals and help them.

My first conclusion is that we need a definition that simultaneously looks at rule violations called objective definitions of violence. Included in that same definition is room for reactions varying from none to positive to negative.

The second general conclusion is that if we want to understand violence in Canadian society in 1986, we can do things better than we are doing them. One of the things we can do is take seriously the fact that the State is implicated in some way other than as passive victim.

The third general conclusion deals with the process of defining and naming. It is really treated as a theoretical problem by many sociologists and by most psychologists, it is treated as a technical measurement problem. It would be better to take the process of naming seriously especially when it comes to highly politicized areas of inquiry such as wife abuse, terrorism and so on.

This third conclusion emphasizes the role of the State. We have the usual triumvirate, the dependent wives, children and old people. There are sections on victims as a whole. Bearing in mind this concern I have about victim precipitation and its political uses, I looked into who could be the victims.

I started off with the Federal-Provincial Task Force on Justice for Victims of Crime. How were they defined presuming there is a link between the definition and that of victimization. It said on page one of the report that "This report confines itself to victims of traditional crimes and does not deal with victims of corporate and white collar crimes, crimes against the environment, racially motivated crime, false arrest and prosecution." It does recommend that further inquiry be made into these areas. I got the impression that corporate crime is not a heavy item on the agenda. If it is not, corporate violence certainly would not be.

I was working on corporate deviance and corporate violence. When I even mentioned the word at the University of Toronto seminar, there was some resistance to using those words. As soon as I mentioned the word, it elicited a political reaction not a technical measurement. Obviously, they conceived of it in some other way, and they saw no link between what I was talking about and what they were talking about. This is the second time this has happened. On one other occasion, I was at a ministry and the present research we are doing connects lawyers and wife abuse.

Concerning lawyers and wife abuse, the political response was that it is not the appropriate thing to do because lawyers are not in the business of abusing their wives. The intensity of wife abuse may vary with whether they saw an adversarial lawyer rather than a conciliatory one. It seems to me that it is a perfectly legitimate question to ask. At least there is a myth going around in this era of marital conflict that lawyers make things worse.

Again we have legitimate areas and people connected with violence which is not always obvious to everyone. It looked like victimization. That was my first conclusion. Maybe it is because only a few people are really involved so you put your talent and energy where most of the victimization occurs. That is not so. I have worked out the statistics on corporate controlling for people not covered by workers compensation, and there is no comparison between corporate violence and street violence. There are massive and routine injuries at work. The difficulties come if you do not conceive of it as violence. That may be a value thing, and logic cannot move values.

This important task force excluded major forms of victimization. We focused our eyes downwards again. It is the nuts and bolts of victimization. That used to be a phrase referred to deviance courses where, if we dealt with sex, we always dealt with people running around washrooms hiding and never with perfectly normal, stable homosexual relationships. There was great criticism against deviance, always drawing attention to the down-and-out.

I conclude that this is what is happening in victimization. There is concern with the perfectly respectable, but much of it diverts our eyes away from victimization where it is victimization from the top down. The provincial task force convinced me of that.

I found a book by two English feminists called *Well-Founded Fear.* It is an important book because although it does not fit well with the positivist, it reveals the truth. It deals with their conception of victimization. They had a little discussion about where you measure victimization in the way that the criminal law can deal with the bits of action and the severity of it.

Their conclusion is that some of the most difficult things that women have to deal with are coercive relationships where the violence goes on and on. It is not serious where bits make up a series, but it is an everpresent feeling of imminent hurt, psychological or physical. These two women feel, taking their measures from the bottom up and letting the definitions emerge from the subjects, that if you measure victimization in bits you miss the point that often victimization of the most desperate kind continues. It is a relationship that goes on.

It is not a relationship where a man and wife are hitting. It is but rather a relationship where the man is abusing systematically at random over a period of time. That would tell me that there are technical problems in how you measure it.

You get abused women telling their experiences. This seems to be a positive step, and I thought if the State is interested and consistent in its treatment of abused women, it will alter its conception of the victim, its definition of the victim when it comes to paying compensation. Because the State admits it has failed a little bit in its duty to protect citizens, we have a Criminal Injury Compensation Board. When I asked them if they keep records on whom they give money to, they replied yes. Do they break down the data that they present in their annual report? This is the Criminal Injuries Compensation Board whose sole area is dealing with helping victims who have been assaulted or hurt.

They present no statistics, breaking it down by victim. The Criminal Injuries Compensation Board's major reason for being is to deal with victims, but we have no statistics published on that.

My second question was what happens if a woman comes and says she has been abused by her husband? I was told she will be treated just as any other victim. They do not have a special victim thing for women and one for everyone else. It starts to be a problem if she is beaten twice.

If she is beaten three times, the problem is heightened. We therefore have a working conception of a victim being defined as a person who is beaten once by the person she lives with and goes away. If you are beaten systematically over time, collusion superimposes itself on innocence. If you are beaten more than once by the person you live with, there is definitely a problem. It is not that they will tell me this. What they told me was that there is no difference in the way we treat victims when they are women who are being abused.

We treat them just like anyone else. But there are definite problems for a woman who is in an abusive relationship which goes on over time. If she is dependent for one reason or another via provincial and/or federal legislation which increases her dependency and if there are no daycare centres for her two children, we would have to wonder what the role of the State is with this woman going to the Criminal Injuries Compensation Board.

I am trying to find some consistency in the approach to the troubles of abused women, and I am finding working definitions which are not consistent with advertising campaigns designed to say we really are concerned. I am not saying they are not; they probably are. Working on definitions of victims and having dealt with definitions of perpetrators, we see working definitions of victims which the State holds to.

My next step is to go to shelters. The third step was simply to link definition, conception and process, and it really is a big deal. There is a vast panoply of conceptions of politics, measurement and money tied into whether you are running couples therapy or not and whether your therapy is segregated gender or not. We are told constantly how different we are from the United States in relation to violent crime. The difference in quantities is of several orders of magnitude.

Some very interesting studies have been done. Violent crime data comparing Canada and the United States was examined by Block et al. Suppose now that we are working with reported data. Accept also that we are dealing with State definitions of crime. When you look at the patterns between the United States and Canada, what has emerged over the past 20 years is not so much the differences but the similarities in the patterning. In the United States and Canada, crime rose in the 60s, and in the mid-70s it went down. A Vesuvius model has been inverted. If it is plotted with dots that are connected, a beautiful cone-shaped model appears.

The Canadian pattern is best described by assault. This is with the category of homicide with strangers getting into fights and ending in killing. It is more than acquaintance or family homicides. This was compared with the pattern in the United States. The amazing thing was the similarity in patterning. They did not explore it, but what it suggests is that there are major differences in policing, laws and sanctions.

What they are saying is look to the economy. It will not be the only answer, but it will provide the setting where the public issue of structure enables you to come down and link that with this fight, in this tavern, where this person died. This person was a cripple. The sociological imagination is a way of theorizing. My conclusion looks at these various areas and at how victims and criminals have been defined. It looks at the program and its relation to victims and criminals we know. Whatever theory we adopt should give some prominence to naming it as an important activity. It is very significant. In preparation for my book, on the day that I was writing the chapter, I listened to how many things had been called terrorist. The Ontario Medical Association's reaction to the government's resistance to its attempt to extra bill was called terrorist. Putting a cyanide pill in aspirins was called terrorist.

I went through a whole list of things particularly the use of words to obfuscate what is a rich area for inquiry. In areas such as spouse abuse, what does spouse abuse actually mean? What does it mean to you? A man and woman hitting each other? Let us call it wife abuse. In most cases the wife is the one getting hurt. It matters. In the whole area of naming, the police make a very interesting distinction. A policeman beats up a snitch that other officers are working with. That is violence, and it is prohibited. That is deviant violence. A policeman beats up a child because he would not get out of the car quickly enough; that is not.

Exploring a little bit further, I discovered a number of rules influence police behavior. Let us take two, my rules and their rules. For a police officer my rules are my group's rules, my peer's rules, the subcultural rules. If an officer violates one of these subcultural rules by structuring violence and not eliminating it necessarily, that is deviant. If he breaks the rules, that is deviant. There is no room for interpretation, meaning or interactions before you assign the label deviant because he broke our rules. What happens if he breaks a rule which is in the criminal code? It is a law. Just because he did that does not mean that this violence was deviant.

He has to be convicted before we will agree he is deviant. Now they move to a subjective definition of deviance. Objectively defined, violence is intentionally injuring someone and in the process violating rules prescribing it. Therefore deviant violence is violence which breaks the rules prescribing it.

Two men each beat their wives very badly. One by the mere fact of beating has violated the criminal code and can be charged. He broke a rule, and that is it. You cannot take a subjective approach. You have to wait for the moral drama to be worked out, wait for the accused, the accusers and any witnesses to assign meaning. As a result of all this indeterminate activity, he may or may not be labelled a wife abuser. This puts subjectively oriented scholars in a great deal of difficulty because they are for women. Subjectively oriented sociologists in the area of deviants are sociologists who are for the deviant, the dependent, the poor.

When it comes to wife abuse, Shur labels women violent. Shur is one of the founders of the subjective school. When it comes to analyzing woman battering he uses Strauss's objective definition of wife abuse. With not a pause, no qualification, I want to show women I am on their side. I am going to switch. He does. On top of everything else, even when you know this is a subjectively oriented scholar, he is not going to accept violence and build theories of it on objective definitions. You come up with a very different theory. If you define violence subjectively, what you are going to be dealing with is that social control causes violence.

That anomalous inversion of the socially controlled violence relation is central to labelling the societal reaction approach. If you deal with it objectively, more often than not you get social control. What the State does is rise as a result of violence and try to control it. There the State social control is the dependent variable. It makes a great deal of difference. It becomes all the more interesting to deal with naming as an important problem because the implications are so important.

I tried to incorporate all these thoughts into what I learned about police deviance. The report of the Nova Scotia Commission is a superb analysis for anyone who believes in a bad apple theory. They have a good apple theory. They are taller, braver and more patriotic than the rest of us, and they have a bad apple theory. We are all really good, but if we look at the commissions of inquiry at Kentville, Nova Scotia, the operation of the complaints office in Toronto, almost two-thirds of the complaints deal with, over their first initial three-year period, violence.

The number of convictions barely reaches two per cent. In the area of corporate crimes, I looked at the Dubin Commission inquiry on hazardous practices in flying aircraft in Canada. The number of convictions was less than one per cent. In this process, there are similarities between policemen and people who run corporations in relation to the processing. Not calling what they do a crime is a big deal because it diverts attention to some kind of less harsh processing. When I looked at the police data in Toronto, there were very few convictions. There are good reasons for this because there are legal reasons having to do with the status of the police chief and the legal status of police officers. All these things explain why policemen do a good job. This is not a statement which necessarily means that they do not.

At the same time, if you look at the legislative matrix for policing, if you look at the processing of their behavior, and if you conclude it is just an accident, you will not get as far as if you looked at the role of police and how the legislation was set up. There is a very good analysis by Robert Reiner at University of Sheffield in England. He shows, at least with the English police, the relative neglect of policing. It is the same thing in the United States and in Canada. This is very poor policing of policing. In Reiner's analysis, this was not an accident. Now let us make the connection.

Here is the unauthorized use of force against this person. How can you connect this with large-scale structural developments explaining police violence? Reiner's attempt took this form. Policemen in England usually come from the working classes. Their job is a job. It is the same with prison guards. A bargain had to be struck. The State and police chiefs had to agree that the price of the loyalty of the police would be non-interference by the State in the policing of policing. Reiner carried this analysis out in England. Now one of the manifestations of the non-policing of policing is the kind of activity that Box described for England which also is described in the United States and Canada by Reiman.

He does the same thing with unionization. Unionization makes the bargain a little bit more tenuous. Then he shows how, given unionization and the autonomy it confers, it widens the gap. It makes the policing of policing even more tenuous. The State is implicated only as a dependent variable.

The evidence over time is that most people have been killed, maimed, hurt, injured, devastated by State violence. Many more have died this way than by the retail violence of the kid robbing the store. This is not to praise robbing grocery stores, but it is just a descriptive statement. Legitimate violence has taken care of most killing, hurting and maiming.

The main thing then is that for most forms of violence, the State is implicated in more than one way. It would improve our understanding greatly if we acknowledge that fact. The most dangerous people do not hurt their caretakers most. If you compare Millhaven Prison and at the rate at which guards have been injured to Freshwater Fish Marketing Company, the latter has a rate of injury of 93%. The rate of injury per worker for prison guards is approximately 13%.

The safest of all are people who work in criminal justice with a rate of 0.13%. With that one person, a pencil could have fallen on him. The rate of assaults at work are massive and routine, and there are lawyers who want to play it down. You take a drink, and you are guilty with your first sip. Then he compares it to someone who builds a 15-storey building. He knows after the fifth storey that many people are going to be killed unless he does something to prevent it. He builds it anyway. This is what happens. If we look at the criminal code and then occupational health and safety, we must ask why drunk driving is a criminal offence, and this is not.

VIOLENT CRIME IN CANADA, THE U.S., AND EUROPE

Paul Brantingham
Simon Fraser University

When we view current situations in the world perspective as well as in the historical perspective, the contemporary Canadian violent situation is not so bad. By whatever means we use to measure it, we have come through in the last quarter century with a massive rise in crime not only in Canada but throughout the Atlantic community and possibly in the rest of the world.

The levels of crime we put up with now are significantly greater than the levels of crime we put up with in the 1950s and the 1940s, but they are not substantially higher than the levels of crime that people had put up with in the 1920s or in the 1890s. They are substantially lower particularly in terms of violence than the levels of crime that people have historically put up with. Similarly, the levels of violent crime that we experience in Canadian society are relatively low on the world scale. We have a minor violent crime problem when we look to the world situation.

In 1984 and 1985, officially recognized violent crimes accounted for about nine per cent of the criminal code offenses in Canada. That number has remained stable for relatively long periods in recent times. That proportion puts us relatively close to the United States where about 10% of their uniform crime report offenses are for serious violent crimes. It also puts us a bit over the English pattern where approximately 6% of their known offenses are for the kinds of violent offenses we report in our criminal statistics.

We criminologists spend a good deal of time pointing out to the world and particularly to undergraduate students and professional audiences that there are problems with criminal statistics. In fact, it turns out that criminal statistics are relatively robust measures of trends, distributions and patterns in the stuff they record and report. It turns out that Interpol data correlate reasonably well with national data. It turns out that all the different criminal justice measures of crime correlate well with one another. It also happens to be the case that, as we probe deeper into our alternative measures using victimization techniques and self-report studies, the correlations, the relationships, the ability of each of those measures to give you a solid prediction of what the other measures will tell you is on a very high order.

There is some reason now to believe that you can use criminal justice statistics to tell what has gone on and what is going on. Using Interpol statistics you can look at the Atlantic community and, using a robust figure like homicide, begin to get a feel for what the distributions are.

In 1982, the most recent year that the Solicitor General's Library had some Interpol statistics available, Northern Ireland led the rest of the Atlantic community with a homicide rate of about 24 per 100,000 population.

Surprisingly enough the United States was not second. It came third after the Netherlands. Canada falls into a broad middle ground of countries along with Italy, Belgium, Portugal and Austria with homicide rates in the vicinity of two to three per 100,000.

England has a much lower rate, below two, and Ireland reports the lowest homicide rate among the Atlantic communities. It is even more interesting if you look on a broader perspective which is much harder to do. For a variety of political reasons, various countries do not report their crime rates to Interpol, and the closest we have come to getting some kind of world picture of what crime is like is a survey conducted in the mid-1970s by the United Nations. They sent out carefully constructed de-politicized questionnaires to all member states and received a good response. A few places such as Soviet Union, China, India, and South Africa that we would like to know about declined. Most member states participated, and out of that we get striking comparative figures if our interest is violence.

On a map constructed of world homicide regions, using the United Nations data from the mid-1970s, we see that the communities of both Australia and New Zealand have a relatively low homicide rate on the world scale. The North American and European homicide rates are about one-third the world average rate. The Latin American regional rate is 20 times the world average rate.

Some African states that report to Interpol give us numbers that look absolutely horrifying. In 1976 Nigeria reported a rate of 81 homicides per 100,000 population, and one country reported a homicide rate of 137 per 100,000 population compared to our 2.7. You could now make similar observations with the United Nations data and the Interpol data. That tells us that in other categories of violent crime we look relatively good as well. In the United Nations survey, the North American and European assault rates were less than half the world average. The sex crime rate was about half the world average. The robbery rates were less than a third the world average, and the kidnapping rate was less than a tenth the world average. Comparisons that go much beyond that begin to break down because of all of the things that criminologists like to tell us about statistics. But at this level they give us a robust measure of what our position is in the world pattern. We have the advantage of dealing with a violent crime problem that is sufficiently contained, and we can think about our options and explore new questions of violence that we have not looked at before and decide whether they need to be dealt with in criminal law.

On a map of the world theft pattern, we find that North America and Europe lead all the rest of the world in theft and fraud. If we have a problem in terms of the quantity rather than the quality of the offenses we deal with, it lies in theft and property crime and fraud, and not in violence measured on the world scale.

I would like to discuss the historical perspective. How are things now compared to the way they were? They are a lot worse now than they were in 1950.

Over the past decade or so crime has become a major issue for historians. Out of the historical research that has been done, much of it in Canada, we can begin to build a general picture of crime in England, Canada and the United States and, to a lesser extent, in some of the European countries over the last 800 years or so. One of the things we can say is that there has been a general decline in the level of violence experienced by European-based societies over the last 700 or 800 years. We have reliable measures that range from the 13th century to the present in England and consistent measures of that time span from other places that tell us that the rate of violent crime is down.

We are very confident about measures of homicide because dead bodies turn out to be very difficult to explain, hide or dispose of. English homicide rates have declined steadily from the 13th century to the beginning of the 19th century. What is the magnitude of the drop? It has declined from about 20 per 100,000 population to something on the order of one per 100,000.

I have a rough comparison which tells us something about the pattern of crime and violence in 14th century England just before the Black Death decimated medieval society and 1977 which happened to be a handy year. What you see is a major shift in the relative proportion of the violent crimes. In the mid-14th century, homicide, robbery, arson and rape together accounted for about 30% of all the indictable offenses. If we take a comparable set of criminal offenses in 1977 and manipulate the figures into comparability, we see that that set of offenses accounted for 10% of the violent crimes instead of 30% of the offenses. That kind of shift in the crime mix has occurred probably most markedly in the last 100 years. In Canada it has occurred since 1886.

The shift in the relative proportion of violent crime is striking. In 1886 violent crimes accounted for 21% of known offenses; now they account for about nine per cent and have done so for about the last 25 years. So we are looking at a crime situation in which we have relatively less of a problem with the traditional violent crimes against a person and more with other things. I can also say that many of the social and demographic characteristics of violent crime appear to be persistent and appear to have lasted in an essentially consistent form over such a long period of time that we can begin to think of them as constant.

One of them is the sex of violent offenders and victims. Violent crime is essentially a male activity, and this is particularly true of homicide. In the 14th century, in the 18th century and today, there are approximately nine male offenders for every female offender, and there are approximately nine known male victims for each female victim. Violent crime is also an enterprise of a somewhat older population as opposed to the children who commit burglaries. The demographics are slightly higher. It is still characteristic of young adults rather than aging adolescents. The shift is somewhat higher.

There is also a link to violence. There is the link of alcohol to violence that we see today. In the 13th and 14th centuries and in the 17th and 18th centuries, all the accumulated data tells us that violent crime revolves around pubs, whiskey, beer and the social interactions that come out of that in a very large way.

There is one thing demographically that has changed. In the 14th century, clergymen, priests and real world equivalents of Robin Hood's jolly Friar Tuck were the major perpetrators, the biggest single occupational group known to commit violent offenses. In fact, much of the battle between Henry II and Thomas of Beckett was triggered over whether or not Henry could drive criminally-oriented priests and violent priests before the royal courts of justice. That has changed.

Contemporary data suggests that the clergy are not now major components of the violent occupational group. That is a change for the better. There has also been a demonstrable change in our general social attitude towards crime. We tolerate it less. Violence is less tolerated, more frequently reported and more frequently prosecuted than it was before. We perceive forms of violence that we were blind to in the past now as appropriately criminal.

The growth of concern with wife-beating and child abuse is a good example of that. In the first half of the 18th century, wife-beating was not considered a crime at all. Although technically there was a way that you could perhaps bring it under the category of assault, people were as blind to that question as we are contemporaneously blind to the question of all the assaults that ought to come off a hockey brawl. We become very surprised if a crown prosecutor lays charges against the Flames or Canadiens. People were equally astounded.

Another recent change is the change in rape laws. Rape, historically, was sexual knowledge by force or threat to a woman other than the perpetrator's wife. A wife had no right to resist. The fact that an enormous amount of violence was used on a particular occasion was seen as unacceptable under the law. We do not accept that anymore. We modified that law. We have gone to a sexual battery statute. If enforcement is not always the way everyone would like it to be, it takes time for the criminal law to move. But like a glacier, it does move. So we have begun to remove archaic limitations to the criminal law.

On the subject of crime waves in the future, one of the characteristics of the historical research has been to establish that there are two kinds of crime waves. One of them is the kind produced by the media when an editor says, "Things are slow... let's find some crime and write it up." And we have a long history of social scientists documenting that happening in locales. The other kind is real. There is a long-term cycle in crime that can be traced for 700 years. It has a roughly measured amplitude, and that varies about 100 years between peaks and valleys.

The English happen to have approximately 150 years of data readily available. Essentially there was a massive peak in crime in England sometime just before 1850. It had been building from sometime in the middle of the 18th century. There was a massive decline in crime which all involved historians and social scientists now believe was quite real. That took place from around 1850 until around 1920, and then there was a rise that began slowly and a massive rise that we have lived through in the last 25 years. That cycle can be projected backwards quite nicely through the data.

It is not very clear what drives it. Demographics fit into it. Changes in the size and rate of growth of population seem to change it and drive it. Major changes in the structure of the economy seem to drive it, and major changes in the structure of the criminal justice system seem to drive it. The 1850 peak corresponds to a massive modification in the structure of criminal justice systems in Europe and North America with the invention of police and the institutionalization of prisons for the first time.

It also corresponds to the beginning of a massive change in the structure of industrial life, and it also corresponds to some demographic changes. The general long-term crime pattern in the second half of the 19th century and beginning of the 20th century in the United States resembles that of the English and of the French as well as everywhere else where the data has been looked at in a serious way. The exception is perhaps with Canada.

With murder in the United States, there was a peak around 1890, one around 1930 and one recently. There may be a reason for thinking that the homicide cycle travels somewhat differently than the long-term major cycle, and there may be about 40 years duration between peaks. Does any of this mean anything other than it is great stuff to examine undergraduates on? Some of the demographic movements include the baby boomers who have moved into their forties, who are slowing down, who are not hanging out in bars at the same rate and who are not getting into fights in the market. There is a much smaller population doing that.

That structural change in society suggests that violence rates, and crime rates in general, should begin to drop and should drop for the next 20 or 30 years. I think it might not happen. There is a countervailing pressure, and it comes from what may be an industrial revolution going on now. We see it in British Columbia at the moment. We have very high unemployment and very real problems in the forest industries. The forest companies have never shipped more lumber.

It is not bad times for the forest companies. In order to compete against the Swedes, the Russians and the American South over the last five years, the forest companies have shaken up their operations and modernized their plants. They can cut more timber with fewer people. There are highly skilled forest workers who are never going to be re-employed in the forest industry no matter how good times get. They become structurally unemployed because they have been replaced by machines and better ways of doing things. The next place it is going to hit is Oshawa. In order to convince us to buy something built in

Oshawa rather than something built in Yokohama, the car companies are going to robots and computers. A large number of workers are going to find themselves structurally unemployed. If we cannot re-absorb them, we have a genuine potential to create a situational opportunity to re-establish the kind of conditions that existed in London before the onset of the industrial revolution, This comes about with a large floating populace of unemployed and unemployable people who are not starving, who receive enough from the productivity of our economy to be able to afford food or whiskey, and they can take their choice. They also have more leisure time to get themselves into trouble. For them, disciplined behaviour, according to the requirements of the law, no longer pays off because they are not going to be employed and earn above minimum wage. If that scenario is correct, we may have a real problem coming from a very different kind of base, a problem that has been experienced in North American or European society for perhaps 150 years.

We therefore have a genuine challenge if that scenario is correct.

INCIDENCE, RISKS AND FEARS: VICTIMIZATION SURVEY FINDINGS

Dorothy Hepworth
Ministry of the Solicitor General

Crime, or victimization as it is called in Canada, has become increasingly popular in Western countries as a way of estimating the dark number of unreported crimes. Because they never come to the attention of the police, they are never included in our official statistics. Victimization surveys have been carried out regularly in the United States since the early 1970s and more recently in the United Kingdom, the Netherlands, Germany, Australia and many other Western countries.

Developmental work for the Canadian survey began in the Ministry of the Solicitor General in the mid-70s with John Evans and Jerry Leger and others at the helm. The basic survey instruments and methodologies were based on work already done on the United States, but they adapted the methodology to make it more suitable to our less populous nation. There is a very good paper outlining the development of the Canadian Victimization Survey which Leger and Evans wrote.

In general terms, victimization surveys can provide a wealth of information on a wide range of issues, and our Canadian version of the survey is no exception. I will focus on a fairly narrow range of information from the survey including perceptions of crime, fear of crime as measured by the survey and the experience of violence from the perspective of the victim. I will also comment on the appropriate use of victimization data in the development of the criminal justice system and on other social policies to deal with violent victimization.

We have so far published six different bulletins on a variety of subjects. The first Canadian Victimization Survey was carried out by the Ministry with the assistance of Statistics Canada in early 1982. During that survey, more than 61,000 people in eight major urban centers were interviewed by telephone. The areas were Vancouver, Edmonton, Winnipeg, Metropolitan Toronto, Montreal, Halifax, Dartmouth and St. John's, Newfoundland.

Our most recent victimization survey was conducted in Edmonton in early 1985. The survey excluded commercial and institutional telephones. We did random dialing to get our subjects, but commercial and institutional telephones were omitted from the survey.

People under the age of 16 were also not interviewed, and their personal victimizations were not reported by anyone else. We have been able to make estimations from our sample of people age 16 and older or of the households with telephones. To maximize the reliability of recall, respondents were asked to report on only those incidents which had occurred between January 1 and December 31, 1981. There are many technical reasons why firm limits have to be set on what the period of recall is because people do not recall accurately or they may have been so affected by a certain event that they do not want to recall. There are therefore difficulties in setting the boundaries in surveys of this kind.

The survey covered eight major categories of crime which included sexual assault, robbery, assault, break-and-enter, motor vehicle theft, theft of household property, theft of personal property and vandalism. I will cover only the first three in this paper. Fortunately, the more serious the crime in this list is, the less likely it is to occur. It is for this reason that it was necessary to draw such a large sample in each of the cities studied.

We occasionally ran out of cases when we tried to make more detailed cross-tabulations and analysis. The number of sexual assaults that we uncovered in one of the cities was so low that we were not able to make any cross-tabulations on the socio-demographic characteristics of the victims. I should also indicate that when we talk about these offence categories, we try as far as possible to make them correspond to the uniform crime report categories so they include attempts as well as completed offenses. We have in the sexual assault category, for instance, incidents of molesting, of attempted rape and of completed rape, and they are all categorized together under sexual assault. The same would happen with robbery or other assaults.

As with other surveys conducted in Canada over the past 15 years, our survey found that most Canadians believe crime is increasing. They are not preoccupied with crime, and they do not perceive it to be a daily threat to the quality of their lives.

When asked whether they felt that crime in their city was increasing, decreasing or staying about the same, about 81 per cent said they thought it had increased in their city. But only one-third believed that crime in their own neighborhoods had increased. So there is a sense that crime is increasing, but it is not really encroaching on anyone personally.

When asked whether they thought their own neighborhood was an area with a high crime rate, only 12 per cent said that their neighborhood had a high amount of crime. Seventeen per cent described their neighborhood crime problem as serious. The others said that it was either average or not serious. The elderly were no more likely to perceive increasing crime in their city or neighborhood than young persons, and females no more than males. I make this point particularly because there has been some discussion about the differences in fear levels expressed by elderly persons and by women. We asked people how safe they felt walking alone in their own neighborhood during the day or after dark. Only five per cent said they felt unsafe during the day, but after dark about 40 per cent said they felt unsafe walking alone in their own neighborhoods. Half of those aged 65 and older felt unsafe, and 56 per cent of all women felt unsafe.

This figure for women rose to 62 per cent for those who had been victimized during the previous year. Only 20 per cent of male victims felt unsafe walking alone in their own neighborhood after dark. We should probably study the pathological lack of fear among males.

We found that with residents aged 16 and older in these eight cities, there were about 70 violent incidents reported to us per thousand population during the survey year. There were 3.5 sexual assaults per thousand population, 10 robberies per thousand population and 57 assaults. All of the sexual assaults involved direct attack. By definition we did not include in this category any sort of threats or obscene suggestions. It had to involve an actual attack. In about half of the robberies and half of the assaults there were threats, and with the remainder actual physical attacks occurred. Weapons were used in about 35 per cent of the personal violent crimes and guns in only about five per cent. Most of the weapons that were used were blunt instruments or other weapons which you would not normally consider to be a weapon. We even had one case in which a dozen eggs was the weapon. Guns are not used very often.

Fewer than half of the violent victimizations, only about one- third of the assaults, 38 per cent of the sexual assaults and 45 per cent of the robberies, were reported to the police. Rates did increase with the extent of injury. Thirty per cent of those who were attacked reported, and 70 per cent of those who required medical or dental treatment reported. The more serious the incident was, the more likely it was to be reported. This did not mean that all very serious incidents were in fact reported to the police.

When we look at the risk of victimization, although women who had been victimized were more likely to be fearful than non-victims, the higher proportion who felt unsafe overall cannot be accounted for by higher rates of personal violent victimization. On average, women were much less likely than men to be the victims of violent crime. For example, men are twice as likely to be victims of assault and nearly twice as likely to be the victims of robbery. On the other hand, women are about seven times more likely to be sexually assaulted. The rate for men was just under one per thousand males; the rate for women, 5.8 per thousand females. It is interesting that our survey is one of the few that actually measures rates of sexual assault in which males are the victims. British crime surveys do not even ask male respondents whether or not they were victims of sexual assault.

When all violent crimes measured in this survey are combined, we estimate that the number of incidents experienced will be 90 per thousand males and 53 per thousand females. There is quite a discrepancy in the actual rate of victimization. I should re-emphasize that for both men and women, violent victimization rates are highest among those who are less than 25 years of age.

Victimization rates for both males and females between the ages of 16 and 24 are more than twice the overall rates for each sex. Risk is highest for those between the ages of 18 and 20 and drops very rapidly after age 24. One can think of good reasons why this age group is more vulnerable. Many are still living at home and under some kind of parental supervision.

Even more dramatically, we find that sexual assaults are heavily concentrated among young women. Sixty-eight per cent of all female victims of sexual assault were under 25 years of age. When we go to the other end of the scale in terms of elderly persons, violent victimization rates for elderly males are one- sixth the overall male rate; for elderly females over the age of 65, one-tenth the average rate. The curve peaks very rapidly at age 24, drops off gradually, and almost disappears at age 65 and older. To those who have criticized our results in terms of elderly victimization, I must concede that we did not interview people living in institutions and therefore might have missed a most vulnerable group of elderly persons.

Other elements of lifestyle, marital status and the number of evening activities outside the home also affected violent victimization rates. Young, unmarried persons who are students or looking for work have the highest victimization rates. Rates also increase with the number of evening activities outside the home especially for males and especially where assaults were involved.

When we look at place of occurrence, although the majority of all violent victimizations occurred in public places, women were much more likely than men to be victimized in their own homes. Looked at individually, 21 per cent of the sexual assault incidents occurred inside the victim's own residence, and 11 per cent either in the home of a friend or acquaintance or in the vicinity of the victim's residence. The remaining 68 per cent occurred outside or in public places.

The victim's home was the location of half of the actual rapes. This is not attempted rape. Over half of the sexual assaults which occurred in the victims' own homes involved intruders; that is, the assailant was not legitimately in the residence nor had he been invited to enter the residence for one reason or another. They may have broken into the residence as a result of a quarrel with the victim. Forty-one per cent of all sexual assaults involved victims and assailants known to one another, and in only seven per cent were victim and assailant related by marriage or by blood. Most robberies occurred in public places, and men were nearly twice as likely to be robbed as women.

Seventy-one per cent of the robberies occurred in public places and 22 per cent in women's homes. By contrast, males were robbed in public places in 88 per cent of the incidents and in their own homes in only five per cent of the incidents.

More than 5,000 robberies occurred after offenders had gained illegal entry into homes. In these incidents two-thirds of the victims were women. Strangers were responsible for 88 per cent of the robberies against males and 78 per cent of the robberies against females. The general picture is that it is most likely to be strangers in a public place, and people are most likely to be unrelated to one another. For women, the concentration of incidents that occur in the home or involve acquaintances is higher than it is for men. Assaults were by far the most common type of victimization experienced by either men or women, and the incident rates as I mentioned before were 79 per thousand for men and 39 incidents per thousand for women.

Women were the victims in 77 per cent of family assaults, in 90 per cent of the assaults between spouses and in 80 per cent of the assaults between ex-spouses. Speaking of domestic assault, there is always some argument side as to whether women ever assault men. It does occur, but it is much more frequently the case where men do the assaulting. Risk of assault was greatest for women who were separated from their spouse at the time of the interview, and this rate was very high, 102 incidents per thousand women. This does not mean that all of those incidents were at the hands of a spouse or ex-spouse. Generally their risk is high. Widowed women had the lowest rate of victimization. Separated women were nearly five times as likely to be assaulted than married or attached women.

It should be noted that the vast majority of assaults against both men and women involved male offenders. Ninety-eight per cent of the assaults against men involved other men, and 89 per cent of the assaults against women involved men. What are the consequences of victimization? Just over half of the victims of violence were physically attacked, and 27 per ccnt of all victims were injured.

Eight per cent were injured badly enough to require medical or dental attention. Only one per cent stayed in hospital over- night or longer, but this amounted to more than 50,000 nights in hospital. Eight times as much time was lost from daily activities as a result of victimization. Slightly fewer elderly victims of violent crimes suffered injury than younger victims. We had initially assumed that if there were a violent victimization, elderly people might be more likely injured than others. Injured elderly victims were twice as likely to require medical or dental treatment.

The incidence of actual attack and physical injury was relatively high among female victims. They were more likely than men to be physically attacked and injured. Actual physical attacks occurred in all of the sexual assaults I have mentioned and in 63 per cent of the robberies. Three-quarters of the assaults by spouses resulted in actual physical attack. In this very intense relationship the number of threats declines, and the number of actual attacks increases. One could then assume we are more likely to hear about the assaults that result in an actual attack than about mere threats.

Sixty-one per cent of the sexual assaults and 61 per cent of the assaults by spouses resulted in injury. The closer the relationship between the assailant and the victim, the more likely we were to have serious consequences.

Aside from the injuries and attacks, we also measured emotional trauma or need for counselling as a result of victimization. We found that the more serious the incident was, the more likely victims were to request counselling for their type of injury. That included male victims of sexual assault for whom counselling and other support services are probably rare.

In conclusion, I feel we have learned much about the context of crime and how it is experienced differently by males and females and by young and old. It is important not only to look at relative risk of victimization when instituting crime prevention and other policies, but also to look at how seriously the incident affects different groups and the social context of their occurrence.

Some very serious incidents are still left unreported, and these must be a source of concern to all of us. Victims of sexual and domestic assault are still reluctant to involve the police either because they fear revenge from the offender or because they are concerned about the attitudes of the police and courts. I would expect that this concern is a declining reason for not reporting it. Concern with revenge from the offender is going to remain a difficult problem.

There are many policy implications for what we are doing. The need for a variety of responses to crime and to victimization becomes very clear. It is not enough simply to make things illegal and require that police enforce the law. We obviously require all kinds of resources so that those who do not feel able to go to the police, or do not feel it would be beneficial, have a variety of resources available to them.

PORTRAYALS OF VIOLENCE IN THE MASS MEDIA

Anthony Doob
Director, Centre for Ciminology
University of Toronto

It is worth asking ourselves why we are talking about portrayals of violence in the mass media. Why is that such a concern for us? The concern is that fear, justified or not, rather than reality will form policy. Policy decisions will be driven more by myths than by what is actually happening in the world. Policy decisions should be made according to more information rather than according to the perceptions that many of us have.

Most of us, even criminologists, gain information about crime from the mass media. Approximately 95% of the public mention media as a prime source of information. Television, interestingly enough, is mentioned most often as a source of information about sentencing.

This is a problem when you consider the role of the media and the appropriate concerns. It is nice to say that the media's main concern is educational, but that ignores the fact that to a large extent it is an organization with interests other than educating. It is interested in selling products and maintaining its audience.

This leads inevitably to a pitfall, simplicity. If the public is informed about something in a 37-second news story, it has to look to simple solutions for complex problems.

When the efficiency of the media is questioned, that question has two different answers depending on whether we are involved in the media or trying to concern ourselves with an informed public. If we are interested in the media, criteria for a successful broadcast may well be in terms of something being interesting, understandable and simple.

There is no simple solution to a problem. There are quite different and important ways of evaluating a question. In some of my research I have shown for example that newspaper accounts of sentence hearings influence the public. The public conclusions could be quite different from the conclusions they would otherwise make. We compared people who had actually seen court documents or transcripts of court hearings to those who had read newspaper accounts and found that the response was quite different.

This is not necessarily a concern of the public. One reporter's response to this was that the reader would be discouraged by technicalities and an editor would cut them out anyway. He is probably correct.

We have to understand these constraints when we are trying to understand why the public believes what it does. The interesting thing is that the public, although it may hold initially a very simple view of issues, can quickly understand and appreciate the complexities of the issues. When the public is asked about the causes and solutions of violent crime, it often does not look initially to the criminal justice system. The public understands that crime is an integral part of society. Looking at violence is really looking at people rather than simply at the criminal justice system. We would like the public to put crime and violence into some kind of perspective.

When we look at what is informing the public, we understand why the public concerns sometimes do not make sense to us. If we look at newspaper accounts of crime, we find that half are violent. Half of that involves some form of homicide. There is very little about victims' independent relationships or corporate actions which threaten lives or well-being. It is not surprising to find that the public equates violence with crime. Only about 9% of reported crime in Canada involves violence. The public seriously overestimates the amount of violent crime. The public believes not only that violence is increasing, but also that violence is involved substantially in those millions of crimes reported each day.

People tend to view sentences as too lenient. When they think about what they mean by too lenient, they think about things involving violence. Yet the public says to the politicians, "You are being too lenient on criminals."

They are thinking about only 9% of those cases. The source of this in the media is clear to anyone who has looked systematically at reporting of individual crimes in the newspaper, radio or television. The kinds of things that one sees leads to the belief that if one wants to be informed about crime, the best thing to do is to stop reading about it.

What is important to remember is that it is not a matter of simply taking a larger sample. The more you read about crime, the more you are going to be informed about it. Because what I am talking about is a population of stories. If we sample them in larger degrees, we are going to become systematically less informed about the underlying social problem or social issue.

The problem is more serious than just the over-reporting of violence. There is some evidence to suggest that the media tends to pick the more serious instances of specific offences. The typical robbery reported in a newspaper, on television or on radio is going to be much more interesting and much more dramatic than an average robbery reported even to the police.

The same thing occurs if one looks at the reporting of manslaughter. What we find is that the most dramatic, disturbing events are reported. It is interesting to note that a substantial number of reports of manslaughter seem to talk about the crime as if it were not manslaughter, but murder. There also exists a tendency of the media to pick themes and develop them. Examples of this include the muggings in Britain in the 1970s and at the same time in New York with crimes against the elderly. Since the Young Offenders Act was passed a couple of years ago, there has been a disproportionate amount of reporting of youth crime. What this suggests is that these issues can become public issues without any necessary reality behind them. They lead to false information and false allocation of time and resources.

The difficulty occurs when we pick up information and urge those who form policy to use it in informing. Violence is easy to report. It is easy to make stories about it. It is easy to entertain people with it.

There is a constant parade of horrible incidents which can be picked out in a society as large as Canada. We have to be careful how we respond. The issue of missing children has the potential of being one where we can be driven in the wrong direction. The concern most people have with missing children is abduction by a stranger and is the least common cause of missing children.

Does the media necessarily pick up this image or this information? Sometimes it does. The problem of missing children is a much more interesting issue if we are talking about abductions by strangers. It is a much more interesting topic than runaways or abductions by parents where there is an issue of custody. If we look systematically at the news coverage of missing children's day in May, we find a mix. Only some stories put the nature of missing children into context.

One radio broadcast discussed the release of 3,500 balloons with pictures of missing children without any mention of what we know about them. A newspaper story contained a long feature about a child taken away from his mother. Only towards the end of the story did it become clear that the father had abducted the child. That does not necessarily improve matters, but it changes the tone of the story and makes the kinds of solutions that you look for quite different.

The problem of understanding violence becomes serious as soon as we get into looking at solutions. The problem is that we have, as has mass media, linked violence to other kinds of phenomena. We have linked violence in many ways to mental illness. We have linked violence to other issues related to the criminal justice system such as parole, mandatory supervision and release on bail. We have linked violence to recidivists. All of these are missing the point. The problem with recidivism is that most people, or roughly half the people before the courts, are there for the first time. In dealing with recidivists we are therefore talking about at least half the people before the courts. We also have to remember that most people who do come before the courts for the first time never reappear.

Eighty per cent of first-time offenders will never come back into the criminal justice system. We have to keep this in context when forming policy. The difficulty is that the usual kinds of statistics or realities are not persuasive enough against the single salient incident. Those kinds of things stick in our minds. Unfortunately, those are the kinds of things which we listen to when we are trying to figure out solu- tions. So how do we approach the problem of violence? It has been suggested that the criminal justice system be used as a last resort in dealing with certain kinds of crimes. The criminal justice system is not the last resort of solutions. I suggest that the criminal justice system has almost nothing to do with solutions to the problem of violence. Looking at comparisons across countries, we find that the situations have not changed for some time. There have been historical changes, but to some extent those historical changes seem to be parallel ones. The criminal justice system is really a punishment system. It selects who needs to be punished and by how much.

That has relatively little to do with the problem of dealing with violence. It does not mean that we should ignore it. I do not see the criminal justice system as a last resort. It deals with a problem different from violence. It deals with the punishment of people who have perpetrated violence. If we evaluate solutions by criminal justice penalties, I think we miss the point. I would be concerned, for example, if we evaluated our system of dealing with pollution, occupational health and safety or fraud and theft according to the penalties that are given out. What we want to evaluate is whether or not change is necessary. That is much more important than the question as to whether somebody was penalized or brought before the criminal justice system. Dealing with the problem is more important than merely punishing.

We do not look to the criminal justice system for solutions, and I suggest three pitfalls to avoid. First, we should not think of crime as violence. Violence is an unusual part of crime and is quite varied. Second, we should not look to the criminal justice system for solutions to violence. We must look beyond to the process which leads to distasteful events. Third, we should not think of solutions to violence per se. We should look for solutions to specific problems and not categorize.

On a flow-chart, drinking and driving merge to create an impaired driver. Impaired drivers are more likely to make errors. With errors come accidents. With accidents come injuries and deaths.

There are therefore six different categories where we can intervene. We can intervene at the drinking level, but we can also intervene in driving by trying to provide alternatives to cutting down on the frequency. We can only intervene with the impaired driver within limits of the criminal justice system. We can intervene in trying to reduce the number of errors people make. For example, a relatively simple way of reducing wandering drivers is to put a white line down the edge of the road. People apparently find it easier to drive between two lines.

There are a variety of things that we can do in designing both cars and roads. Going beyond mere accidents, we know a variety of ways to avoid deaths such as with the use of seat belts or air bags. If we concentrate on the criminal justice system, we are concentrating only on one part of that whole process. We are concentrating on the driver after he has become impaired.

Looking at violence today we must deal with the structure of the specific kind of problem, not with violence per se. We cannot rely solely on the criminal justice system because it has a very limited role in controlling people's behavior. We must look at the troublesome problem itself. If we do that, we may be able to at least move in a useful direction.

PART III

PERSPECTIVES ON THE CAUSES OF VIOLENCE

PERSPECTIVES ON THE CAUSES OF VIOLENCE: THE BIOLOGICAL PERSPECTIVE

Lionel Tiger
Rutgers University

My paper will deal with the whole issue of the body and the physicality of social life as it involves violence. The macro-theory or macro-approach that I will focus on takes as a point of departure the individual organism, the individual person.

Homo Sapiens are highly gregarious mammals. Our great skill is in social life with our evolutionary triumph involving very complex adaptations to new social, economic and geographical situations. The whole issue of human social life can best be seen in a respectful manner as well as occasionally awestruck. Jacques Moneau, the French geneticist who won a Nobel prize for his work on DNA, wrote in a book "tous àtre vivante est aussi un fossil. Everything that lives is also a fossil." It is the fossil I would like to talk about.

Human cultures always seek to distinguish themselves from nature. Inevitably a judge, when sentencing a particularly miserable malefactor, will say, "You acted like an animal." There is that notion of the animal that lurks beneath the human, and we seek to repress that or to deny the salience or the vivacity of that animal form of life. This exists even in our terminology. To talk about biology becomes almost intrinsically either political or controversial. I am sure one can gain a degree in any of the social sciences in this country without having to take a single course on any animal other than Homo Sapiens.

Our notion of what constitutes social behavior in its most elaborate sense is highly focused on Homo Sapiens. This is perfectly understandable, but there may be reasons to go elsewhere to get some sense of the location of behavior and its motivation. My paper carries two basic themes. One is my focus on the function, cause or impact of violence on the reproductive system. I am going to use the function of Homo Sapiens in the context of the reproductive system.

As Darwin pointed out, the reproductive system essentially made us. We are the product, the end result, of an infinite series of matings that took place over millions of years and which produced that complex DNA molecule of which we are the fossilized remnants.

My other basic theme deals with irrationality. I will talk about another language, another form, another perspective, another means of rendition for which we hardly have any good vocabulary. That is why we can only understand certain things from music, films, plays, dances or paintings. But I am talking not about logic where an individual makes a series of logical, clear-cut and formal relationships between one stimulus and another, but rather about a peculiar sort of arrangement of stimuli that we can see as bio-logic.

The body is not a neutral instrument. It does not simply take stimuli and produce responses. It is not an empty black box. There is much going on in that black box. For example, the brain, which we customarily associate with logic, is swimming in a sea of neurotransmitters. There are countless things, some only discovered in the past five years, that are consistently shaping the manner in which the brain is able to act. We do not have a clue about the impact of some very low level phenomena on our behavior. For example, Richard Michael and Dorothy Sumpay at Emery University Medical School reported in a recent issue of the American Journal of Psychiatry that the battering of women increases in the summer. That would suggest that people either feel freer and easier in the summer, or there is more tension in the air because of the heat. Their hypo- thesis is that bodily heat itself may have an impact on the neurotransmitters which affect aggressive behavior. Since we know there is an annual cycle of violence, there might be something happening along these lines.

I am going to discuss briefly drugs and alcohol. A study in the June 3 issue of the New York Times reported that with 14,000 arrests, 60% were found to be using drugs generally and 25% were using drugs at the time of arrest. What is extraordinary is that 60% of the cases involved forgery committed by drug users. There is something very powerful about substances brought into the body because of the impact they have on the body. This includes the brain.

My earlier interest in this subject has to do with the explanation of gender. We know that sex and violence are very closely linked. Males are nine times more likely than females to commit homicide and to be the recipients of homicide. That is not accidental because the neurophysiology of violence is very closely related to the neurophysiology of sex. The circuits are so closely identified that often we cannot distinguish between them. It is understandable that provera which affects the endocrine system has been used to subdue bellicose males. It affects the basic wiring of the organism, the machinery and this non-neutral territory.

The relationship between sex and violence existed during the Paleolithic period when we were hunters and gatherers, when we had a certain amount of real danger in the universe, when we had real violence to deal with, when warfare or fighting was quite frequent. There were no police and none of the effective mechanisms that we have created over the past years. There was a relationship between sex and violence because sex could be the result of a successful act of violence. This was not necessarily over a female, but rather with respect to other men and with respect also to the whole hunting and gathering ecology. There are endless cases of males whose initiation ceremonies, such as the scalp myth of the American Indian, involved committing an act of violence before entering the world of manhood. This was also the world of reproduction.

We are currently in a phase of history in which the wealthiest and most productive communities are the least reproductive. For the first time, a species is not converting resources into offspring. It is a genuinely new period of human bio-history.

There is a long tradition in neurology of researching people who committed violence due to medical defects, physiological or neurophysiological defects. Frank Elliott of the University of Pennsylvania Medical School rejects Aristotle's distinction between mind and brain. He mentions a study of 286 cases of upper middle class Americans which investigates episodic discontrol. He found that of these cases which he collected over 11 years, 102 had involved some specific brain injury before the episode. Ninety-four percent of this entire population had had some neurological defect, either acquired or developmental. In another reference published by Dorothy Lewis, Professor of Psychiatry at the New York University Medical School, 9 out of 13 men and two women convicted of murder had severe apprehensible medical problems neurophysiologically. Essentially there is something wrong with them by the standards of normal neurophysiology.

I suggest that when somebody commits violence or homicide there may also be something inherently wrong with him. It appears that since the brain is the managerial organ of the body, it is the prime place for a problem to originate.

We can get a sense of what happens when we watch the effects of drugs and alcohol on the brain. It is widely known that approximately 55% of car accidents occur during or after the use of alcohol, and we know that alcohol incites fighting. We also know that from 60% - 80% of wife abuse cases are associated with alcohol use. There is something about alcohol that reduces control over our behavior. These are controls which directly affect the brain, and they are imports into the body which can cause the body to act abnormally.

A most interesting finding was that 60% of forgers use drugs as part of their life experience. Forgery is certainly one of the most logical of crimes. The individual has to have a real sense of relationship between means and ends, has to have a distribution pattern such as accomplices, has to be able to run a Gestetner machine and has to be able to do all things that are appropriate for a good forgery.

Drugs mimic what we now begin to realize are natural opiates in the brain. Morphine replicates the endorphins which are naturally secreted by the body. We produce these substances and have receptors for them and what many of these medically useful and illegal drugs do is mimic that natural pattern. In a curious sense, what we are doing with chemistry is enhancing the capacity of the brain to have certain responses, but we do not any longer depend on our own production of these substances. We can buy them. We can import them into the body, and that is why we get addicted.

The brain goes wild because all the receptors are working overtime, and the rest of the body follows suit. People enter a treacherous state of complete loyalty to a chemical substance. I am pointing out that crime, an analogue of violence, seems to be associated very frequently with alcohol and drug use. There is a possibility that much of this behavior is the result of some disruption in the body. We must then question our abilities medically in anticipating the existence of violence and dealing with the consequences of it. People today are more aware of their behavior in a way that is unprecedented in North America.

That may make it easier for us to look with some respect and sympathy at those people who have disrupted their own bodies by importing these substances, and it may allow us to help them without being so critical. We cannot be blind to the fact that they are experiencing an advanced form of cellular disrepair.

One of the most useful contributions to modern biology has been the concept of reproductive strategy. Adam Smith, one of the protagonists of the study of productive strategy, has talked about how individuals economically were able to calculate marginal advantages and marginal costs. Everybody was a small firm assessing the implications of all his behavior in a very sophisticated manner. In biology, animals have reproductive strategies although they do not have the calculators nor the know-how. But they do it. I will explain certain ways in which this happens. For example, take the langur monkey in India. There is a characteristic pattern among the langurs in which the dominant male has sexual access to the females, and he controls the community. There is only one male who is an adult in the community. Once a male is deposed, a new male arrives and very quickly kills the suckling young that are already in the community. There are two implications here. One is that they are not using resources, but the other is that after suckling the female starts cycling again. As long as she is lactating she will not go through ovulation and hence will not be able to reproduce his offspring. This is not something we can identify with rationally.

This was astonishing when first discovered by a man named Bruce. The Bruce Effect in rodents is if a pregnant mouse is brought into physical contact with a male other than the one she was fertilized by, she will spontaneously abort. The same pattern has been found in Mustangs. There is a remarkable kind of reproductive strategy or pattern which tends to affect the genetic flow of a particular community.

Now let me discuss humans for a second. It is customary when the police come to investigate an abuse, the father is implicated although often the culprit is the stepfather. This was essentially first discovered and effectively refined by Martin Daley and Margot Wilson at McMaster University. In a study of 88,000 cases, they made a distinction between abused children and neglected children. Neglected children tended to be associated with low economic status. The greater association for abused children was with family composition, natural parents versus step-parents, rather than with economic levels.

This is again a fundamentally important movement from a productive system to a reproductive system. The wicked stepmother is really the wicked stepfather in this context, and the danger must be made known. The stepfather is in a particularly volatile situation particularly when the children are under four years of age.

After the age of four, the volatility and the danger decrease for the offspring. With a new boyfriend or stepfather, statistically speaking a child is at risk. Most people carry on loving relationships with their stepchildren, and it works fine. I am really talking about the exceptions here.

In conclusion, there are things that are happening in the reproductive system that may have some impact for the criminal justice system in broad terms. I refer to the considerable decline in the reproductive rate of this community and the considerable increase in the breakdown of the traditional family structure.

Single, unmarried males without children are not actively involved in fathering and are among the most volatile categories in terms of criminal justice. These men do not have intellectual defects but are functionally or socially not in the reproductive system in the way that other males are. What we are beginning to see, because of the low birthrate and the fact that females can now control the reproductive process through contraception, males are alienated to a certain degree from the means of reproduction. I see an equivalent problem with people who are reproductively unemployed because not only has the male function been completely changed, but also for the first time in biological history one sex can control the destiny of the reproductive system.

This is again totally new, and only since 1963 to 1965 when the pill became available did females have that option. Now females have that option and are exercising it. One consequence by definition is that males have less access to this system simply because females have more. We are entering a new kind of reproductive demography. This demography in particular will affect younger males, relatively unattached, who find that one form of either self expression or activity may be to conduct acts of considerable violence.

The new landscape then in terms of prevention has to deal not only with productive equity, but also with reproductive systems. We may have created a community in which people are reproductively unemployed, and we do not have the faintest idea what the long-range consequences of that situation may be.

PERSPECTIVES ON THE CAUSES OF VIOLENCE: THE SOCIO-POLITICAL PERSPECTIVE

Edgar Z. Friedenberg
Dalhousie University

Violence is not a major feature of Canadian society, but Canadians perceive it to be a serious and growing problem. Their anxiety leads to further constraints on behavior in a society already over-controlled.

There are two major assumptions about violence in contemporary Canadian society which differ from conventional wisdom.

The first of these assumptions is that violence is immoral because it violates its victims. Violation need not be a physical act nor even an overtly aggressive act at all. These acts are intentional, but they are not regarded as violent in our culture. Donald Marshall, falsely imprisoned throughout his youth for the murder of his best friend, is the product of a series of remarkable irregularities in police procedure. He was also physically abused while in custody, but that is a separate offence.

My second assumption deals with how the State is the most significant source of violence in the world. The violence is often physical of the most brutal kind, torture, bombing, burning villages. One century ago, Max Weber defined the State as being a monopoly with a legitimate use of violence.

Today we would question use of the word legitimate. Bombing raids and invasions against friendly states are not legitimate. Covert actions to destabilize them and unlawful acts by public authorities are also not legitimate. They are just plain acts of brutal violence. The State has become a common criminal, terrorist among terrorists. I see no reason to defend this evil monopoly.

It may be argued that in Canada, the State is hardly a major source of violence. This is not Sri Lanka, South Africa, Poland or El Salvador. Our conviction that Canadian authorities seldom indulge in violence against their subjects remains valid only as long as we continue to define violence as physical abuse. It is not completely valid.

Canadian authorities are by world standards seldom physically abusive. Violence committed by the State is still the most threatening of all violations as the victim is essentially defenseless and powerless. The courts are reluctant to find the administration of justice brought into disrepute by its own minions.

Our current obsession with violence both conceals and expresses a much more valid source of anxiety. What worries so many people is the loss of authority in social institutions, the home, the courts, the church and the police. This is happening, and it is making a big difference in the way people live.

Thomas Hobbes would not have liked it at all. He was rightfully convinced that order is a precondition to freedom. He was also convinced that, given the choice, most people would prefer order to freedom. He was also convinced that the State was at least a dependable source of order and therefore essential as the guarantor of whatever freedom circumstances might permit.

It is surely evident today that the State has become the source not only of violence, but also of the worst disorder. The government of South Africa could not control the violence of its own police even if it tried. It is not trying very hard. We blindly accept the proposition that real governmental reform is impossible in Haiti, Central America or in the Philippines because the military would not stand for it.

The governments of the United States and the Soviet Union systematically sabotage the efforts of their client states to rid themselves of murderous regimes. The government of the United States proclaims and exercises its right to support the overthrow by force and violence of any government threatening its own national security. The government that imposes the greatest threat to American national security, and everybody else's, is its own.

The government of Canada moves unobtrusively as a good neighbor should. The State in 1986 is no reliable source of public order. This makes it less than evident that a good Canadian is eager to oppose violence and support law and order. As legitimacy declines, challenges to it become more frequent and more severe, but they also become more difficult to assess.

Overt acts of physical aggression committed by private individuals individuals acting without authority can be serious. But there are many possible offences in contemporary Canadian life more threatening than conventional violence.

There are many common grievances more dreadful than the prospect of an encounter with some ruffian. Hamlet is useful in illuminating what violence is and how to respond to it. He never assumed that the State could be trusted to serve as a defender of peace and justice. The fact that it could not was the very heart of its difficulties, and he never assumed that the world was a safe haven for himself or for anybody else. To Shakespeare, violence was merely what powerful people used to achieve their ambitions.

Politically, Shakespeare was conservative and maintained a consistent preference for legitimate and wisely exercised authority. Most of his plays deal with abuse by inept or corrupt officials. He was never skeptical nor cynical about the need to accept established authority to maintain social order. He also knew that power was gained, and authority maintained, by violence. Once plucked from the barrel of the gun, all power assumes a patina of respectability if you can keep it. Shakespeare, a prudent student of the dynamics of dynasty, could draw his case material from the Plantagenets and tell sad tales about the death of kings. To condemn Brutus, MacBeth and Othello as murderers, we ignore the tragic flaw that destroyed each of these very different men. It diverts attention from the deeper meaning of who they were and why they did what they did.

Thinking seriously about the nature of evil, we cannot allow ourselves to be squeamish. There is reason to assume that physically destructive and intentional acts by unauthorized personnel constitute a uniquely serious social evil.

If we accept the pretensions of the modern liberal democratic state which embody the will of the people and express their consent to be governed, we legitimate its monopoly of violence. We make those who breach that monopoly enemies of the people. If we accept these pretensions, we have a right to be concerned because private violence seems to be increasing. There are no such things as uniform crime statistics. The threshold of perception at which a specific act becomes pre-perceived as criminal is too influenced by political factors.

When sociologists turn their attention to the reported increase in violent crime against the elderly in New York City, they find it to be an artifact. It is attributable to an increase in police vigilance in response to media coverage of horrifying cases. Many more incidents are reported and publicized by law enforcement officials intent on proving they were there to serve and protect. This leads to more media attention and reported incidents and establishes a vicious spiral that leaves senior citizens fearful of the streets.

Sometimes an increase in violence represents an improvement in the status of victims who could previously have been assaulted or murdered without becoming a statistic. The increase may be real, but it is limiting in that it represents the beginning of the end of a particular kind of victimization. This is what seems to have happened in the lynching of Blacks in the southern United States 50 or 60 years ago. It is also involved in current domestic violence against women and children as their assailants indignantly get in their last licks.

Identifying a social group as a prospective victim of violence, is a sign of progress. If there has been, as Amnesty International is maintaining, an increase in the prevalence of torture, there has also been a corresponding decline in its legitimacy. The victim is as helpless as ever. If he survives, he is more likely to indict his tormentors, and they are more likely to find themselves ultimately in the dark. None of this can be much comfort to those who become victims of mindless or wanton violence. But the violence that preoccupies us is not wanton, mysterious or unpredictable. It might more properly be called random in the same sense that branding a movement of molecules in a fluid is random. You cannot predict which molecules are going to strike others, but you can certainly predict a pressure within the whole entire system. You can predict with total accuracy that turning up the heat or confining it more closely is not going to help.

The factors that contribute to the prevalence of conventional violence are hardly inscrutable. If you wanted to design a social system that would be prone to maximum internal strife, what would you build into it? You would build long-term structural unemployment in a context that makes self-esteem a function of affluence. It would be an economic system closing down entire towns and dealing savage blows to entire provinces and breaking up the communities.

We all know the recipe already. What we lack is the political will to change it. We continue to cling for fear of getting something worse. It is the fear that the history of social change, and especially revolutionary social change, is justified. There is a certain perspective to be gained by recognizing how little of our anxiety about violence results from any principal objection to violence as such. It expresses our concern about whether our world is becoming increasingly violent. The distribution of violence throughout that world is certainly changing, and violence itself is taking on unaccustomed forms.

If we are to live together with less fear and greater mutual trust, we must come to understand the relationship between violence, power and order that prevail in every society and respond to them with greater candor. We must guard against mistaking the defence of privilege and tyranny for precautions against violence. As we see our cities saturated with riot police and our freedom of movement abridged over and over again, we must wonder what level of protection is appropriate. I wish we could be guided by a revised Hippocratic Oath, "Thou shalt not kill, but need not strive officiously to keep alive." We cannot be blind. We submit to a great deal of coercion in the interests of security.

We tend to proceed on the assumption that greater security for one means greater security for all. Sometimes it does, but often it does not. Violence is the fundamental issue in any political system. It would be constructive to confront it without hypocrisy.

PERSPECTIVES ON THE CAUSES OF VIOLENCE: THE SOCIO-LEGAL PERSPECTIVE

Hans Mohr
Church Council on Justice and Corrections

Our mainstream socio-legal perspective is grounded in the same views as the socio-biological and socio-political ones. Our socio-biological views are mainly grounded in a theory of evolution, a theory of competition and selection which elevates violence to a natural principle. Our socio-political views have moved from consensus to conflict with violence as the main arbiter. The basis of the modern concept of law has long been recognized as the threat to inflict evil on those who will not obey. These views cannot be expected to yield solutions for our concerns about violence.

The concept of cause has a very limited meaning when applied to a phenomenon such as violence. Violence is defined by undue application of force and undue intrusion on some form of integrity, value judgments. This paper explores the formation of such judgments which are mainly represented by what we call social science and legal doctrine. It will try to establish that causes and cure are of the same mold feeding a cycle of violence.

The widespread concern about violence in Canada at this time is not so much a matter of actuality, but rather it is a matter of deep uncertainty about the nature and control of aggression internationally, nationally and in the sphere of intimate relations. This concern is valid because if it is not addressed, it will bring about what is now mainly feared. The paper will examine those facets of our major traditions which have indeed given grounds and reasons for non-violence, recognizing our propensity for aggression and our lust for power.

The concerns are serious. "It was the view of the [John Howard] Society that the fear of violence in Canada was generating increased attention to the phenomenon of violence which in turn was causing yet more fear". This cycle of fear has an effect on the type of programs which develop and has an effect upon legislation of recent years. The daily dose of media reports, an increasing number of special studies and pronouncements and the increasing urgency of calls for strong measures against violence on the home front as well as in national and international relations make the point. Many of these measures are as violent as the phenomena they are supposed to combat, and they are part of the same mold. What tends to differ are the justifications.

This paper is supposed to add to other views a socio-legal perspective. It cannot do this without reference to the other views and the values they express. What we call legal is a specific form of expression of societal values. The paper will argue that legal measures and their justifications, although normative rather than empirical, are now based on the same rationale as other sciences which purport to tell us not only how we live, but also how we ought to live. Like the other sciences which so deeply determine our public and private views, legal concepts, institutions and methods are part of the cycle of violence rather than a response to it. The paper will further argue that the base assumptions of modern science and modern law are grounded in violence, that they are largely the cause of our concerns and not an answer to them, and that we have to turn to other forms of knowledge and other understandings of justice to come to terms with evil.

Violence, in whatever form we may see it, has become a dominant and dominating theme of the perennial concern about good and evil. The discourse, however, is mainly a discourse of evil in which the good is seen as the absence of evil. The official answers we arrive at are those of repression. All moral traditions have an understanding not only of the primordial character of evil and disorder, but also of the good and the meaning of peace. These are not residual categories, but accomplishments of truth, justice and love.

The very word violence has consistently carried two connotations. One connotation is the undue application of force, (1. vis, violentia); the other, the undue exploitation of some form of integrity such as misuse, ripoff and rape (fr. viol). We do not get a notion of violence from the application of force or the exercise of power alone, not even from exploitation because we may also exploit opportunities. Even these neutral words have come under suspicion as has everything else that claims to be value-neutral. For some, an expression such as Armed Forces does not yet raise the spectra of violence; for others, it does. That one man's terrorist is another man's hero is only denied by those whose own integrity is threatened. Although assault is defined in law as the application of even minimal force (touching) without consent (the expression of integrity), there are many exceptions to this standard such as disciplining children and arresting persons. The point is that violence is not defined by acts but by value judgments. To arrive at a socio-legal perspective, we thus have to examine the values on which our social and legal theories are built and determine our public judgments.

The original title of Konrad Lorenz's book on Aggression is The Evil So-Called (Das Sogenannte Bose). As a natural scientist, an ethologist, his observations tell him that aggression serves a purpose, the maintenance and evolution of a species. In this we can find the basis for the assumptions which inform almost all of our mainstream theories from the biological to the political. Good is what is good for us. Who us is, especially in the human context, is generally ignored. For Lorenz, Nature provides aggression as well as inhibition, and although he recognizes that Man has transcended Nature mainly by technology and has become dangerously self-destructive, he ends with an Avowal of Optimism to trust the truth of Nature. "I might even say that I regard it as inevitable, provided the human species does not commit suicide in the near future, as it well may. Otherwise it is quite predictable that the simple truths concerning the biology of mankind and the laws governing its behaviour will sooner or later become generally accepted public property..." Not only is it a curious proviso for optimism that we may well commit suicide, but one is also shaken by the naivety of the trust in the truth of science which he does not recognize has already become public property and has made possible the means of wanton destruction.

Lionel Tiger, after having examined the nature of human groups and their hierarchies, devoted a whole book to optimism which he subtitled The Biology of Hope. It turns out not to be a biology although it uses biological metaphors, not even an anthropology as we understand this word today, but the quest for a mythology which could make sense of the human experience.

Strictly on the biological level there is no basis for a concept of violence nor of hope although once armed with higher order interpretations, we can see all kinds of violence in Nature. It all depends. The cat seems to have a great deal of fun with the mouse before eating it; the mouse, less so. Since we are more partial to cats than to mice, we are not inclined to interpret their gruesome game as violence or sadism. We tend to be less neutral when the cat goes after a bird we like. And we abandon natural theory altogether when the neighbour's cat goes after our own. We no longer speak of natural selection, the survival of the fittest and evolution in this case. We aim a kick at the neighbour's cat which is sure to incense the neighbour.

The making of scientific theories and especially their use is not that much different from this account. Our major biological theory is the theory of evolution, evolution by competition. Shortly after Darwin and on the basis of a similar set of observations, Kropotkin offered a theory of co-operation in Nature. Darwin has become a household word and is taught to innocent children. Kropotkin has not, and we only slowly begin to develop a notion of ecology. Racial theories may be out of favour now, at least in some circles, but they are entirely compatible with a theory of progress from lower to higher. It is an empirical fact that white Western Man has unleashed the secrets of the atom, and the black African has not. Surely that should give him some rungs on the evolutionary ladder.

Stark evolutionary notions, have been consistently mitigated by notions of adaptation. But even there we tend to discover a bit late the inherent violence of the procedures we are sold. The record of biological interventions to achieve adaptive behaviour is now well established.

I have made these forays into biological views and their social applications not to condemn them but to bring before us what we ought to know by now. Modern science cannot distinguish between good and evil, knows nothing about the integrity of human beings and of what is due or undue. It is indeed value-free, but its application is not. This is not only true for the physical and biological sciences and their technology, but also for the social and political sciences to the extent to which they share the same assumptions, the same rationality and the same will to power and control. It also is true for modern law which too has claimed value-neutrality, as paradoxical as this may be.

Whether law is seen and experienced as order or as violence depends, as in science and technology, very much on where one stands, who one is and what power and legitimization one has at hand. We are still adding order to law to arrive at our ritual formula of law and order. Although we generally tend to treat them synonymously, the difference was quite clear to those who fashioned the modern understanding of law.

John Austin, often referred to as the father of positive law, developed his major work at about the same time as August Comtes, the father of positive social science. For Comtes the only legitimate authority was science; for Austin, the sovereign state.

Comtes says that we think it to be impertinent if anybody claimed to have knowledge of physics or astronomy without having studied those sciences. Thus, social knowledge as a matter for experts is legal doctrine. All Comtes grants to members of a society is desire, but they can have no legitimate opinion about its fulfillment unless they are scientists. Austin states the same basis for law which for him is predominantly a command.

And although desire can be assumed to be distributed by Nature and circumstance, command and the correlative duty to obey are clearly not. Laws and other commands are said to proceed from superiors and to bind and oblige inferiors. He is quite candid in saying that superiority is not defined by precedence or excellence, but that "the term superior defines might." So, right is might. The purpose of law is to work out the principles and the generality of rules, and the duty of its agents is to enforce them in individual cases. This is what has come to be known as the rule of law, and its basis is the threat of punishment even though Austin did not like the term punishment because it lacked generality. Since command is the essence of law, it is based on the authority to inflict evil. This alone distinguishes law from other rule-making activities. And it alone has the privilege of violence. Doing good became the domain of the Comtesian experts.

I have used Comtes and Austin not only because they have shaped our basic assumptions of what is social and what is legal, not only because they express them more clearly and with greater candour than subsequent mystifications allow, but also because they were still aware of what their project and the project of their time was. It was to extricate us from the mythical- religious-irrational conceptions of morality and justice. Comtes propagated a religion of rationality.

Positive law has, for good reason, consistently tried to separate law from morals but never conclusively. The last great law and morality debate following the Wolfenden Report said that at least some areas of morality ought not to be the business of the law. Lord Devlin answered this concern with The Enforcement of Morals. There is no longer an equivalent debate following the Badgely and Fraser Reports. Although Fraser still recognizes and agonizes over some limits to law, Badgely does not seem to have any such compunction. The experts will do what the law cannot because the law will enforce their opinions.

Comtes still called his final major work Systeme de Politique Positif ou Traite de Sociologie Instituant la Religion de l'Humanite. Positive politics as the religion of humanity is a combination from which both science and law have freed themselves. It is a humanism only for those who take their ideology for granted, and are prepared to legitimize their violence on those grounds. This is very visible on the international plane and less visible in the national sphere, especially in a country like Canada which has no real conflict of ideologies and which has been largely invisible in the context of intimate relations.

What we call the Enlightment has replaced religion and morality by science and legality, the perennial signs of a waning religion that can no longer uphold a moral order, only enforce it. We say that research has shown when we want to defend a value. Whenever we want to make it stick we say that there ought to be a law. We have redefined God as the State who will take care of us from cradle to grave and punish us when we misbehave. We have recast the human being as the individual who can only be understood as a scientific subject and be controlled as a legal person. All this demystification turns out to be a deification of instrumental rationality, of means without ends. And it is clear by now that violence has not decreased. This century, if it is not the last, will stand as yet another symbol of unmitigated violence.

Every tradition of any depth has accepted violence as a primordial fact. Every tradition has fashioned a response to it. It is the response which makes visible what we mean by human. In the major traditions which have formed the Western mind, the Greeks have given us a core concept of measure and truth (althea); the Hebrews, a core concept of justice (tsedek) and peace (shalom); Christianity, a core concept of love (caritas). We recognize these mainly today in their modern edition of science, law and welfare. This edition may have gained power but lost a sense a signification. To declare violence as senseless because we cannot face its truth, to judge it without asking what it signifies and to excuse it as a reaction or a mistake are ways of hiding rather than disclosure. They not only hide the primordial violence which the Greeks have signified as tragedy, the Hebrews as fear of the Lord and the Christians in the cross, but also the secondary violence of our response. It is more pervasive today although without a context of meaning. Yet we find violence immensely exciting and attractive as long as it is confined to page or screen, happens far away and to other people and does not disclose our participation in it. The greatest anguish of victims of violence and those close to them is the discovery that they are capable of the same murderous feelings the offender has expressed. Neither scientific insights nor legal procedures, nor welfare measures, nor all the tricks we have in our socio- legal bag are likely to even touch these feelings. These manoeuvres are the defenses of strangers who want to see a precarious abstract order restored and yesterday's news story forgotten. It leaves a residue of unease and too many unanswered questions.

Our goal focuses on helping all Canadians to understand the nature of violence and dangerous behaviour and to help us to cope as a society with the phenomenon. So far, the phenomenon has been delegated mainly to social and legal experts. This paper has attempted to show that the sciences and the law these experts depend on is itself deeply implicated in violence. There must surely be other values in Canadian society which can be given visibility. The very concern about violence speaks of that.

We cannot change our social and legal institutions before we become aware of the values they reflect. We have to seriously consider that what happens in a society and between societies is not accidental or arbitrary. This holds true with the creation of perverse minds rather than with the inevitable outcome of perceptions we hold in us and between us. It is clearly false consciousness to complain about violence, sexual abuse and pornography while refusing to recognize their endemic status in scientific theories as well as in popular consumption. It will not do to be outraged about violation, about the play of power and powers, while maintaining a belief in the survival of the fittest, in the kind of production and reproduction in which the means are private and presumably controlled by the fittest and in a law which legitimizes and institutionalizes those beliefs. We cannot maintain our belief in a free market when few are free to make a living independent from established modes of production. There can also not be a sexual liberation without re-examining the social values formed by modes of reproduction. The law does attempt to limit obvious evil, but it does so in refusing to recognize that crimes are only occasions when a deeper evil becomes visible. Legal means are now largely means of repression, of the threat of greater evil. Law thus violates its own intrinsic mandate of laying out before us the reasons for the evil it is asked to judge.

One wonders how a society such as Canada has come to be restricted to a common source of values derived from science, law and politics in their narrowest meaning. Canada is not alone or even exceptional. This phenomenon can be seen in all developed societies, and it is generally associated with the vague term Modernism. By developing societies we mean a development in this direction. Where older value sources such as those embodied in religion, are still public rather than private, active rather than passive, they tend to become associated with law and politics and tend to do their bidding. Christian and Moslem mainly mean warring factions as do Protestant and Catholic and forms of Catholicism which support progressive or repressive regimes. Israel has become a national state. Closer to home, the moral majority which is neither moral nor a majority pushes for power in the legal and political arena. We have achieved all the worst scenarios that Hobbes has painted for us, the war of all against all consolidated in the Leviathan, the national State, the monster that threatens to kill us all. The God of our religious tradition truly appears to be dead as Nietzche has prophesied.

The humanistic tradition derived from the Greeks has not fared much better since its official rebirth in the Renaissance with the wisdom/knowledge of Rome. Its liberalism and tolerance, the main value claim of the rising middle classes, the liberation of the individual, the doubly negated emptiness which sees freedom in the disposing of values which bind us which sees these values only as limits and not as the core of our human destiny have finally been over-reached in Post-Modernism.

If we are indeed serious about rejecting violence as a means of meeting our human destiny. We have to seriously search for and address ways of non-violence. This is hardly possible as long as we maintain a conception of being in the world which in itself is based on violence. As long as we believe in and teach the kind of biology, behaviour science, sociology, political science and finally the kind of law we have, non-violence simply does not make any sense. The best we can do is to shift the legitimacy of violence from one group to another, from citizens to professions, from individuals to the state which in turn redistributes it. This is clearly visible in the circularity of what we call the criminal justice system.

Even a recovery of the deepest accomplishments of the traditions which formed the Western mind is in itself no longer credible after the Church blessing of weapons and humanistic performances in concentration camps. There are new beginnings. The struggle in biology is not between evolutionism and creationism but between an individualistic biology of competition and an ecology of interrelation. Even physics, the most atomistic of sciences is reconsidering its understandings. The pressure does not come from some humanistic piety but from the very real and visible effects of the exploitation of Nature derived from a theory of dominance and domination. This is not from biblical creed but from the kind of greed which converted the very word domination, namely householding, into overpowering. We also begin to speak of a human ecology which recognizes that a phenomenon such as violence is not just the attribute of a specific individual, but it is generated by forms of human interaction. A behaviourism which exhausts itself in the repression of individual expressions of violence without addressing its collective generation is at best the proverbial finger in the dike; at worst, additional violence.

Similar developments can be discerned in the social and political sciences and even in law. It is there that the tension between received notions and their critical evaluation produces the strongest tensions. It is also there that we have the greatest impasse because of the new recognition that social and legal knowledge does not exist outside of an ideology and value commitment. The impasse is not only visible in the competing interpretations of left and right, capitalism and Marxism, both materialisms which hide or distort their Judeo- Christian origins, but in a waning liberalism, a humanism of Greek descent. It is in the socio-legal field that the modern conception of science can be most clearly seen as deficient, and yet law and society are also the fields which are most deeply anchored in the text and texture of tradition. Attempts at overcoming this impasse can be seen in the efforts in giving ground to a new pluralism, in deconstruction which treats texts as a totality to be reinterpreted by hermetic means and in liberation and reconciliation theology. Institutional practices are still largely untouched by these efforts.

The Canadian Charter of Rights and Freedoms is a perfect example. It starts with a short preamble, "Whereas Canada is founded upon principles that recognize the supremacy of God and the rule of law." This is the first and last time God is mentioned, and we are left wondering what the principles are that recognize His supremacy although the supremacy of the rule of law is spelled out in some detail. The Charter then "...guarantees the rights and freedoms set out in it subject only to such reasonable limits prescribed by law as can be demonstrably justified in a free and democratic society." The fundamental freedoms which follow are in any case the kind of liberties traditionally associated with liberalism which let us think what we like as long as we do what the law tells us to do. Rights are expressed by democratic rights only in the absence of serious conflict. Mobility rights, excluding the needy, and legal rights which refer to principles of fundamental justice remain like God, ambiguous. Finally, in the expression of equality rights, the disjunction between fundamental principles of law and social reality becomes obvious. Subsection (1) insists that every individual be equal before and under the law, and subsection (2) recognizes that some are less equal than others, and the law should not stand in the way of attempts to improve their lot. The point here is not to praise or to damn the Charter, only to show that abstract concepts such as rights, liberty and equality which have at least a 200 year history of legal and political institutionalizing behind them, do little to assist us in the interpretation of social behaviour.

How would those principles that recognize the supremacy of the rule of law help us in dealing with them? They are clearly not free to engage in the alleged behaviour because it is proscribed by law. How is this law demonstrably justified in a free and democratic society? Not even incest has been a criminal offence in most common law jurisdictions until relatively recent times (England 1908) not because it was not seen as an evil, but because there were serious questions whether the criminal law was able to a deal with such behaviour.

There is little recognition left of the limits of law, particularly criminal law and what it can achieve in terms of social ordering. The presumption of innocence, so important for our legal process because it puts the onus of proof on the accuser and thus provides a measure of freedom from legal interference, has the opposite effect on police behaviour. This is evident especially with the behaviour of the ever increasing policing agents such as school counsellors, child welfare workers, public health officials and private ones too since they are under orders to report. By the time a case comes to court, there is hardly a social presumption of innocence left, and even an acquittal will socially amount to little more than not proven guilty. There is no reciprocal liability on the policing agents for the disorder they may create or enhance short of intended individual malice.

Are there no historical or contemporary examples of confessions and retractions of this kind made in the face of authorities concerned about our salvation or about the public good? The point here is not only just the possibility of tragic injustice but also the systemic and systematic imposition of an order upheld by the threat of violence. What has been exposed as an exaggerated fear of violence and victimization in Canada may well be the expression of a growing apprehension which realistically perceives the threat even though it misinterprets its nature. Scientists and practitioners, most of whom are paid by the State, must ask themselves to what extent they have been fostering this misinterpretation.

PERSPECTIVES ON THE CAUSES OF VIOLENCE: THE SOCIAL PSYCHOLOGICAL

Brendan Rule
University of Alberta

Both scholars and the public are concerned about interpreting declines in certain types of aggression. Psychologists have been studying for many years the factors that instigate aggression. Within social psychology there are a variety of accounts ranging from broad-based instinctual theories of aggression to those focusing on acquired drives, conditioned reflexes and, more recently, cognitive variables.

In 1939 the frustration/aggression hypothesis was proposed and was the major focus of socio-psychological research on aggression until 1960. Earlier notions from psychoanalytic theory carried the proposition that frustration, defined as the blocking of an ongoing goal-directed behavior, produces an instigation to aggression directed mainly toward injuring the person perceived to be the cause of the goal blocking.

This instigation to aggression was anger, a drive or force that energized aggression. In the early 1960s however, many leading scholars began to question and express dissatisfaction with the frustration/aggression formulation. These authors recognized anger as only a setting condition or a facilitator of aggression which required external stimulus events to prompt retaliation. The shift from an attention reduction model of aggression to one emphasizing the role of external factors led to two different theoretical perspectives. One was based on classical conditioning; the other, on instrumental conditioning. Berkowitz, one of the leading scholars, stressed the role of environmental stimuli which pulled the aggressive response rather than pushed it from within. He argued that highly aggressive cues or stimuli in the environment, such as seeing a gun in the holster of a policeman, elicited impulsive aggression. Albert Bandura, another leading theorist in the early '60s, deviated further from the frustration/aggression theory by rejecting frustration as a necessary condition for aggression and by introducing environmental and cognitive factors as important influences on aggressive behavior.

His emphasis was on observing aggressive models such as the media as major determinates of aggressive behavior. The focus on external stimulus conditions and the rejection of attention served as a background for an emerging general approach. This has now implicated physiological arousal and emotional states such as anger and cognition, the thoughts people have in expressing aggression.

Issues that have been addressed include experiencing anger, the influence on anger and aggression, exposure to additional sources of environmental stress and how this thwarting of frustration influences aggression. The common approach that underlies the current treatment of each of these issues deals with a person's cognitions or ideas which mediate the experience of physiological arousal or emotions which in turn affects the subsequent levels of anger displayed.

First I will review the learning models that focus on external situational conditions which determine the acquisition and the maintenance of aggressive responses. I will also discuss the role of internal factors such as anger, attitudes and cognitions as they affect aggression.

Finally, I will discuss the multi-determinate nature of aggression and the implications of these different positions where the control of aggression will be presented. In this paper, aggression and violence are used interchangeably and refer to actions intended to harm another person. Violence often denotes a greater intensity of harm. Many contemporary theories of aggression have placed emphasis on learning factors in producing aggression. People imitate what they see others do. They imitate the aggression seen either on film or in real life.

In his now classic work, Bandura demonstrates that people mimic aggressive behaviors. In controlled studies, children who watch aggressive characters on television are more likely to display aggression towards their playmates in natural settings than are children who view non-aggressive characters or shows. Similarly, angered young adults are more likely to be physically aggressive toward a stranger after they have seen a violent film. Presumeably, observing media violence reduces a person's inhibitions by showing how desirable or effective aggression can be. People also learn intricate skills. Observing live models and people in crowd situations and riots has also been shown to reduce inhibitions of the onlookers.

Viewing aggressive pornography increases the willingness of college men to express aggression towards women but not against men. Both anecdotal evidence and a considerable amount of laboratory research have documented how observation of violence influences the acquisition of aggressive responses. Studies done in Britain in 1958 and 1960 show that in many naturalistic studies the observation of television does not seem to have an impact on aggression.

Although imitation may reduce inhibitions and may push someone towards aggression, other conditions are important in influencing aggression. These other conditions may have more impact and contribute more to the display of aggression. Because aggression is multi-determined, the influence of any one factor may be obscured in natural settings. Potential media influence can be offset by factors such as reinforcement by parents or peers. It is not surprising then that many studies in natural settings which lack experimental control over extraneous factors may fail to show that exposure to media violence is not related to aggression.

Reinforcement is clearly a very potent determinant of aggression. It has been shown that if aggression is rewarded and approved, such reinforcement will increase the likelihood of aggression. Numerous studies have documented this. Approval by a parent, friend or a person nodding his head in agreement with an aggressive action can be a very powerful determinant of aggressive behavior. In various subcultures, aggression is praised.

In Canada we condone hockey violence. There are now hockey videos containing hours of taped fights. Yet it has been demonstrated that people are less likely to be aggressive if the cost outweighs the benefit. Cost refers to sanctions such as social disapproval. These sanctions are against aggression and are reflected and expressed in our social norms. People rarely hit their neighbor's child although they may hit their own.

Sanctions help to prevent violence. The magnitude of the punishment or the probability of being caught show that the cost will outweigh the benefit. Unfortunately, in many family abuse situations, the private nature of the family reduces such social control. This raises the effects of physical punishment. This is a cost in reducing aggression. What about the effects of physical punishment as a parental disciplinary technique? It turns out that the threat of physical punishment diminishes aggression only under highly specific circumstances. It will reduce aggression only when it is immediate.

Physical punishment as a disciplinary technique not only does not suppress aggression, but it also usually increases it. There are many reasons why physical punishment increases aggression. Punishment is an aggressive model. Punishment supports the idea that retaliation is accepted. It establishes and maintains the "eye for an eye" norm. The evidence supporting these ideas comes from many laboratory and field observational studies.

In summary, the social learning perspective has allowed a greater understanding of the external conditions that promote violence. Outside the laboratory experiments, there is evidence that violence begets violence. Children of violent parents are more likely to attack their siblings. Lack of punishment teaches them that aggression is an effective response.

The second major contributing set of factors are internal conditions that promote the expression of aggression. These include attitudes, cognition and emotions such as anger. People learn from a variety of sources such as the media that violence is an acceptable way of life. Television, books and newspapers show violence as a way of solving problems and achieving goals. Much of this violence is justified; police are praised, and the good guys win. But such justified aggression actually increases the likelihood of aggression. The goal of the broadcasters, to show a positive moral base, is non- existent.

It is clear too that society's norms favor aggression in a variety of other ways. Not only do people observe violence on television, but they also learn from friends and family that there are positive norms for expressing aggression. It has been said by some writers in the area of family abuse that a marriage license is a hitting license. We know that people talk about sparing the rod and spoiling the child. We also hear that it is fine to be aggressive to keep one's wife in line. Interviews with concerned people show the strength and the prevalence of such norms in contemporary society.

In a laboratory experiment where an aggressive sexual film was shown, the men believed that women enjoyed being overpowered by them. Viewing aggressive pornography strengthens the myth that women enjoy rape. In general, people learn that aggression is acceptable in a wide variety of circumstances. If people hold these beliefs, they are more likely to express aggression in both its milder and more extreme forms. They are also more likely to be tolerant of aggression in other people. In addition to acquiring attitudes that reflect acceptance of aggression, people gain ideas about what is normal in an aggressive sequence of events. In our current research, university students were asked to list 20 events, moods, feelings, thoughts and actions which occur in a typical act of aggression.

We also asked them to do the same thing for marital disputes and parent/child aggression. People are remarkably consistent in the scenarios that they describe although each type of aggression differs in minor ways. The descriptions for a typical act of aggression seem to reflect a street fight. The marital dispute focuses on anger and interactive verbal and physical aggression between spouses, and the parent/child aggression reflects punishment. The terminology differs, but the elements described are very uniform. The pattern involves frustration, anger, emotional expression, verbal and physical aggression.

What is striking about our descriptions is how uniform they are with both men and women. Whether people learn these scenarios for what is normative about aggression from the media or from their own experiences, it is clear that people hold a very consistent unified view about what normally occurs in aggression. In fact, much of this data shows us that the public, the ordinary person on the street, seems to have a very clear idea about what aggression is.

We are studying this because we are interested in looking at how people's conceptions of aggression affect their interpretations after viewing television or after reading news accounts. Our view is that their memories are likely to influence their own behaviors in actual aggressive encounters.

Finally, a wide variety of stressful conditions instigate aggression. Despite earlier emphasis on frustration, our research shows that frustration does not produce as general an effect on aggression as was originally proposed, and that is partly why some of the theorists in the 1960s began rejecting the frustration/aggression hypothesis.

We have shown that frustration increases aggression under two conditions. The first is primarily when a person perceives the frustration as arbitrary or intentional. If people are frustrated and are blocked by someone else in obtaining a goal, they do not become angry and do not express aggression if they realize it was an accident. The problem arises when people perceive that somebody else was deliberately frustrating them. The second condition is when strong and persistent frustration instigates aggression. In the area of family abuse, it has been documented that poverty is associated with abuse. This relation is correlative but may be compounded by other factors. It is plausible that the extent of the frustration induced by poverty contributes to the display of aggression.

Emotions and generalized arousal may be induced by a variety of sources other than frustration and insult. Extreme arousal can be experienced through vigorous exercise, stimulating drugs, loud noise, excessively hot temperatures or exposure to erotic materials. These sources of arousal may contribute to the development or the expression of aggression. In our own work we have suggested that general arousal or general emotions may trigger aggression if aggression is the dominant response in the situation or if the arousal experienced is labelled as anger.

If a person is exposed to adverse noise in the company of someone he does not like, he or she is more likely to be more hostile and/or aggressive with that person. If a person is mildly insulted while engaging in strenuous exercise, he might label his arousal as anger and be more aggressive. The research in this area shows overall a complex pattern of results and clearly shows that conclusions have to be limited by certain conditions. It should be obvious by now that we view aggression and violence as multi-determined. There is no single instigator of aggression. External factors such as weapons or exposure to violent films can increase aggressive responses.

Reward or social approval for aggression increases the likelihood of aggressive responses. In addition, internal conditions such as one's attitudes, thoughts and the norms that sanction aggression promote the display of aggression and violence. Moreover, the degree of stress and frustration affects aggressive reaction.

Given this state of affairs, it should be quite clear that the control of aggression and violence is multi-faceted. Although it is multi-determined, we can still control it. Although family abuse has declined, there are still sufficient cases of aggression to work on.

There is no reason why we should treat social problems differently from medical problems. But what do the social/ psychological theories say about the control of violence? First, social learning analyses indicate that external control is effective. It is possible to teach people and instil in them the notion that aggression is wrong. Instead of promoting violence as an acceptable way of life, we can teach other ways of coping with problems and obtaining success.

Second, rewards can be given for alternative responses such as co-operative, sympathetic and helpful behaviors rather than for hostile and aggressive ones. For example, non-aggressive and altruistic models can be presented in the media, and reinforcement contingencies for expressing hostile aggression can be altered. This technique has been very successful in Gerry Patterson's Nursery School situation. The recent paper by Strauss indicates that the heightened awareness and the sanctions for family abuse may be factors that have affected the overall incidence of abuse.

Third, if people are aroused by a variety of factors in their environment, it is possible for them to learn that alternative responses to this arousal can occur. In other words, we could re-channel arousal and emotions. People can learn ways of dealing with their frustrations other than emotionally, and they can learn to attribute their frustration and insult to other things. People may adopt cognitive strategies and coping mechanisms to deal with their emotions. In some cultures it is clear that the reaction to anger and insult is not aggression; it is passivity.

Programs have recently been instituted in high schools to provide social training skills aimed particularly at delinquent adolescents or at highly aggressive adolescents. They have been shown films, and in these films they have been taught to reinterpret otherwise frustrating events and otherwise anger-inducing events so that they do not become angry. They have been taught that if they do experience anger, they can channel their responses in other directions.

Our work in the field of attribution clearly indicates that people, even highly aggressive people, can learn to make appropriate interpretations of what would otherwise be thought of as insulting and frustrating events in their lives. They can learn to be sensitive to the appropriate cues or stimuli in the environment and distinguish righteous indignation from unjustified anger.

Anger can be controlled through a variety of techniques. We have shown that there are a variety of factors that instigate aggression, with implications for control. One such factor is physical punishment at an individual level which does not reduce aggression except under very special conditions. Unless it is swift and strong, physical punishment backfires and is more likely to increase rather than decrease aggression. We have examined the catharsis effect. Since Aristotle, people have suggested that exposure to emotional material such as tragedy would purge the person of affect. They would come away limp, not be able to experience affect and consequently would not be aggressive. Psychologists have attempted to verify this idea by suggesting that people who observe and/or express aggression will relieve their tensions and subsequently be less likely to be aggressive if they are not otherwise provoked.

Research in general has not supported this idea. Usually the expression of aggression does not reduce aggression except in some laboratory studies under highly specific conditions. With the catharsis effect there is no support for the idea that expressing aggression reduces aggression. There are not widespread or general catharsis effects, and so it would be very ineffective to try to use observation of aggression or expression of aggression as a technique to reduce it. From our theories and research we have found a number of conditions that promote aggression, and we know that there are a number of conditions that can be imposed by parents, teachers and professionals to control aggression. We certainly know some of the techniques that are not effective.

Theories of aggression and social psychology have shown how cognitive and emotional factors contribute to aggression. Research and laboratory and field settings have shown which factors effect instrumental aggression, aggression aimed at obtaining a goal other than injury, and which effect angry aggression, characterized by the desire to hurt another individual.

Although we social psychologists recognize there may be temperamental factors that underlie aggression, our focus on learning and on cognitive variables offers hope for control of aggression. Such control occurs at the individual level as well as at the group level. Specific areas must be considered to see the range of the principles developed from our theories and research. Wife abuse, child abuse, sexual abuse and homicide are specific problems to which certain of our principles may be more applicable than others. The interplay and exchange of knowledge between practitioners and researchers in academic and applied settings is essential in finding solutions to problems such as aggression.

PART IV

UNDERSTANDING TYPES OF VIOLENCE

SEXUAL ASSAULT

SEXUAL ASSAULT

Vernon Quinsey
Institute Phillipe Pinel, Montreal

My paper covers two subjects. The first concerns rapists and child molesters. People who study sexual assault and obedience do not necessarily have inappropriate sexual interests and do not necessarily approve or condone the behavior they study.

I want to discuss rape from a variety of perspectives. The first is biology. From a biological perspective rape is reproductive behavior. Any reproductive behavior affects evolutionary history. The unit involved in evolution is the gene and not the person. We usually think of people as being selected for fitness and reproductive success. In actual fact, it is more frugal to think about the unit of selection or the unit that natural selection works on as being the gene. It is obvious from that perspective that an activity like rape has reproductive consequences. With men, differential reproductive success is achieved through coercive sexual activities. The point here is that the reproductive interests of males and females do not always coincide. They can be different from a genetic point of view. From a male point of view, a male can have an indefinite number of offspring, but the number of offspring a female can have is strictly limited.

This has profound consequences when one thinks about the types of sexual or reproductive strategies that males and females can employ to ensure that their offspring are going to be represented differentially in the next generation. I use strategy not in the sense that our ancestors ever thought of these things in a conscious way. I am talking about behavioral strategies or behaviors.

To exemplify this, I mention the Mexican scorpion flies. The males will exude an attractive chemical to females. Females will buzz in, and the males try to have an offering. They will have a large or small insect on a salivary mass. This is what they call a nuptial offering. The males gather these insects from spider webs and often get eaten themselves. The female is only interested if there is an offering. If the males are not successful, they attack the female. Their specially developed physical structures allow them to do this. You can see the evolutionary pressure here. This actual physical structure evolved to allow this behavior to occur.

Most males and females do not enjoy forced mating. We see from an evolutionary point of view that it is in the male's interest to revert to coercive mating strategy. Those males that do will survive differentially. Their offspring will survive differentially in the next generation. People are like scorpion flies, but from a biological point of view genetics operates in exactly the same way.

Coercible mating strategies are common in a variety of species. Mallards, for example, form pair bonds where both the male and female invest time and energy in the rearing of offspring. Under certain conditions there is coercible mating among mallards in which the females are severely and physically damaged. These kinds of behaviors are related to things such as overcrowding and to the dominant hierarchy of males and their partners. They have clear influences in terms of male reproductive success.

Turning to animals that are more closely related to us, we look at wild chimpanzees. We do see coercible mating strategies, but less frequently. In the chimpanzee social organization, males are highly territorial. They are hostile towards neighboring groups of chimpanzees which are related biologically. Females are in a territory. The males control the territory where they have achieved differential reproductive success.

If we look at human sexual behavior, we are struck by its diversity. Some elements in human sexual behavior are relatively invariable. One example is the forming of pair bonds in every society. This is something that both the male and female invest time and energy into and rear offspring. The male is relatively certain of biological paternity. This is characteristic of all societies.

With the male strategy, the way to reproductive success is to have genes differentially represented in the next generation. This can involve forming a pair bond and having sexual activities either of a coercible or a seductive nature.

From an evolutionary point of view, the only thing that is relevant in reproductive behavior is success. Success is defined by the percentage of genes represented in the next generation. That key phenomenon has to be related in some fundamental way to all human sexual behavior.

There is no social/biological theory of sexual behavior or coercible sexuality that has been worked out to date. From a biological point of view this genetic calculus has to be taken into account.

I turn now from a biological perspective to cross-cultural phenomena. There have been many studies of rape frequency in various cultures throughout the world. The most outstanding finding is the large variance in the frequency of sexual assault. There is a lot of variability. Most of the earlier literature has been of a case study/ anecdote type. It is very difficult to know what factors are associated with either a high or a low frequency of rape within a given society. More recently there have been systematic studies where people have surveyed large numbers of cultures and have tried to identify the predictors of the high frequencies of rape. There have been two surveys in particular. The surveys were conducted from very different points of view with similar results. We are confident with these findings.

The first study found that high frequencies of sexual assault were related to a variety of variables. One variable was the fact that when a man and woman marry, they live with the male's relatives.

Fraternal interest groups are groups of men related biologically who exert power in society. The existence of these fraternal interest groups was correlated with the frequency of sexual assault in a sample of these cultures. Another variable was feuding.

Another variable was punishment for sexual assault. Where severe punishment decreased, sexual assault increased. There was an interesting interaction in the data. Punishment severity was only relevant when there were no fraternal male interest groups. In other words, if fraternal interest groups existed, all the variants were cancelled.

The other study on this variety of cultures found a group of very similar variables related to sexual assault frequency. The practice of raiding other groups for wives was one of the variables. The largest correlation was with the degree of acceptance of interpersonal violence in the culture. Male ideology focuses on toughness where the males are warriors and are proud of it. There are frequent wars among neighboring groups. There is a lack of female power and a predominance of gender separation. Of all these variables, the one that captures most of the variants in sexual assault frequency is the degree of interpersonal violence in the society. Again we see this phenomenon where there are groups of men organized essentially for the application of force. There is much warlike behavior going on. Sexual assault frequency seems to correlate very highly with this set of variables.

Turning to industrialized societies in the West, we know that sexual assault and rape is a problem. The frequency appears to be rising. A large amount of sexual coercion cases reported in victimization studies is short of rape. Dating situations seem to include pressure to engage in sexual behavior.

Sociological studies of this phenomenon indicate that of all the rapes reported, about 16% result in conviction. The probability of reporting is affected by social class. People in a lower social class and ethnic communities are less likely to report, and there is less likely to be a report if the victim is related or has some relationship with the offender. These behaviors in the United States tend to be inter-racial. They differentially occur in the evenings and on weekends. There is evidence that this behavior is predatory in the sense that rapists will seek out an opportunity, a vulnerable person. The most beautiful study of this was the Toronto Transit Strike Study. When the strike was on, many people, particularly females, were hitch hiking. The number of rapes of females in automobiles went up by a factor of nine during the strike.

Interestingly enough, there was no increase in the overall number of rapes. There are therefore people who are essentially predatory and are looking for easy victims.

There are many differences between multiple and single offender sexual assaults or rapes. If we look at multiple offender rapes in comparison to rapes involving a single assailant, there is a sharper clustering on weekends and evenings. More often alcohol is involved. The offenders are younger. They are more likely to come from ethnic backgrounds, low socio-economic backgrounds. They are less likely to have previous histories of sexual assault or even other offenses involving personal violence. The victims are less often intimate. They are usually unknown to the assailants. The behavior is more likely to start in the streets. The victim will be contacted in the streets and taken elsewhere. There is greater force involved. These sexual assaults, perpetrated by groups of men, are quite different from sexual assaults perpetrated by single offenders both in the characteristics of the assault itself and the characteristics of the perpetrators. This is a different phenomenon. It is more a social phenomenon.

There is evidence of there being a great variability in rape rates over different places in Western societies. For example, Switzerland is low; the United States, high.

I am going to discuss now studies of ordinary men who are not known to be sexual assailants and variables that might be related to the propensity to commit a sexual assault. To understand this logic you have to remember that sexual assailants have to be recruited from some population of people. What groups are they likely to come from? Are there individual differences? Is there variability among ordinary men that would make them more or less likely to commit a sexual assault? The question must be raised as to whether punishment is a deterrent to this sort of thing. The people who do it tend not to be the kinds of people who have had much sexual experience. They are the kind of people who would endorse what are believed to be mistaken views about rape itself. They have some strange ideas about sexual assault. In the laboratory situation, these people are quite different from other men.

If a rape situation is described to these people, they show more arousal than people who do not endorse this kind of thing. This indicates there may be some sexual interest in coercive sexual activity. All this data and all things related to beliefs about rape show much variability among normal men.

We know that people identified as sexual assailants are differentially recruited from those people who have committed sexual crimes in general. They tend to commit more serious crimes. They are more likely to commit an offence against an unknown person. These are the kinds of things that influence victim reporting practices in prosecution.

There was an early study done on men who repeatedly committed sexual assaults. They were found to be quite different from rapists who had committed one offence. They had had more pre-puberty sex. They reported many problems with their families. The salient finding was that these men were the only people in the sample who reported interest in sadistic fantasy.

We know there is much variability among sexual offenders and rapists themselves. What is needed in this area is some sort of taxonomy of sexual offending so that we can see what kinds of individuals we are dealing with. They are not at all similar. For example, one type of sexual offender is a person who has engaged in a sexual murder. Sexual homicide is an extremely rare event. You are more likely to be hit by lightning than you are to be murdered in a sexual assault. The characteristics of these offenders are quite striking. People involved in this type of behavior tend to be introspective, withdrawn, have no previous criminal records, are loners and have marked interests in certain kinds of things such as anatomy textbooks, detective magazines, forensic medicine. They very often get involved in trades where they might be an undertaker's helper or a worker in a stockyard. They are seen as slightly effeminate. Many of these people have rehearsed their crimes before they actually commit them.

With sexual assailants, recidivism increases with the frequency of previous offending. This is a general rule in criminology and here as well. The probability of recidivism with rapists does not decline quickly with age as it does with property offenses. It is clear that some of these offenders are density offenders. They rape at high frequencies over long periods of time.

In the area of child molestation, I will begin with some anthropological work done in New Guinea. On the coast of New Guinea people live in small, marginal societies. The societies are marked by much gender antagonism. There is strict separation of the genders. Men live in secret societies. There is an emphasis on headhunting and warfare. About 15% of these societies are involved in ritualized homosexuality with young boys. This practice involves initiation and is a structured behavior. It is condoned.

In northeast New Guinea a boy, when he is seven years old, will be taken to the men's place, and the beginning of his initiation into the men's society begins. The belief is that this boy has to be fed semen orally. The boy enters this situation and phallates the older boys and men. This behavior continues until the boy becomes a teenager, and the roles reverse. This is a peculiar age-graded, asymmetrical behavior.

There are many beliefs concerning the significance of this kind of behavior. Although this obligatory homosexual behavior is actually prescribed, there is still an element of erotic attraction. It is well known that these boys are sexually or erotically attracted to these men in these secret societies. And apparently vice versa. It is a very interesting phenomenon. One of the things of interest is that some of these men are supposed to stop this behavior when they have children of their own. Some of them have marked difficulty in doing this. Boys are valued for their attractiveness and youthfulness. They are seen as being more attractive the younger they are. Women are not seen as attractive.

One of the mechanisms of interest here is that these are small ecologically marginal societies. The way you get a wife is through sister exchange. The sister exchange mechanism involves either equity or debt. You either have a sister to exchange or you do not. The feeling is that this ritualized homosexuality is a covenant or an agreement that keeps the sister exchange mechanism intact. The ideal inseminator is the boy's sister's husband. The rules of the society shape this behavior.

What I am writing here is very similar to the situation in ancient Greece where there was an interest in young boys. Boys were prized for their sexual attractiveness. The ages were older. They were interested in boys who were pubertal, yet unbearded. There was a warrior cult. There was low women status. The male warriors would become involved with these boys sexually and would tutor them.

Over time this kind of behavior, the sexual use of boys and later the sexual use of girls, became frowned upon. The penalty for sodomy in medieval Europe was burning. In medieval Rome, for example, there were brothels of boys and prostitution of young girls even though these behaviors were being investigated by the Inquisition and punished very heavily. Behaviors in different societies might change in frequency, but they continue.

In modern Western society these behaviors are crimes. They are viewed as illegal and often immoral. It becomes a question of explaining why these kinds of behaviors persist and what the characteristics are of people who engage in these behaviors. There are two things that are very important. One is a sort of failure of socialization on the part of some individuals. That is more important in terms of sexual assault such as rape than in terms of sexual assault of children. The other important variable is sexual interest in these kinds of activities. This involves people who engage in sadistic sexual activities, sadistic sexual fantasies. They masturbate thinking about them. Very often they are obsessed with them. People who have sex with young boys or girls are very often differentially sexually aroused by this category of person. They actually prefer children. The ideological and theoretical question is one of explaining how these preferences arise.

SEXUAL ASSAULT

Patty Begin
Department of Justice

Here in Canada the criminal law is legally extended to all jurisdictions. This precludes a controlled population for the purposes of establishing a comparison group. As literature has indicated, the inability to introduce a control group into the study has brought a number of shortcomings in measuring legal impact. Behavior discovered in the research process could appear to be the result of the law. It could also be due to circumstances or factors that have occurred independent of the law. There are a host of factors both non-legal and extra-legal that could influence or affect behaviors of victims of sexual assault, criminal justice personnel and offenders.

I do not think we can ignore the changing status of women and the advances made by them as well as the effect this has had on them in terms of being victims. Visibility and the heightened awareness have developed with respect to victims of crime in general and to female victims of crime in particular. In 1985 at the seventh United Nations Congress, the agenda dealt with female victims of crime. One of the topics was sexual assault.

Within the police force, there are sexual offence squads. These are groups of investigators whose sole job is to investigate complaints of sexual abuse and sexual assault. What has developed is an expertise in gathering evidence as well as in the whole investigation process. Within some Crown offices there are specific prosecutors who handle the prosecution of sexual offence cases. They deal with the victim from the preliminary hearings to the end and have developed an expertise with respect to interviewing and preparing the victim for trial.

Another factor that could have an impact on a victim's behavior is the establishment and expansion throughout Canada of sexual assault support centres.

There is a trend that has developed in the United States and the United Kingdom to increase the use of prisons in response to violent crime. These and other factors make it possible for behavior consistent with the sexual assault legislation to occur irrespective of the law reform.

I would like to mention the evaluation plan. The objectives of the evaluation research are fourfold. First I will describe how the law has been implemented and how it works in the various segments of the criminal justice system. Then I will assess the impact of the law on a victim's experiences, particularly his experiences with the criminal justice process. Third, I will attempt to assess the impact of the law on the criminal justice system in terms of added practices as well as on the effectiveness of repressing sexual assaults. Fourth, I will attempt to identify the unintended impact the law reform may have had. For example, shortly after the law was passed in Ottawa, two women were rendered witnesses. One was a victim of a sexual assault. She refused to lay charges. One of the arguments brought forth by the Crown in justifying the decision to compel her was the new law and the protection it was attempting to extend to victims and therefore their responsibility under the law.

I do not think it would be possible for us to assess the impact of the law in a straight statistical way. This is so because laws are very different. The definition has changed. The groups to whom legal protection is extended have changed. The penalty structure has changed, and the procedural rules and rules of evidence have also changed. I feel confident we will be able to assess what the legal impact has been by documenting quantitative information related to complaint and case characteristics, reporting, founding, charging, conviction rates and sentencing patterns. We will collect qualitative information relating to experiences, perceptions and attitudes. We will also collect a mixture of quantitative and qualitative information relating to the implementation of the law. Our intent is to gather both primary and secondary data. There would be a mix of quantitative and qualitative methods that would describe both the process as well as the outcome of the provisions of the law. I hope that by reaching as many data sources as possible we would enhance the validity of the study findings. We could then draw conclusions with respect to what the legal impact has been.

How the research has been organized is as follows. The major aspect is on the field research component. This will take place in six sites in Canada. These sites are Vancouver, Lethbridge, Winnipeg, Hamilton, Montreal and one jurisdiction in the Maritimes to be determined. These sites were chosen to reflect the regional characteristics of Canada. The terms of reference and the final decision on research sites were derived from a federal provincial cooperative effort. A research advisory committee in each of the jurisdictions was comprised of Crown, police and sexual assault workers.

The research will take place over a 10 month time frame. It will involve the following components. One will be court observation which will occur over eight months with a provision for follow-up of those incomplete cases commenced within the time frame. Trained observers will sit in both preliminary hearings as well as in sexual assault trials. They will record information on basic issues dealing with cross-examination and rules of evidence. In addition, they will collect all relevant contextual information regarding cases, charges, decisions, camera hearings and the trial outcome. The focus will be on cross-examination of the victim and the rules of evidence. In addition to court observation, we will also conduct a file review of criminal justice system files such as those of the police, the Crown and the courts. This involves a before and after data search respecting information on both rape as well as on sexual assault cases.

Although there was a variety of historical circumstances in the period leading up to the reform of the rape laws in Canada, there is no comprehensive systematic research program developed to collect baseline information from which to measure impact. This will be something we will be doing within the context of the evaluation research itself. The plan will be to collect information from the criminal justice records and from sexual assault centres which deal with the two years prior to passage of the law and three years after its implementation in Canada. We will conduct both structured and unstructured interviews and will use questionnaires. These will be administered to criminal justice system personnel, the Crown, the police, judges and defense attorneys. We will also interview sexual assault centre workers and victims. What we want to gather from these interviews and questionnaires is an understanding of the impact of the law. Wherever possible, we will attempt to assess the attitudes and perceptions of these people with law reform experience. There will also be more qualitative assessment of what was going on in the pre-law reform period and how these people feel about the impact this law has had.

The area on victims caused much reflection and thinking. We had a feasibility study done for us which addresses the practical as well as the ethical considerations. Victims of sexual assault were interviewed in an attempt to make contact and to assess their experiences. We interviewed those victims who would be identified during the court observation component of the field research. When their cases reached completion, contact was made with the victims either through the Crown office or through the police force. Victims were informed of the study and were asked if they would be willing to participate. We realized that on the basis of this we would only be interviewing victims who had reported the offence to the criminal justice system and had decided to talk to us. We would not have a randomly distributed sample of victims of sexual assault. Given the practical as well as the ethical concerns while attempting to make contact with victims, we decided this would be something we could live with. It would nonetheless contribute significantly to the study.

With respect to the non-reporting, we certainly hope we will be able to get a handle on that through the review of the Sexual Assault Centre files as well as through interviews with Sexual Assault Centre workers. We realize that if victims have chosen not to contact the Sexual Assault Centre, not to report to the police and not to have their cases go through the criminal justice system, we will not have access to those victims. It is a concern but nonetheless something we will live with.

In addition to the field research component, we will also be conducting a series of other studies. One will involve a time series analysis of uniform crime reporting data on indecent assault particularly indecent female assault such as rape. The three tiers of sexual assault covering a 15-year period will be covered. Basically what we are hoping to do is assess trends with respect to reporting and charging practices over that period. In the early 1970s, there were a few changes or amendments to the rape law. With the abolition of the rape offence and the introduction of the sexual assault law, we will hopefully get a sense of trends and perhaps be able to draw some conclusions with respect to impact. The interview data and the qualitative data will help us interpret these findings. We will also conduct a monitoring of court decisions.

This study will involve a socio-legal analysis of legal issues which have emerged in case law since the passage of the sexual assault legislation. The main focus of this study will be the impact of the Charter on case law decisions and on any established precedents which would have emerged. To date, there are not any established precedents under the new sexual assault legislation. There certainly are several pending both at the provincial and federal levels.

We will also do a number of smaller but important studies. One would involve an examination of the impact of the law on corrections as well as on parole. This would mainly look at population or offender characteristics and the possible changes in admission and types of persons admitted to correctional institutions. With respect to parole, because the laws is only three years old, we may in fact not find that there are too many people who have come before the parole board at this point. We will also do a study using Statistics Canada data to examine the incidents of murder that have occurred within the context of sexual assault. This will be through an examination of the data that the homicide program at the Centre for Justice Statistics is developing. It would indicate if there were other offenses being committed at the time the homicide occurred.

This evaluation will represent the first national sexual assault study to be done within the Canadian context. In reviewing the few evaluations that have been done to date on rape law reform in other jurisdictions such as in the United States and Australia, I feel this study represents the most comprehensive approach in assessing and evaluating the impact of the law reform.

PART V

UNDERSTANDING TYPES OF VIOLENCE

VIOLENCE IN CORRECTIONAL INSTITUTIONS

ASSAULT-TREATMENT FACILITIES

Ron Langevin
Clarke Institute of Psychiatry, Toronto

I have travelled extensively across the country looking at various facilities. Interestingly enough, in comparing maximum security hospitals with maximum security prisons, I found that the better prison facilities are better than many of the lesser maintained hospitals.

The thing that is most offensive particularly about Saskatoon is the perimeter security. There is a double link fence with all kinds of sensing devices for intervening, and there is a truck that drives around the outside. Armed guards travel around the perimeter of the fence. If anybody actually managed to get over, he would presumably be shot at. These are prisoners escaping, not patients escaping.

Many of the fine staff there do not like this mentality, but it is something they have to live with because it is a penitentiary. Inside, it is very modern. It is a very attractive, architecturally attractive building. There is a big distance between the building itself and the fence. If you did manage to escape from your ward and run for the fence, the difficulties you could face there would be huge. It is a circular arrangement with a central courtyard and a bell tower. Apparently they had some trouble with that tower because the lights on the top made it resemble a tall building.

On the trip across the country, I then moved from Saskatoon to a hospital setting in Edmonton. Of all the facilities I have visited, this was the best model. It is a new building, and the front door does not look like it belongs in a prison.

My feeling as I went around was that somebody will probably escape one day. There is nothing pre-selected about these people. They are not screening out the bad guys and sending them somewhere else.

One of the best ways of maintaining security in terms of weapons inside is to make sure anybody who goes through the security area passes the metal detector. The best way to get around it is to build the metal detector into the doorway so people have to go through that way. The front gate is all wired with electronics.

The most secure ward is very different from our secure ward at Oakridge. The rooms look like a college dorm. If a patient is thrashing around, he is put in a separate room. The general atmosphere resembles a hospital more than a prison cell.

There is a nursing station with a 360 degree view. It is basically for staff and is a bit more comfortable. This is something that Oakridge does not have. The attendant staff or line staff have nowhere they can go other than to the visitor's area for relaxing conversation.

The occupational therapy and teaching facilities are very extensive and in large rooms. There is a large gymnasium and swimming pool. This takes a lot of money. If you think about the criminals as patients, these facilities should be expected. Many other prisons have good facilities like this.

We also visited Abbotsford and the Riverview Hospital. Abbotsford is a regional treatment centre in the penitentiary system, and Riverview is a secure hospital. Although somewhat old, Riverview has a much better therapeutic atmosphere.

Broadmoor, the oldest of the maximum security hospitals in Britain, has an old world philosophy. They do not like people going around taking photographs.

Broadmoor was one of the earliest criminal lunatic asylums in Britain. It dates back many centuries. It was originally Bedlam, which was Bethlum or Bethlehem Hospital. The building, formerly a hospital for criminal lunatics, is now the Imperial War Museum. This hospital is very much like Oakridge which dates back to the last century. The staff consists of nurses. It is approximately one hour from London, but it is not so remote that it has some of the staffing problems that Oakridge has.

Britain went through the crisis of what to do with these people a good decade or two ago. There were reports like ours being made on a regular basis describing the place as being in terrible shape, overcrowded and mismanaged with patient abuse. Successive government reports recommended reducing the number of patients by building another facility and placing some of the patients who did not need to be there back into open hospitals again. We could see a number of parallels to what was going on at Oakridge. I visited it partly out of interest because I was in forensic work before I left Britain in 1976.

They are going through some substantial changes of the kind that we ought to be going through here. Not only have they reduced the number of patients by opening another large and very impressive maximum security hospital in the north of England, but they are planning to knock down large sections of Broadmoor in order to rebuild for a larger population.

There is a lot of reconstructive work going on. A lot of staff attitudes are having to change in a hurry, and there is a very exciting mood there. One of the impressive things was that they had a workshop laboratory where they were experimenting with new materials to construct safe rooms. One of them was made entirely of plastic so a very violent patient could not harm himself. There is a lot of experimental work going on, and I think our government could do very well to capitalize on this because the work is already being done.

One of the most famous inmates at Broadmoor was Daniel MacNaughton who tried to kill former prime minister of Britain Sir Robert Peel and shot and killed his secretary instead. He was found not guilty by insanity and was confined originally at Bethlum. He was then sent to Broadmoor when it opened in the middle of the 19th century. He eventually died there. These people remained for long periods, and originally they died there. There is a little graveyard in the grounds and there are many famous names on the tombstones.

At one time the hospital, which was built for 500 patients, had close to 900. It was desperately overcrowded. Broadmoor, unlike many of the other facilities including Oakridge, has a mixture of patients. They are separated by male and female wings. The female wing tends to look more homey.

Even at Broadmoor, they have extensive recreation rehabilitation workshops, and they do contract work there. They are close to a city of 9,000,000 people so that kind of contract work is easily found. There is a little store were patients can shop. When you think that this is one of the older hospitals in Britain, and you compare it to the facilities that we have here, I think it is really quite striking.

In financial terms, as we went around these places, we knew that one of things we wanted to recommend for Oakridge was that they should rebuild. In the British system, people were talking about $50,000,000 equivalent, and that was a few years ago. I recommended that if we had to rebuild Oakridge in Ontario, it would cost $100,000,000.

Broadmoor reduced its number of patients by building another facility at Park Lane in Liverpool. There are many advantages to starting from scratch like this. Renovating and changing a place that is well established, you find an enormous number of difficulties. When you are starting fresh, many of these problems can be resolved.

The other way the British tried to resolve the problem of overcrowding was to bolster the number of medium security places throughout the country. It took them a generation to start building these places, and even now they are not finished. We saw some excellent medium security facilities throughout the country.

It is worth mentioning money all the time because Ontario is not one of the poorest places in the world. Britain is certainly in financial difficulty, and they are having to pump central government funds to build these facilities. Something desperate would have otherwise happened. Here too we wait for something desperate to happen before things change substantially, before the amount of money that is really required is handed over. Often governments will provide you with the capital costs, but then the money dries up. These places cost enormous sums to establish and run.

The entrance to Park Lane looks like a fortress. The perimeter is very secure, but inside it too has a very different atmosphere altogether. The buildings are bright and modern. It has a very open atmosphere, and at the time that I was there they had 300 patients although it is built for 500. Their most secure ward is for the very violent patients. They are very secure rooms with little panels enabling them to turn off electricity and water.

Another advantage which they have is that they graded levels of security which again is characteristic of many of these facilities. Instead of just keeping people there for years, they actually plan for the patient's release. They were actually able to identify patients who could easily manage in a less secure setting, and they started to set them up in small apartments. Most of these patients welcome this idea. It is a very important part of their rehabilitation.

An important point to mention here is that with a large number of psychiatrists dealing with the severe mentally ill, you end up with a very chronic, burned-out population in this kind of hospital. In the medium security units, the people get better quickly. There is a high turnover rate.

There is a parallel system. Short-term patients tend to go to the medium secure units, but the people who are going to be incarcerated for longer tend to go to the hospitals. The special hospitals no longer think of those medium secure units necessarily as places to where their patients will go when they are well enough to be released. They started to have their own rehabilitation in part. Park Lane has an enormous rehabilitation program.

When I talked to colleagues in the United States who knew the maximum security hospital system, I selected various hospitals which I thought would have a representative population similar to our own in Ontario. Many states now have to upgrade or to rebuild facilities.

Chester Mental Health Centre is about two hours from St. Louis, Missouri, but it is actually in Illinois. It was rebuilt around 1976 and is on the banks of the Mississippi River. It is very much like Oakridge with a beautiful environment and pretty countryside, but it is a rural farming community. There are other institutions nearby from the Illinois State Penitentiary system. The Illinois State Penitentiary is an awful place.

The part that we selected was called Menard Correctional Centre which is a treatment centre within the prison system. This was literally row upon row of cages filled with crazy people, and it was just appalling. The guards were walking around with rifles, and there were high fences with coiled wires. It looks just like a concentration camp.

The parallels with Oakridge are very close. They had enormous problems getting psychiatric staff at this hospital. They relied heavily on consulting staff which is a recommendation made and implemented at Oakridge. Instead of expecting to recruit people to come into the middle of the countryside to live which is very difficult to do, they make use of regular consultants.

They also have a de-medicalized organization. Many of these patients may be chronically assaultive, but doctors have not done very much to help these people. There is not a lot they can do. They had non-medical unit directors.

People in the United States have told me many times that when you are setting up new facilities, you have to really think about the security aspects all along. You have to have lots of different people coming up with security issues from many angles.

The first thing you have to remember is the population of patients in these facilities. They are very unattractive to mental health professionals. It is partly a fault of the training programs which do not emphasize this kind of work and partly because many psychiatrists would say, "Well, what could I do for these people. I am trained in psychotherapy or drug therapy, and there is nothing that I have for these people that would make any difference." It is unattractive to mental health professionals.

Admission to these facilities is typically non-clinical. If you are found not guilty by reason of insanity, that is a court decision, and your treatment needs may have nothing to do with that decision. The clinicians who are providing the treatment have no great control over who comes in. Also, they have no control over the discharge or release of these patients.

There are patients in Oakridge who clearly have recovered from their mental illness relatively quickly, but they are held onto because they have murdered. It would be difficult to transfer them into a more open facility after six months. This is a reality. Also, the discharge decisions are often based on the supposed ability to predict dangerousness. Dr. Webster is an authority on the problem. He has said in courts many times that no matter how confident we are in being able to predict, the evidence is against our being able to do so. Yet the decisions about whether these people are going to move on are based on recommendations from clinical staff.

What has become more complex in recent years is the right to treatment vs. right to refuse treatment. When is it a behavioral management program treatment, and when is it simply a ward routing? Prediction of dangerousness and other kinds of issues must be considered.

One of the most common problems with some of these facilities is geographical remoteness. If the idea were to put these people out of sight and out of mind, that is what they have done. It is very difficult to get staff to work in these facilities if they have any level of training. There exists a level of professional isolation. A doctor or psychologist tends to be cut off from centres of learning. In several of the facilities we visited, there is no integration with a university which is often what people want.

One of the features is a line staff sub-culture. There is a sense of them and us. The patients are them, and we have to protect ourselves against them. So they all band together, and this can lead into one of the other problems such as patient abuse and extreme kinds of therapy. When there is no outside influence on these kinds of behaviors, this sort of thing can happen. In an isolated hospital, the staff is a closely knit group with no influence from other professionals.

They tend often to be neglected physical facilities. Offenders are not a top priority with others. Many people say that offenders deserve what they get, and often governments behave the same way. They deprive these facilities of funds which leads to neglect of physical facilities. The public is more interested in hospitals and cancer research than in mentally abnormal offenders. Many of these poorer facilities thus look inward. They have no interest in the outside world. The outside world often just leaves them alone.

When I talked to psychiatric colleagues at the Clarke Institute, they said, "Oh yes, Penetang is a wonderful place. It always takes my patients." The problem is they have never been there. Lawyers too are unfamiliar with Penetang. It is important to know what kinds of places mentally abnormal offenders are going to be housed in.

The poorer facilities also tend to be preoccupied with security almost to the point of an obsession. They tend to be basically custodial care. They tend to have an absence of any graded level of physical security so that the whole place is secure, and there is no means of giving the privilege or greater freedom within the maximum security environment. Physically it is not possible.

There also tends to be an inappropriate matching of therapies with the patient. If the philosophy of the hospital is group therapy, then all the patients get that regardless of what their particular needs are. People are sometimes sent there inappropriately because there is a big gap between an ordinary hospital and a secure hospital. Nothing lies in between. Afterwards, many of the patients in these hospitals are not prepared for a transfer either to the street or to a less secure setting.

Of all the places I have visited, Park Lane in Liverpool is one of the better large facilities, and the one in Edmonton is the best in Canada. This is not only because of its physical appearance, but also because it is close to Edmonton. In fact, there is a bus stop right outside the hospital. It is a centre with other psychiatric facilities. It is in the Alberta Hospital which is a large provincial psychiatric hospital. It now has university affiliation. The most important characteristic is that it has multiple levels of security from maximum to minimum in the physical building itself. It also has an integrated outpatient follow-up in the community. It has a whole continuity of care, and the system is a very impressive one.

VIOLENCE IN CORRECTIONAL INSTITUTIONS

Marnie Rice
Penetanguishene Mental Health Centre

My colleagues and I have just completed a 10-year study of assaults in our institution. Although assaults have increased, our staff training program has done much to keep the increase at bay. The majority of assaults seem to occur when patients are crowded together with little structured activity and when staff demand activity from them. One particular time is just after meals when patients are milling in corridors. These are high frequency times for assaults as well as times when staff are in the process of directing patients to do various things. That is another high time for assaults. Although a small proportion of patients account for a large majority of the assaults, there seems to be no clear idiosyncratic pattern to the assaults of these individuals. You cannot find any one particular pattern with their assaults. The most logical interpretation includes the interaction of environmental and internal factors rather than something about patient pathology.

When the patient aggressors were asked about the reasons for the assaults they usually said that they had been provoked in some way. Either they had been provoked by the staff or they had been bothered by another patient. The reasons they gave resembled the reasons you would expect males anywhere to give for their assault behavior. Staff tended to report no reason for the assault. When staff were the victims of assault, there was less agreement about the reason for the assault.

Our results led us to believe we might be able to help staff to learn ways of dealing with this. We have been running a course since 1980 at both the maximum and minimum facilities of our mental health centre. Most of the direct care staff who have worked at our hospital for five years have taken the course at least once. The course lasts for one week. We originally ran the course in groups of eight to 10, but now we run it for groups of 14 to 16 at a time. The course is divided into three parts, assessment, classroom and stimulation. The security and calming portions of the course we call our preventing violence portion. In these portions of the course we discuss how staff can prevent violent situations from arising. Restraint is used during a crisis. Interviewing and mediation are techniques we discuss as follow-ups.

In the security part of the course, we discuss different levels of security, maximum, medium and minimum. In some cases of maximum security, we found internal security to be very tight. In other places maximum security mostly means providing an extremely secure perimeter with less control on the inside. In medium or minimum security, perimeter security may or may not be emphasized, and there may be more or less internal security.

We discuss various aspects of security and the advantages and disadvantages of each. We discuss static physical control. Certain physical features of the institution help to maintain control. At times staff physically lay hands on patients to control them, or they might use restraints to control patient behavior. Medication is often used as a method of control. With situational control in our institution, we have ways where high privilege patients are allowed access to different situations.

Interpersonal control deals with ways of talking to patients and interacting with them as a method of control. It is conducive to the development of self-control. Self-control is what we are aiming for in the patients. Our ultimate goal is to have patients control their own behavior.

The next section of the course deals with calming. We discuss things that can be done on an everyday basis to prevent patients from becoming agitated. We use an escalation process where the patient moves from a calm state to an anxious state to a hostile one.

We break each topic down into a step-by-step procedure. The steps that we break each segment down into are observation, preparation, approach, action and follow-up. The things they think about at each of the steps is different. For the calming part of the course, the observation phase has the staff identify and make a list of the sorts of situations that might cause a patient to become slightly anxious. They try to identify why patients might be feeling anxious. They also list the behavior cues that might indicate to them that a patient is slightly anxious. In the preparation step for the calming procedure, we discuss safety.

The next step involved in the process is approach. In the approach step for the calming, we consider voice tone and quality. We talk in a gentle and low voice which will calm the patient. We consider various body postures.

In the action phase we consider what we might say to the patient to try to have a calming effect. We use open questions to get the patient talking. The next step is follow-up. In the follow-up phase we continue to observe the patient. We communicate through progress notes to other staff.

In the next segment of the course, we discuss defusing. By defusing we mean techniques used as a last resort to avoid physical contact when a patient is in a very hostile state. The emphasis in these situations is on techniques to gain and maintain control of the patient's behavior. We are no longer interested here in calming the patient down. It is mostly a matter of gaining control of the situation. Personal safety factors are important in this phase of the procedure. We go over the statistics from our assault studies. We go over the types of situations.

We classify each incident as either a restraint or an assault. What we found was that significantly more days were lost due to restraint incidents than assault incidents. We found that the more serious incidents were not assault incidents at all, but they were rather restraint incidents. These are cases where staff initiates physical contact. In cases where staff lost time from work due to injury, that injury involved the back, knee, neck or shoulder. These incidents were more likely to result in lost days as opposed to incidents involving the face, nose and fingers.

We found also that the more the injury was due to direct patient action, the less serious it was. It was less likely they would lose days from work if the injury actually occurred as a direct result of the patient action.

In each portion of the course we use a number of videotapes as examples of good and bad ways of carrying out these procedures.

Part of our course is conducted in the gym. We discuss methods of patient restraint, ways to escort patients under restraint, ways to restrain patients against the wall. In some areas of our hospital, the preferred technique is to get the patient down on the floor. We found in our study this is where staff would most likely be injured. We advocate restraint against a wall whenever possible. We also go over self-defense techniques such as how to defend oneself against grabbing attacks, striking attacks, offensive techniques and techniques of going into the patients room. We do not advocate entering a patient's room. Many of the injuries at the beginning of our study occurred when staff entered a patient's room. We advocate that they should never go into a room to get a patient. In our institution all patients have individual rooms.

In the final section of our course, we have staff participate in various simulations. For two half days we have them role play actual situations. We begin our simulations with a hostage- taking situation because it grabs the attention of our participants. The simulations are done in an empty ward area in order to maximize the likelihood of using these skills when back on the ward.

We have evaluated our course by using four different types of measures. The first type of measure is the use of questionnaires which our staff fill out after they take the course. Feedback has been positive.

Another questionnaire we used was called the on-board-job- reaction test which asks how comfortable they feel dealing with upset patients. The next type of measure that we used was the measure of skills. We measured how skilfully the staff could actually handle difficult interactions with patients. We also had a videotape test. On this test we had a number of scenes presented on videotape. Staff was asked questions about the way staff had handled situations.

We also measured their knowledge of physical skills. We had a written test to test their physical skills. We also had an actual live physical test in which some of the trainers would pretend to be patients attacking one of the staff participants in the course. The staff would have to restrain them or use some self-defense technique, and they were scored. Our studies show the importance of the course as it results in a drop in the number of assaults. It also has shown to be effective in decreasing the number of days lost.

ANGER MANAGEMENT

Louisa Gembora
Millhaven Institution, Kingston

Millhaven is an S-6 institution which means it is the highest level security for a general population institution. Beyond that, if a person consistently demonstrates aggressive acts and is assaultive, he or she is then placed in the special handling units. Millhaven once had one of these, but eventually it was moved out. There are specific institutions designed for these inmates.

I certainly believe there are interventions or treatments that work with certain types of offenders who have problems with anger and aggression. Therefore, I do not believe in the philosophy that nothing works. You do have to select your group. That makes a big difference in the success or failure rate. In terms of this type of intervention, we are at a very preliminary stage where the assessment and evaluation techniques are very primitive. For someone like myself trying to do some kind of treatment, I am hampered by the lack of such techniques. That points to a need for good applied research. Working in a prison, I find there are very limited resources to do that. We clinicians rely on individuals who do the hard core type of research whether it is from universities or from special treatment centres.

When I do intervention I am often lucky to have an intern with special funding. Generally speaking, it is done on a one-to-one basis or in a small group where I am the only therapist present, but I have a clerk who may be able to assist me in preparing materials. I have gradually developed a package I am comfortable with in this particular institution.

When I consider what type of inmate I am going to work with, I wonder about questions concerning anger, aggression, rage or adverse treatment. With adverse treatment, the individual has a history of very aggressive and assaultive behavior and a history of being resistant to any kind of change or help. The person I prefer to work with is someone who will come to me and mention his or her problems with anger. Surprisingly, some of these individuals I work with do not have institutional histories of being assaultive. They have told me how scared they are with getting out in two years. I start asking questions. What I see are people perhaps very close to being batterers, scared and unwilling to admit it. They are unwilling to deal with it until finally for some reason they are close to being released. Some of these individuals are not seen as aggressive. Others are certainly the type who have very poor control over their anger. They are irritants.

Very few of the people I have actually treated are individuals involved in a lot of serious assaults. Those assaults tend to be very infrequent. After a few years, after the parole board has turned them down and after they have been turned down many times on transfers and stuck in Millhaven for five to 10 years, they finally question receiving a transfer. We start looking at why, and it is this kind of threatening, assaultive behavior that they have. I do not see many from that group.

How are you going to assess? Which are you going to take? What type of instruments can I use? A lot of paper and pencil tests are very easily manipulated by these individuals. Even when they say they have a problem, they still know it is not socially appropriate to go bashing people over the head. They know it is not appropriate to verbally threaten. I have seen the pattern where a person who has a very serious problem controlling his anger comes out being quite average on a number of measures before this kind of treatment. At the end of the treatment, he is up. For a researcher, that is puzzling.

In my research comparing these two groups, I did get some distinct differences between people who said they had chronic anger problems and those who did not. The interesting thing even here is that criminal history did not distinguish between those who had a chronic anger, a chronic aggression problem, and those who did not. The only thing that really did distinguish the two was the institutional history of assaults or verbal threatening, verbal behavior.

There is a desperate need for more research in this area. There is a need for research on the social norms of acceptable levels of anger expression. What are the differences between genders? What are the differences between what is appropriate for males and females to express? There has not been enough research in this department.

How do social pressures and social expectations change the actual behavior of men and women when they do express anger? What are the differences in styles of expressing anger? Not everybody expresses anger overtly. One form of anger is where you do not show it. You are passive and just hold it in. It chips away at you. Possibly, it will raise your level of arousal, and then one day some trivial incident will lead to an anger outburst.

Another form of anger is the resentment style, a passive/aggressive style of expressing anger. In ordinary anger you start shouting and yelling. Your gestures increase in intensity. A survey done a few years ago on 1,000 people stratified for age, sex, race and socio-economic status, found that 80% of those people reported they used an old style of coping. We need a lot more information on that.

In my research on individuals in the non-anger group, half of them were serving life sentences. That again asks the question of whether someone who commits murder is necessarily going to be dangerous and assaultive in the future.

Within the last few years we have seen that models of behavior and of emotion are becoming more complex and are not simply stimulus response reactions. How people evaluate a situation and appraise it becomes extremely important. I think a lot more work has to be done comparing individuals with or without temper problems. How do people interpret a provocation or a stress differently? Why did that one inmate interpret a greeting in such a provocative manner?

Sometimes in our daily lives we have rotten weeks. It is Friday, and we know the weekend is going to be filled with chores. We are irritable and annoyed. When somebody makes a simple request, we react. There is no break between someone who has a chronic temper problem and becomes assaultive and when we are under tremendous amounts of stress ourselves. Our arousal is high. We no longer have the ability to make the kind of cognitive interpretations that are healthy or appropriate, and we lose our temper as well.

When I first started doing intervention, I tried to do a very quick program and found that it was not effective. By the end of the eighth week, the individuals were just beginning to tell me what was going on in their heads and how they were actually behaving. The interventions that I then started were ones in which I would spend as long as four to eight weeks in a very didactic, detached approach. I would bring in video tapes depicting anger-provoking situations which would generate discussion or debate within a group of five to eight inmates. How do you think this guy reacted in this situation? Was he assertive or aggressive? Was he passive? When is it good to be assertive? When is it good to be aggressive? This didactic educational approach would get them to start giving me their norms of what is appropriate and inappropriate.

One of the criticisms that inmates often made was you have to be aggressive in this institution. Everybody expects it of you. In prisons, people do expect a certain amount of aggression. Perhaps that is another myth about prison because I would point out to them that the other inmates are not aggressive, and they are considered powerful individuals in the institution. Their style of solving conflicts, of reacting to provocation is similar verbally to ours. They will not show their anger necessarily. They will not threaten nor punch somebody out. I started asking inmates to give me models. That helped a great deal. Instead of telling them their thinking is crazy and illogical, I would take a different tack using questions. If they mentioned, for instance, that guards and staff were out to get them, I would ask how come they are still alive. How come these good things have happened? If you take the assumption that this world is evil and antagonistic, then how come these other good things are happening? How come that guard did such and such which was positive? How come the nurse did that? I ask them to explain it. Slowly, one begins to chip away at some of these very illogical, very distorted perceptions.

Again, in the research that I did looking at these two groups, the group that had a chronic anger problem clearly made more distortions. They made attributions or omitted things which were not in the situation. They walk in seeing the world in a particularly pre-set fashion. How do you then change that type of perception in a person like that? That is where the treatment has a great deal of difficulty.

I spend a great deal of time working at that type of cognitive thinking and appraising. There is very little one can do to change a prison. A prison has a certain physical environment you cannot change, and it has a certain social, sub-cultural environment you really cannot change. You can give the individual who has a temper problem, an anger problem or an aggression problem an opportunity to learn some self-control. This is the little carrot that I hold out. We will not change the prison. We will not change where they live. The only thing we can do is help them change themselves so that things do not bother them any longer.

That concept is very important. It is like teaching relaxation. If you simply teach a relaxation technique, they are graded doing it when relaxed. If you start asking how to apply that relaxation technique to situations of provocation, you are not only teaching relaxation, the application of the relaxation technique, but you are also teaching a certain amount of self- control. Rather than reacting when aroused, they concentrate on their breathing.

There is a great deal of controversy over whether one should use an intervention that is cognitively oriented or behaviorally oriented. People use appropriate measures in each department, and then they say that they used these behavioral measures and were able to change behavior. Recent research has shown that if you use a behavioral measure, you see changes in cognition. If you use a cognitive measure or a cognitive intervention, you can also see changes in behavior. At this stage it is very unclear, when using a particular treatment, what area of arousal, the physiological, the cognitive or the behavioral, you are actually affecting. It is also unclear what the consequences of that are. It is very muddled.

I started off in a very detached fashion, getting those inmates to tell me what is right, what is wrong. How does one best deal with that provocation situation on the video tape? I have enough different opinions in that little group of five to eight people to ensure a good debate. They start sharing experiences of their own on what worked and what did not.

Recently I have tended to place more emphasis on the cognitive end. With training behavioral skills, often these individuals can perform that particular assertive or appropriate behavior. If your goal is to convince them of an urgency, say that. Say it is urgent. Say you are upset if they do not cooperate. What is your goal? Saying what your goal is can be viewed as either a cognitive intervention or possibly a behavioral one.

Research that certain people have done in the area of information processing seems very comparable to research done on individuals making decisions whether to be assertive or aggressive. When they appraise particular situations, they are either threatening or non-threatening. I am slowly starting to look at the field of information processing to see how they are evaluating, how they are measuring anger and aggression. I think that is an area to look at very carefully.

I have seen inmates make significant changes in the way they behave. Not surprisingly, those changes have taken a great deal of time. Some of the individuals I first started working with when I arrived at Millhaven five years ago are at the point where they are feeling pride, and they are no longer verbally abusive or threatening. The program they may have been involved in or the individual counselling that they may have received from me has taken a very long time to have an impact. It is a gradual change. I feel hopeful because I have seen these changes. Even if it takes three or four years, we should not become discouraged because we can offer them hope, give them encouragement to keep trying. We do see changes.

ANGER MANAGEMENT

Art Gordon
Regional Treatment Centre, Saskatoon

It is uncertain whom we are really talking about when we talk about the violent offender. What sort of individual are we focusing on? Some people have considered the violent offender as the individual who has committed a violent offence. The murderer is clearly a violent offender. The rapist is a violent offender. Someone who has committed manslaughter is a violent offender. Someone who has committed break-and-enter is not a violent offender. The problem I have with this is clearly that these individuals have committed an act of violence. We know from the research that these individuals are not necessarily going to be the individuals who present ongoing aggression while incarcerated.

The other way of looking at the violent offender or the aggressive offender is to look at his ongoing behavior while incarcerated and perhaps prior to his incarceration. We are going to look at the major problem of violence within prisons. Even there we can break down different categories. We can say that we are going to focus on the individuals who commit severe, extreme acts of physical violence. The individual who stabs another inmate is a violent offender. The individual who takes hostages and who kills guards is a violent offender. These are the individuals who are committing the most severe acts of violence within the institution. They are clearly a very problematic population and yet make up a very small proportion of it. These incidents, as severe as they are and as traumatic as they are both for staff, inmates and the system, are not very frequent.

We can look at ongoing aggression and look at less severe forms. We can look at the inmate who is involved in assaults against other inmates. We can also look at the inmate who is very verbally aggressive. What names can do is create an environment of very high tension within the prison. They very much limit the sort of programming and atmosphere you can provide for any rehabilitative programming. Verbal agression can have a very severe impact on the individual who is aggressive. That can be another form of the aggressive inmate.

Another very important category is the individual who is not terribly aggressive while incarcerated but seems to have this anger building in him. The anger and resentment builds up inside but is not eventually expressed. You are not even going to notice the guy is there. Again, we can talk about this as a problem in anger and aggression, but we are looking at a very different individual than the one who blows up at you every time you say good morning to him. I am not sure at this point who we really should be looking at, but I do feel we have to start paying attention to type casting when someone says the violent offender. That is a label. That is a nice category, but I am not sure that it means the same to everyone. I am not sure we are looking at the same sorts of individuals to explain their behavior in the same way. I am also not sure whether the treatment and management approaches are going to be the same for these different sub-groups.

One last distinction is the differentiation between the hostile and instrumentally aggressive act or individual. Instrumental aggression is aggression committed with a specific, usually concrete goal in mind. If you have the job in the laundry, and I want that job, I am more likely to get it if you are found dead with a knife in your back than if I just sit and wait for you to retire. That is very clearly an aggressive act. It is done in order to achieve a very specific goal. Certainly, it occurs within our institutions. The hostile, aggressive individual tends to be much more impulsive, and aggression seems to be designed to reduce aversive states. If I insult you, provoke you, ridicule you, you may retaliate in order to reduce the unpleasantness. Generally, the unpleasant state that you try to reduce is anger. These individuals tend to be much more impulsive. What triggers their aggressive outbursts seem to be rather trivial. You really cannot see why they are doing it. These are the individuals I am particularly interested in. These are the individuals who wish to change, who see their behavior as being inappropriate. They view themselves as being out of control with their behavior and wish to get control.

The individuals using aggression instrumentally often are doing it deliberately. If they are getting what they want, why should they change? They are generally much less open to the idea of changing their behavior because they do not see it as being problematic unless they get caught. In terms of treatment and research, we really have to start defining the sub-groups in some meaningful way so we are not looking at an extremely heterogeneous population.

In terms of treatment, we can be much more flexible. In my treatment program, we tend to focus on the very volatile, impulsive aggressor, the individual who is blowing up three or four times a day but not necessarily physically. He is always getting into verbal fights, verbal altercations, a lot of threatening behavior, throwing things around the room. He has been involved in physical altercations, but that is not his typical form of dealing with things.

We are looking at the hostile, impulsive individual. The way we classify him is fairly basic, and I am not entirely happy with the way we do it. We generally go on the basis of the institution recommendation. Someone says this guy is really flipping and you have to do something with him. He has to see his behavior as a problem and be willing to do something about it.

It is important that our treatment is based on some theoretical understanding of the problem we are looking at. That is where it is important again that we define our sub-groups very carefully. I think it is important because a lot of the therapeutic approaches you take are going to be dictated by the theoretical model that you assume underlies the behavior. You can approach therapy in a much more sensible, logical way rather than throwing things together and hoping something hits.

It is also important because we have these programs springing up in many institutions across the country. It will help us evaluate both our understanding of aggression and the programs themselves if we are very clear on what we think is going on and why we choose certain treatment approaches. We can therefore look at things comparatively.

The model I use is based primarily on a model suggested by Daulf Zinmen in his 1979 book. It is essentially a social learning model of aggression. Zinmen suggests there are three basic components that interact and control whether or not aggressive behavior will be displayed. The first component he looks at is a learning component. Here he suggests, as many other social learning theorists do, that we learn to respond to specific situations in specific ways. Our behavior comes under the control of cues in that situation, and we have learned through modelling and reinforcement to respond to those cues in fairly predetermined ways. The suggestion from this may be that the aggressive inmate may not have the skills to deal with provocative situations in a non-aggressive manner. If he feels insulted, rejected, put down, belittled, he may not have the ability to confront the situation without retaliating. That is a reasonable assumption that we can test out. In fact, we have tested it out or are beginning to. Indeed, we have a behavioral role play test which presents the individual with a series of two-stage role play situations. He is given a scenario. He is prompted, and he has to respond to it.

We generally find that the more aggressive inmate tends to behave more aggressively in dealing with these situations. Given the artificiality of it and all the limitations, he tends to behave more aggressively. Do it the way the straights in society would have you do it. He is able to adjust his behavior and reduce the aggression to the point where he is equal to the non-aggressive inmate. He seems to have the ability to perform pro-social responses when certain constraints are put on him and when he is geared in that direction. We have only started looking at that. The aggressive inmate may not be able to conceive of the range of responses and response alternatives that most of us can in dealing with a specific situation.

It does not appear from our very early evidence that the aggressive inmate is grossly deficient in terms of pro-social skills. Nevertheless, many of our guys do have great difficulty dealing with specific types of situations. One of the ways that we gear our treatment is through an assertion training package which looks at specific situations, usually things that are happening to him during his ongoing living at the Regional Psychiatric Centre. We do a lot of role playing to try and help him develop alternate strategies to deal with specific situations. We try to carry this beyond the formal treatment session where the treatment staff will do role playing as the guy has just yelled and screamed at them. They calm the guy down, and they get him to repeat it. It is a sort of overcorrection model.

The second variable that Zinmen suggests is cognitive mediation factors. We have to make sense of our environment. We have to interpret what is going on. I worked with a guy when I was back at the Regional Psychiatric Centre in Kingston who came from Millhaven where the guards were not very nice to him. The guards at the RPC were much more reasonable. He would walk by them in the morning, and one friendly guard said good morning, and this guy had a fit. He felt provoked because that friendly greeting was perceived by him as a taunt, as a challenge, as a threat.

The first thing we have to do is make sense of the input we are getting. Is it provocative? Is it neutral? Is it friendly? Is it antagonistic? We have to be able to identify it once we have defined the situation. What are the alternatives we have to deal with in this situation? What is appropriate? What are the environmental constraints? If you come up and insult me, and you stand 4-6, I may consider aggression as retaliation a lot quicker than if you stand 6-8. I have to consider the consequences of my action. What is likely to happen if I do this? What is likely to happen if I do that? It is very complex cognitive processing that we do very automatically. We do not really pay a lot of deliberate attention to it.

The aggressive inmate may be particularly deficient in one or more areas of this cognitive pathway. It seems that the aggressive inmate chronically misinterprets apparently neutral cues as being very provocative, very threatening. Once we have made that decision that we are being threatened, that is it. It does not matter whether we are right or wrong. As far as we are concerned, we are right, and now you have to deal with the threat. One of the things we have to try to get guys to do is challenge their assumptions and perceptions particularly the key ones that leave them feeling belittled or rejected or threatened. Go up and ask them, "What did you mean by that?" "I felt really hurt when you said that. What did you mean?" It is very difficult for some of them, but it is important that if they are going to become angry, they do it where it is appropriate.

Ninety-nine per cent of the time they are getting angry over their misperceptions. We have to teach them to problem solve, to think about what they can do in this situation, to look at their alternatives. We have to teach them to look at consequences, anticipate what is likely to be the outcome. It is especially important to get them to be very goal-oriented. Your classification officer has refused to support your pass. What is your goal in dealing with that person? If your goal is to get even with him, the easiest way to accomplish that goal is through aggression. If your goal is to try to get him to change his mind, you better figure out strategies to achieve that particular goal. That is something these guys are very poor at. Their behavior looks very bizarre to the bystander. This guy is weird. You never know when he is going to blow, or why he is blowing. Internally, if you can look at his cognitive processing, his behavior is totally logical. What we think is an innocuous cue is a very threatening cue. What we say is, "How could you do that? You know he is never going to support you now." The guys go to the parole board, and they tell the parole board exactly where they can put it. Their goal at that point is to get back at the parole board for the way they perceive the parole board's behavior. They have forgotten the goal of increasing their chances of getting out.

We started trying to look at some of these cognitive processes. How do people interpret the social environment? Do the aggressive inmates tend to have a different style of doing it? Are they deficient in this area? Part of the problem we are coming up with is what sort of measures do you use?

The third factor in Zinmen's model is the crucial arousal factor. If we are at an optimal point of arousal, all of these cognitive processes worked up to their maximum capacity. Once you push arousal increasingly higher, these cognitive processes tend to break down. They become much less sufficient.

If you are much less likely to correctly perceive situations, then you are much less likely to consider alternatives or consequences or make a rational decision about your behavior. Under high levels of arousal you bypass the cognitive controlling mechanisms, and you go right up to the most overlearned response you have. We know that for the aggressive inmate, if you just say respond as it feels most natural, their predominate response is an aggressive response. Under high levels of response of arousal, their behavior almost becomes reflexive. It is poorly planned and impulsive because it is simply being driven by the arousal straight to automatic responding.

Clearly, we have to start working on reducing the arousal, getting the individual to start monitoring and managing his arousal. This presents all sorts of problems because we can do relaxation training, stress management training, and these guys are very good at relaxing when they are already relaxed. What is more problematic is when the guys on the peaked scale do not know what to do or how to do it. I think we have to start working with the individual in that high arousal stage and get him to develop, build in trained coping strategies at that point, get him to reduce his arousal. The main thing we tell our guys not to do is deal with a situation when your arousals are up because your ability to think, to communicate and to respond is impaired. You are reducing your chances of solving it. Whenever possible, your first and only goal has to be to get your arousal down. Afterwards, think about the situation. Work it out. Approach me.

These three factors are the three we see interacting to control aggression at any given time. We are looking at whether or not the habitually aggressive inmate is particularly deficient in one or more of these areas. Our theory and our treatment are primarily focused on issues from each area. Certainly we do an individual assessment on each guy, and this gives us a framework of where to look in diagnosing behavior.

PART VI

UNDERSTANDING TYPES OF VIOLENCE

THE VIOLENT FEMALE BEHAVIOR

THE VIOLENT FEMALE OFFENDER

Louise Biron
University of Montreal

It is interesting to note that the woman is not always the victim. She commits violent acts as well. In Canada, there were 6,613 women convicted of a violent offence in 1984. In comparison to men, it is much smaller. There have been several studies of women who commit violent acts. The only detailed study that we came across was by Ward, Jackson and Ward. That study was made in 1969 and was a study based on documents on file and not on personal interviews.

We interviewed 19 women, and I will give a condensed version of these stories. I do not want the condensed versions of these stories to be unique or extreme cases that show that nothing is that simple or that clear. It is important to get some methodological background on this study so you can understand where it comes from.

When interviewing the 19 women on this subject, we used the criminal code to limit the study. We kept murder, manslaughter, robbery, assault, threats, hostage taking and kidnapping, and we excluded from the study women who had committed violent acts against members of their families or within the context of a love relationship. We also excluded women who had any kind of mental problems. The interviews were carried out in French. The contacts were made personally by meeting the women and then explaining the research and asking who would be willing to volunteer. We got women from the Tanguay [Institution], from halfway houses, a prison for women in Quebec and some from the parole files. People would call them and ask them if they would at least accept a telephone call from us. In this way we would come into contact with the women and explain the research, and they would accept or refuse to participate. We also made a point of not having any of these convictions prior to 1980.

Of the women we interviewed, none were on parole, two were in halfway houses and eight were in prison. Eleven of the women were convicted for armed robbery, five for manslaughter, two for attempted murder and two for kidnapping. The sentence for these women varied from six months to seven years. Three of the subjects were under 21. The majority were between 21 and 25. In the extreme bracket, there were two who were between 36 and 40 years old.

Although most of the women interviewed had had previous contacts with the penal system, five had had no contacts either as adults or as juveniles. This was their first contact with the penal system.

The study was based on interviews. The interviews lasted approximately two hours. We had an interviewing schedule, but it had many open questions. We did have a lot of material on these women. It did cover all aspects of their lives. We were not just looking at how they committed that offenses, but we were looking at, retrospectively, their families, their school backgrounds, their friends, the jobs they held and previous delinquency. A lot of the delinquency we heard about was self- reported delinquency that was not found in the records. We were able to confirm that what they told us could be found in the records. We were not taken for a ride. The results were presented in a retrospective way. It was obviously presented as the women who volunteered the information saw it and chose to report it to us. The research results were drawn from their own stories.

Most of them grew up in large families of four children or more. There were not necessarily two parents. They had stepmothers or stepfathers, and they had incestuous fathers. The median income was close to lower middle class. There were extremes here of the very rich and the very poor. The father or whoever replaced him during childhood was seen mostly as a provider with the whole family depending on this person. When the father is ill or out of work, the social welfare takes over. The father image was a relatively negative one. He was seen as authoritative, brutal in some cases, critical and hard.

It is amazing to see how much difference they see with their mothers. The mother was usually seen as a warm, affectionate, weak, dependent victim. Even for the women we interviewed, who found that their parents were fine. There remained this constant feeling of not really being quite understood. We pursued that. We felt that not being quite understood meant not having enough freedom. All of them complained about being confined, coming in at regular hours or doing chores that they did not want to do. They would have preferred to be free to go to places and hang around with friends. They felt very limited in that way. Running away became a solution. Eight of the women we interviewed had run away. Others were running away because of too much discipline or too little. Others ran away because it did not really matter because the supervision was so low. Amazingly enough, they still felt the need to go back to that family. Parents required financial support which meant that the girl would stop school and get a job to help the family. For the majority, school became so difficult that they dropped out. It became a vicious circle. They would not have motivation.

Most of the women we interviewed had a very low educational background. Only one of them made it to grade 12. Five women never went beyond primary school. Money came from either selling drugs, prostitution, shoplifting and the like. Partying and socializing with friends was more fun that anything else.

There was only one girl who described herself as having a straight friend. The straight friend meant that she lived with her family, went to school and did not hang out in the bars all the time.

Some of the girls had to learn how to defend themselves when they were young. Some remember fighting in school yards.

Half of the women who start using drugs and alcohol for fun become addicted. By the time they reach adulthood, these girls have a serious problem with drugs and alcohol. There is a link between being a drug user at an early age and dropping out of school at an early age. There are also serious health problems with the drug or alcohol problems, losing weight, shaking, and severe cases of anemia. There is also a money problem. The money comes mostly from selling drugs. They hang out with people who are older and more experienced.

After looking at the adolescent years, we noticed that many of the things these women had been involved in were very similar to that of a normal, teenage person. The only difference was the intensity with which they were living this problematic situation.

THE VIOLENT FEMALE OFFENDER

Christine Power
Correctional Service of Canada

In thinking about violent female offenders, I first thought about the definition of the female offender. Is it a woman convicted of a violent offence or is it a woman directing violence towards herself? As far as incarceration goes, it is interesting to note that in a majority of cases with females as well as males, the more violent inmates are more often the ones with mere property offenses listed against their record.

It is recognized that violent female offenders have been victims of sexual or other types of abuse. Although there is no hard data to substantiate this, practitioners do agree that a number of female offenders have been victims of violence at an earlier age. Because many women have been victims of domestic abuse, their violent crimes are situational such as with the murder of a spouse. These women are not seen as violent within the institution. They are usually good inmates and excellent parole candidates. Of the 36 inmates incarcerated for murder convictions at the Prison for Women, only one is considered a violent offender.

Female offenders are not feminist. They are more inclined towards classic, traditional roles. They find themselves involved in crimes for economic reasons or as accomplices. In an offence, women are most often followers and are financially and emotionally dependent on their accomplices. Only in terrorism do women seem to play a dominant role in violent offenses. This has been especially true in the past few years.

Addiction also plays a role in violence involving women. The cause for the addiction is either alcohol or drugs. The loss of inhibitions while under the influence enables many women to commit violent offenses.

There are many reasons why women commit violent offenses. The number of violent female offenders is still very small. Women, rather than men, tend to suppress their frustration or violent tendencies and turn them inwards. This may become a nervous condition or mental illness. In extreme cases, the result is slashing or self-mutilation.

There are fewer than 250 federal female inmates in Canada. Only a small number of them are considered violent. Only four or five are identified as management problems within the prison for women. They have been convicted by the courts usually for property offenses and are now inmates in a federal institution. In administering the court sentence, the correctional services must control offenders and help them at the same time. We attempt to balance the degree of control with the offender's ability to assume responsibility for her own behavior. We must identify the needs of the offender and develop ways to enhance the possibility of her living a law-abiding life. Each case within the institution is handled on an individual basis. Each inmate is assigned a case management officer who is responsible for needs analysis and for program planning.

Trained psychologists and psychiatrists work with the management team. Sexual assault therapists work with sexual assault victims. Many self-help groups exist such as Alcoholics Anonymous and Set and Step which is an inmate group. Ten Plus Fellowship, a group of women serving 10 years or more, assists other women to cope with lengthy sentences. These women have also been involved in a program educating juveniles in high schools.

Women in need of acute psychiatric care are placed in the St. Thomas Hospital in London. The treatment centre at Kingston Penitentiary is a program for men and women with behavior disorders. The prison for women has five beds on that unit. They are completely separate from the males. Admission to the treatment centre is at the inmate's request for a 30-day period. Initiatives have also commenced within Correctional Services for programs dealing with aggression and its relation to emotion and frustration. Aggression control programs at the prison for women operate out of the treatment centre.

They are already incarcerated. They have to go out into the community. The community agencies, in cooperation with Correctional Services can go a long way in assisting violent female offenders. I think they have a wider scope in which to work to assist these offenders. I think the community agencies work much better with these women who serve several short sentences. They help to break the cycle of violence, to determine the reason for their anger, to work to get them back into a reasonable lifestyle where they can live within the community.

THE VIOLENT FEMALE OFFENDER

Darlene Lawson
Executive Director of the Elizabeth-Fry Society, Toronto

Over the last 10 years I have worked with people who have histories of violent behavior, particularly with women. I have come to believe that a major factor underlying much illegal and violent behavior is a feeling of anger. It is a derivative of hate, jealousy and frustration. It is interesting that, given the social and political reality of women based on gender, class and race, one might expect the higher degree of violence against others perpetrated by women motivated by anger. For example, over two-thirds of single people in Canada who are poor are women. Ten per cent of families headed by a male are within poverty, but 50% of all families headed by a female are poor. One in four elderly Canadians live in poverty. Sixty per cent of these are elderly women, and four-fifths of them are widows.

Increased technology costs jobs to women, and by 1990 it is estimated that a million jobs will be lost to women due to technological change. Over 25% of all the women in the labor force work part time. Of all part-time workers, 72% are women. Part-time workers earn only 79% of the hourly wage of full-time workers. Women comprise 75% of all minimum wage earners. They earn an average of 55% of what men are paid. The average male high school dropout earns over $1,000 a year, more than the average female university graduate. There are only 15 out of 282 federal members of Parliament in Canada who are women.

Nine out of 10 women with an alcoholic husband stay with him. But nine out of 10 husbands with an alcoholic wife leave. It is estimated that a woman is raped in an urban centre in Canada every 17 minutes. One out of four women have their first sexual experience by force under the age of 16 at the hands of a family member or someone close to them. One out of 10 women who live with their spouse is beaten by him. The percentage of women who, during their life time, will not experience sexual assault, attempted sexual assault, sexual harassment, battery or incest is only 7.8%.

Despite these facts, few women commit behaviors which are illegal, and very few behave in ways which are violent against others. The average number of adults in prison in Canada on any given day is about 27,000. Of these, only about 600 are women. In 1981, 48,690 men were charged with violent offenses. This is 19.1% of the total charges against men. Only 5,117 women were charged with violent offenses which is 10.2% of all charges against women.

This low incidence of crime and violence among women is partially due to the continuing social, political and economic structures which continue to socialize women into roles of mother and wife, nurturer and caretaker. These are turned into passivity, dependence and acceptance. The other part is that these social structures also set up role and behavior expectations for men and women in terms of how we deal as genders with anger. Women are encouraged to be in touch with their feelings and to be feeling individuals. I think that probably more women spend more time trying to be in touch with how they feel and why they feel that way.

Unresolved feelings of anger is the root of much violent behavior. It is far less acceptable for women to externalize these feelings of anger verbally or by striking other people. On the other hand, there have been lengthy periods of history when it has been quite acceptable for men to use force to maintain their position of authority with servants, spouses, children and parents.

Women have historically turned unresolved anger inward. They experience self-hate which manifests itself in mental or physical kinds of illnesses. While both women and men might be victims of violence as children, male victims often become perpetrators of violence. Women as adults often find themselves in a continuing cycle of victimization as battered women and prostitutes. It is also interesting that out of the very few women in Canada who are considered to have violent histories, many of them also turn their anger inward in terms of slashing themselves and self-mutilation. I think the criminal justice system is ill-equipped to deal with people who have these unresolved feelings of anger.

Two conditions have to exist in order for an act of violence to occur. One of them is a predisposition towards violence, and the other is the trigger situation. Whether it is turned inward or outward, it is destructive because the individual is not aware of what the root of that anger is. There is independent motivation without conscious reasoning. Almost all female violence is reactive, spontaneous and not conscious. It will be more or less serious in its potential depending on how much pent up rage a person has developed through her years of experience and her particular social context.

Various situations can trigger off this kind of anger. It is a very individual situation as to what will trigger something off. For one woman it may be one too many beatings. For another it may be sexual advances by a man in a bar. For another woman it may be a denied telephone call in an institution. For another it may be incessant demands from a baby. We have to look at the predisposition in the first place and then the possible triggered situation because it differs with each individual.

I am not discussing violent people per se. It will become more important for the community to help develop proper responses because there are people who have a predisposition to violence who, in certain situations, can be violent. It requires an incredible amount of resources to help that person begin to understand where the anger is coming from. When the cognitive part of the body comes into play, we have choice. Otherwise, I think choice is a very relative concept. We can only make choices among things that we know exist and that we feel we have some kind of access to. The flipside of that is responsibility. We can hold anybody responsible for anything he does. The criminal justice system certainly does that.

I work with The Elizabeth Fry Society of Toronto, and we have been working the last few years with a number of women who have violence in their backgrounds. We have been trying to create an intervention strategy based on these kinds of concepts. It has been very successful, but it requires an incredible amount of resources. We were lucky to get some money from the Ministry of Correctional Services to provide 24-hour staff support to a couple of women who had lengthy periods of incarceration and violence in their backgrounds. We tried to implement a training process helping them to identify their feelings. They then were to look at a range of options of behavior. It worked. This is perhaps a good way for a society to spend its money.

THE VIOLENT FEMALE OFFENDER

Julie Darke
Queen's University

There is pressure to conform to a fundamentally destructive female stereotype. Women who do not conform to that stereotype are faced with all kinds of social punishments from a variety of sources. Women who do conform to the stereotype are conforming to a standard that affords little personal power. Traditional women are highly vulnerable and dependent on men both physically and emotionally. They are particularly accessible and vulnerable to victimization. They are in a position to aid in the commission of crimes they would not otherwise participate in.

Women who do not conform are considered deviant and socially marginalized. For example, a variety of behaviors considered assertive in men are considered aggressive in women. In the past, women who expressed clearly justified anger were considered pathological in psychiatric literature. That kind of expression of anger had been attributed to masculinity complexes or to the angry women syndrome.

In addition, non-conforming women have their sexuality and their femininity called into question repeatedly. We have all heard of a woman referred to as less of a woman. Somehow she is more masculine.

Basically these are some of the problems that face women as they are socialized and as they grow up. All of these difficulties, pressures and inequities are exacerbated by racial and class factors. Out of 30 women in our research, 24 or 80% had been sexually assaulted as children. The majority had been repeatedly assaulted in childhood, and 75% of those cases involved prolonged abuse. The repeated assaults ranged from several months up to 15 years. All but two of the assailants were men. Of the 34 males, nearly half were fathers or stepfathers. Seventy-two per cent of those women who were repeatedly assaulted over a long period of time were assaulted by their fathers. Other assailants included brothers, uncles, grandfathers, friends of family.

The two female assailants were teenage cousins. The single female victim had also been previously brutally battered by her father. For both single and repeated assaults all of the assailants were family members or friends of the family except for one. There was one stranger involved. Approximately 80% of the women in the sample were sexually assaulted as children by someone they trusted in a position of tremendous power not only in terms of being an adult but in terms of the power that family relationships give.

In addition to sexual assault, nearly one-half of these women reported having been physically battered as children. Again, a majority of assailants were men. All but one of the males were fathers. The five women who were batterers as children were all mothers. Two of these women acted on their own. The other three acted in conjunction with the father.

As adults, 25% of the sample were sexually assaulted one or more times. All assailants were male, and over half of the assailants were friends or acquaintances. Another one-third of the sample were, as adults, battered repeatedly by their male partners, husbands or steady boyfriends. In total, 90% or 27 out of 30 of these women experienced sexual and or non-sexual abuse or violence at the hands of men.

The psychological effects of this kind of victimization results from three sources. They are obviously the abuse of self (the pain, the fear, the humiliation), the socialization of women and the reactions of society to the victimization of women. It is generally acknowledged that the closer the relationship between the victim and the offender, the more traumatic the incident is for the woman.

There are a number of common reactions to this kind of victimization. Anger is primary especially when we keep in mind that females are not raised to acknowledge nor to show it. Expression of anger is punished more in females than it is in males. Our difficulty with anger in terms of labelling, acknowledging and expressing it is just one piece within a larger picture. Women are taught to be more passive and more self-sacrificing. When I looked at the sample of women in terms of their assertiveness, 93% showed passive behavior, flipping between fairly passive and aggressive rather than assertive behavior. Difficulties with anger in terms of assertion was probably the clearest. It was the area of most difficulty for these women. It is important to note that the effects of incarceration and perhaps commission of the crime itself cannot be easily separated from this finding.

Victims of sexual and or non-sexual violence are justifiably angry for all kinds of reasons. They are angry at their assailants for the violation and at their children because of a violation of trust. This betrayal of trust has a profound effect on the victim's ability to trust again. It is not surprising that many of the women in the sample have difficulty with intimacy on both a sexual and emotional level. Sixty per cent reported sexual fears.

Victims of sexual assault are also angry with their assailants for being forced to be silent about their own abuse. Some are threatened with death or beatings. They are told that they would break up the family. They would send Dad to jail. No one would love them. They are told they would be blamed. Victims are angry for being subjected not only to sexual abuse but sometimes to physical battering. In some cases, there are other restrictions on their lives. For example, many sexually abusive fathers socially isolate their daughters. They are not allowed to go out. Their interaction with peers is severely limited. In addition to disruptions in school and with peers, there are difficulties with sleeping and eating. Sexual assault or non- sexual victimization in childhood severely diminishes the child's sense of control and sense of safety in the world.

The understandable fear and anger of the victim tends to generalize from her assailant to other men. Women talk a lot about the control that men have over their lives and the subtle and explicit sexual harassment they experience before or after the assault. They are constantly reminded of the actual assault. There are key elements in common there.

Approximately 90% of this sample reported a conscious fear of, or disdain for, men in general. Victims experience anger with their families for not knowing or doing something about the abuse. Some women reported their abuse to police and were brought back home. In the case of child victims, they have to live with their rapists. Some women in the sample went to court and were provided with no protection. They were either not believed, or their trauma was minimized. Even if they were believed, little concrete steps were taken to protect them. Unfortunately, a lot of this anger and the negative social attitudes result in women being angry with themselves and blaming themselves for what happens. Very often they blame themselves for being females, for having these bodies that get them into trouble. They blame themselves for not being able to stop the assault or reporting or not reporting it.

Anger is an understandable and valid response. For most women, what makes it unmanageable and unresolvable is that it is rarely ever validated. These women are repeatedly not believed, the trauma is minimized, and the assailants are protected. Because they are women, many are told to forget what has happened rather than to try and understand it.

Given the justifiable reasons for anger, it should come as no surprise that 73% of these women have problems with anger control and personal aggression. They have periods of explosions. The tendency of women on the street is to suppress the anger until there is an event that triggers some kind of lashing out or explosion. Some may allow themselves to express their anger only under the influence of drugs or alcohol.

We should also not be surprised that some of these women defy the law. Think of the woman who goes to court as a 17-year-old seeking protection and is sent home to live with her rapist. The rapist defies the law in a more premeditated fashion than others involved in other things such as armed robbery.

The third major area I want to discuss is self-worth. Because of socialization, the specific histories of these women and social attitudes, a woman's self-worth or self-concept is seriously affected by sexual and non-sexual assaults. Ninety- three per cent of the women, 28 out of the 30, evidence low self-esteem. Again, the effects of incarceration and perhaps commission in the crime cannot be factored out without a careful control group. Consider the messages females get in childhood about good girls. Good girls do not lie. Good girls do not have sex. Good girls do not get angry. Victims of sexual abuse are forced to have sex. They are forced to lie. They have good reason to be angry. This seems to have a significant role in lower self-esteem. Self-blame is a prominent characteristic.

Survivors of sexual assault tend to blame themselves for all kinds of events beyond their control. When angry, particularly with themselves, some attempt to diminish the emotional pain by expressing that anger inwards. Approximately 43% of the sample have a history of slashing. Some slashed following the actual assault in childhood or during the teenage years. Some slashed after nightmares of the assault. Some slashed after they themselves were interpersonally aggressive. Approximately 80% of the sample have an adult history of depression, and 67% have a past history of suicide attempts.

Lack of trust in others, lack of trust in oneself and low self- esteem are feelings of powerlessness and lack of control. Incarceration can be expected to increase those feelings of powerlessness. Female violent offenders are not raised to be as socially powerful as men. The standard for women relative to men is more passive and more dependent. Women are trained not to be aggressors but victims. Blatant victimization such as sexual assault further immobilizes and controls women in very concrete ways. During and following the assault, there are few options for girls and women. After the assault, women are literally silenced by their assailant or by cultural messages that tell women that they will be blamed if they talk about it.

These feelings of powerlessness follow child victims into adulthood and adults for many years. Women very often feel they are crazy and not in control. They feel out of control in terms of their lives. Often there is a fear of losing internal control. They are afraid that they are going to explode from pain. They are afraid that if they start to cry they will never be able to stop. There is a fear of losing control during nightmares and a continuing fear of men and repeated abuse.

Some of these women resort to drugs and alcohol which give an illusion of greater control. Approximately 77% of the sample have a drug and alcohol problem. To alleviate feelings of powerlessness, some women take on the facade of being aggressive and invulnerable. This facade is traditionally male in a lot of ways. It may be seen as the only alternative for some of these women breaking from a stereotypically passive and vulnerable female role.

I want to talk about treatment. From what we know about socialization in these women's histories, their difficulties cannot be viewed as simply a result of personal inadequacy. Given that, treatment approaches should be consistent with that analysis previously given which is essentially a feminist analysis. Feminist therapy is the approach that I use. It seems to be the only approach that adequately addresses the issues that have been discussed. Feminist therapy differs from conventional therapy in both content and process. A lot of time is spent linking the women's personal experiences to the social context in which those experiences happen. There are some fundamental assumptions about women which are different in feminist therapy than in conventional therapy. The process is different. Power and balance between the therapist and the client are minimized through a variety of methods in order to decrease their likelihood of a dependent sort of relationship in order to avoid recreating the power imbalances that exist in many male/female relationships. It is to empower the client. It is a much more self-respectful process for women. It is much more likely to lead to self-directed choices and decisions. The goal is to give the client the skills to make herself her own therapist.

From the evidence, a lot of female violence appears to be attributable to male violence and male cultural dominance. A woman's accepted dependence on men frequently results in her participating in crimes she would not initiate or perpetrate on her own. Repeated victimization can lead to women exploding with rage far in excess of that warranted by the immediate situation but entirely consistent with the cumulative effects of repeated abuse. The lack of appropriate services for victims of violence, the unsatisfactory response of police and courts and negative societal attitudes further victimize survivors of assaults. Prevention then necessitates social transformation from a male dominated society to one in which women share equally social, political and economic power. I am not going to hold my breath waiting for that day. Until then there are some self-evident ways we can help out. It includes funding rape crisis centres and interval houses, changing the responses of police and courts to victims of violence and of course considerable public education on these issues from children's and women's perspectives. We need to remove the cultural forces that glorify and encourage male violence, to eliminate the media images that portray women as sexual commodities to be used as less than fully human beings. The options for girls and women need to be expanded particularly with women in conflict with the law. Many of these women have already made non-traditional choices. There is very little support for that either inside the prison or outside. We need to provide those services and skills to maintain self-directed and independent lives.

PART VII

UNDERSTANDING TYPES OF VIOLENCE

FAMILY VIOLENCE

FAMILY VIOLENCE

Murray Strauss
University of New Hampshire

My paper discusses the amount of violence in American families. In 1975 my colleagues and I did a study based on 2,143 families nationwide; in 1985, another study with 6,002 families. In order to make comparisons with the '75 sample, we used only 4,032 because the '75 sample, unfortunately, was limited in several ways. It included only children aged three to 17 and excluded single parent families. It is therefore deficient in studying child abuse in the States. The '85 sample included groups that were not included in the '75 study.

In order to collect data, we used the conflict-tactic scale (CTS). It consists of a list of things that people can do when they have a conflict with another member of the family or are just simply angry. It begins with very innocuous associations reasoning, in verbal aggression and finally in acts of physical aggression. The physical aggression is divided into ordinary violence, pushing, grabbing, shoving, slapping, throwing things, and severe violence, kicking, fighting, punching, hitting with an object, beating out, threatening with a knife or gun.

The next stage in severe violence contains the basic child abuse and wife beating. With violence between husband and wife, almost 16% of American couples experience at least one violent incident. With severe violence, the rate is 6.1%, and these are merely couples who responded to us. At the same time, it is difficult to measure these rates because most assaults do not result in injury requiring medical treatment.

The severe violence rate is 11%, 6,900,000 children who are severely assaulted by a parent, kicked, bitten, hit with objects, attacked with weapons. There is very little disagreement that kicking, fighting and stabbing are included here, but there is disagreement about whether hitting with belts and hairbrushes is. For half of all American children, this does not end until they physically leave home. It starts in infancy and continues for 18 years. It also turns out that children are the most violent people in the United States. Violence against a brother or sister is 80%. In 36% of the cases, severe violence occurred. The important point here is that there is just a lot of violence in American families. I arrive at the conclusion that for typical citizens, their own home is the place where they are at the greatest risk of being physically assaulted. This can mean a slap or murder. Women have relatively little risk of being assaulted outside their homes.

If we want to deal with the larger questions of violence in society, the family is an important place to start. We understand why there is so much violence in the family. Although the family is a loving place, it is also a violent group. The family is a group which has a high level of conflict built into it. There is more to disagree about within a family. Men and women have different perspectives, and there are different generations.

Every study that we have done on male dominance in the family shows there is more violence in the type of situation where the husband presumes to be the head of the household. Egalitarian families have the lowest rate of marital violence.

There are also explicit cultural norms which permit, or even require, physical violence in the family. This is evident in the parents' rights to the children. This has also been affirmed recently by many court decisions and statutes in the United States on Child Abuse which give parents the right to use physical punishment on their children. In Sweden they have passed a law where physical punishment of children is illegal. There is also the marriage licence which is like a hitting licence between spouses. There are other male-dominant situations in which there is conflict but these are not norms. Our university departments are fine examples. My department, after many years, finally has one woman member of the faculty.

Why do we have norms within the family that tolerate and, in some cases, almost require physical force? The reason why families tend to permit physical force is because families inadvertently train their members in violence. It starts in infancy where a parent will use a gentle slap to stop a baby from doing something. The problematic aspect is that it teaches kids more than just not to do something. It teaches children that those who love you are also those who hate you. And this is the lesson that starts in infancy when the earliest layers of personality are developing.

The big surprise to most people was that we found a substantial reduction in the rates from 1975 to 85 in child abuse as well as in spouse abuse. We saw a 47% decrease in child abuse. Child homicide rates for infants and toddlers and wife beating went down during that period, shown in the vital statistics of the United States. We must remember that our data is based on interviews in which people told us about these violent acts. Not everyone is willing to report.

In the United States, as probably in Canada also, there are now thousands of child protective service workers who simply were not there in the early 1970s. They are inadequately trained and overloaded. Nevertheless, most child abuse cases respond to even inadequate intervention. Similarly, in the United States there has been a huge growth in family therapy and marriage counselling. Membership in the American Association of Marriage and Family Therapists has, I think, tripled within the time period of this study. We are on the right track, and we should double the effort in order to deal with these cases.

FAMILY VIOLENCE

John Robinson
London Police Force

The young Anglican theologian, graduating from university, was making his first speech in the cathedral. Of course, there they call them servants. When it came time for the service to begin, the dean came to him as he wandered around the church vestry and asked, "What is your problem?" He said, "I just cannot go out. I am far too nervous." The dean said, "What you do is take a glass of gin with you when you go to the pulpit. People will think it is a glass of water. Whenever you feel nervous take a sip of the gin." So he did, and the service went on. Typical of the Anglican Church, after the service he was shaking hands with everybody as they were leaving. They were congratulating him on his enthusiasm and delivery. When everyone had gone, he said to the dean, "I guess I did not do too badly after all." The dean said, "No. But I think you should go back and reread your history." He said, "What do you mean?" The dean said, "David slew Goliath; he did not beat the shit out of him!"

I think sometimes we do get caught up in old history and are afraid to look at the future. Contrary to what many people believe, the criminal justice system has a unique and primary responsibility and authority to intervene decisively in family situations to reduce violence. This is not enough because without the necessary resources including shelters for women, programs for those who are battered, easy and quick access to legal advice and the courts, the efficacy of that criminal justice system will be severely undermined. Most people in society view the criminal justice system as being punitive and insensitive to the needs of the victim. In some cases it is appropriate, but even the judges can be trained.

The police, as initial responders to calls for help, must be trained to be more sensitive to the underlying issues of family violence. They also must be provided with support from their superiors, their ranking officers and leaders, the Crown Attorney, the courts, and, most importantly, the community. If they are to meet the expectations of both the community and the victims, they need support and resources.

The family is certainly not a new phenomenon. Only in the last 10 to 15 years has it received due attention. As the victims, generally women, are becoming more aware of community resources, they are finally standing up and saying, "No more! We want to do something about it!"

We are also beginning to realize the inadequacies of the criminal justice system regarding wife battering. Until recent times, most victims believed that by charging their partner they would be kicked out of their homes with no place to go or with lack of financial resources to raise their children. This is not as necessarily true now as it used to be.

With the increased resources within the community, the old myths are being dispelled. The criminal justice system has not responded to change as quickly as the victim has, but there are signs that even the wheels of justice are starting to move in the right direction. The new approach by victims and the community at large has itself created an obvious need for action by the criminal justice system. When I talk about the criminal justice system, I always look at the police force.

The criminal justice system for most people is very complex. It can be divided into two readily identifiable sections, action and disposition. Action includes the event and requires the victim or someone else to call for help. The investigation for the response is not enough. To temper the violence for the moment does not satisfy the role and expectations of the victim. Where appropriate, the police should arrest and should prepare the charge and the information for the court.

In the disposition section of the criminal justice system, the court function includes accepting charges, an issuing process. In Ontario, that is the role of the justice of the peace. The prosecution is by the Crown Attorney. People do not need their own lawyers.

The attitudes of the first section, action, can easily be overcome by clear direction within the police community. For example, a direction was issued in May 1981. It was followed up by the Solicitor General in August 1982 and then by the Attorney General. However, clear direction alone will not foster spontaneous change of attitude.

The change in attitude of the second section, disposition, is one of positive action. A 1985 study done in London revealed that reducing violence was more often achieved when police laid charges than when the victim laid the charge. In seven out of eight cases where the victim was adamant not to lay charges, the violence was greatly reduced or eliminated.

It is important to look at the attitude of the court. The laying of private information by the victim requires more time and effort by the justice of the peace than if the police were to lay it. The police condense the information and present it more quickly and efficiently.

If the police officers do not follow through on their mandate, the victim should have quick and easy access to the justice of the peace to start the process. To provide that access would be supporting the victim when he has reached the stage of action rather than being a negative response resulting in possible inaction.

Assaults require as much preparation and energy by the Crown Attorney as do more serious crimes. If we can deal with crime effectively at the minimum level, we will not have to worry about the maximum. The defence counsel will inevitably try to play down the event or even deny it happened. Such a stance tends to reinforce the abuser's feelings that he was entitled to do what he did. It also gives the appearance that the court is not really dealing with a crime but a misunderstanding between two people. The defence counsel has a duty to his client to present his side of the evidence in the best light, and I see little hope in changing that attitude. There is therefore more reason to emphasize those segments of the system where we can have some influence.

That leads us to judges who must be more than impartial assessors of facts. It is their duty to reflect the wishes and concerns of the community. They must be sensitive to the stance of the community in determining the proper disposition in the finding of guilt. The insistence of the Crown Attorney to proceed to trial must eventually convince judges that the community views assault as crime even if it occurred between husband and wife. Our 1985 study revealed that victims report less verbal and physical aggression from their husbands irrespective of a finding of guilt. Although they may not be found guilty, the violence is reduced.

The sentencing process must also reflect the concerns of the community. In some instances the judge will request a pre- sentence report by a psychologist. In preparing the report, the psychologist or probation officer must be very careful not to impose his or her attitude about the right of the abuser to use physical force in his relationship with the victim. If probation is granted, it must be actively monitored and the conditions closely scrutinized. Where there is a breach, a charge should be laid otherwise the violence will continue. I have reason to believe that this is not happening. The probation officer needs to keep in touch with the victim as well as the person being supervised.

It is important to have some mechanism to show that it is being followed through. Merely issuing a directive to your officers is not enough. At the outset, in 1981, we had a great deal of resistance despite the fact that in the first four months after the issue of the order charge the rate went up 2500 per cent. Part of that was that they knew they were being watched and monitored. The whole process is one in which we are trying to sell our officers on the efficacy of it. We sell them on it rather than direct them. We get better compliance this way and certainly a much better criminal justice system.

This direction is being supported in varying degrees across Canada by Attorneys General and Solicitors General. Crown attorneys are starting to take action. Our office takes a very firm stand against withdrawing charges. I believe victims are often coerced into asking that charges be withdrawn. If the Crown says no, at least the Crown and the police appear as the bad guys in the operation. I have had many cases where victims would come in wanting to withdraw the charges because the officer's attitude was not helpful.

Madame Justice Beverly McLachlin of the British Columbia Court of Appeal did make some statements in a decision about whether or not the victim should be forced to testify. In her opinion, a rule which leaves the choice of testifying against the spouse to the victim is more likely to be productive of family discord than to prevent it. It leaves the victim or spouse open to further threats and violence aimed at preventing him or her from testifying. She goes on to say that if the offending spouse knows that the victim has no choice but to testify, he or she is more likely to be deterred from committing crimes of violence. It is important that we commit ourselves to implementing change and providing resources to the criminal justice system.

FAMILY VIOLENCE

Linda Light
Federal/Provincial Working Group on Victims

Is it really to the victim's benefit to have a consistent charging policy in place? In British Columbia we have had a proactive policy in place which has aimed for consistency for two years. We found some evaluations and monitoring of that policy over those two years, and there are not many surprises in the results. We have seen very clearly that the problem in making the policy work is victim reluctance. The evaluations have confirmed that, but we have to start by looking at a system that is victim-oriented right from the beginning.

I am the victim coordinator for victim services in British Columbia. The reason that this proactive policy has been carried out by a victim services coordinator is because it starts from a victim's perspective. There is a danger that we might lose sight of that by demanding that a charge always be laid, and it must be consistent across the board. We have to temper that with reality and with what is best for the victim. We have to ask ourselves why we want charges laid in every case where there are reasonable and probable grounds. Why do we want these cases dealt with by the criminal justice system?

We have to look at making the criminal justice system a helpful one for both the victim and the offender. We have to look at victim services. We also have to look at treatment for offenders. This is especially important when victims are reluctant to become witnesses because they do not want their husbands or boyfriends to go to jail. It is in their interest to have offender treatment. They are more willing to enter the system if they feel their partner will have some chance of rehabilitation. When we are looking at specific kinds of services necessary for offenders and victims, we need to keep a larger perspective in mind to ensure we do not get lost in some other goal.

In British Columbia we developed this policy for both child abuse and wife abuse. They are different policies, but they have much in common. We were starting from a perspective where the social services crisis intervention approach, taken earlier by the police and seen as a very progressive policy 10 or 15 years ago, has not worked. There was evidence that it was not working, and we wanted to try something different. We wanted to try this proactive charging and arrest policy and then keep a close watch on it. We were not simply going to put it out there, let it run and then forget about it. We were going to keep a close watch on it, revise the policy and provide support for it. We did revise the policy, and it has been published. This has raised our credibility within the system.

If we look at ways we can make the system helpful to victims, we have to first look at integrated policies that are victim- oriented. We have to look at comprehensive justice system policies, and we have to look at justice policies that are related to the other systems of health, social services and education. We need integration both within the justice system and among these systems. We then have to look at services.

In British Columbia we started out with an integrated comprehensive policy without any money. We have worked so far with very little money and have been criticized for that. How can we develop a policy that is going to get more cases into the system without any victim services to back it up? We knew how, and we developed this policy right at the beginning of a restraint program. If we had waited for victim services, we would never have gone forward with the new policy. We went with the policy first and subsequently instituted victim services later on.

We are now at a stage where we are able to provide services beyond just a policy. The kinds of services we are looking at are services that can be delivered by justice system people in the course of their work, making the justice system more helpful by providing information to victims and by providing increased pre-trial contact. We had asked that the Crown hold interviews with victims well before the trial date. We found that was not happening in many cases. Probably in most cases they were not able to interview the victim before the trial date, but we found that it seemed to be making a difference in self-report by the Crown. The Crown's pre-trial interview was making a difference in increasing the number of victim-witnesses who were willing to come forward. Some people were saying there was not enough manpower to allow this. We said no. We can see in the small portions of cases that it seems to be making a difference. In our revised policy that instruction is strengthened.

These in-system, day-to-day things that the justice system can do in the course of its work are important although manpower is short, and the Crown is overburdened. We simply have to make this a priority if the system is going to institute a comprehensive policy on wife assault and child abuse. We have to be prepared to make choices about where we are going to put manpower and energy. I think information can be provided. We know from victimization surveys that the victim needs assessments done mostly by the federal ministry.

The greatest need for victims is receiving information about the progress of their cases. We know that can dispel anxiety. A woman who is educated about the system will be less apprehensive about entering it. We know that can be done with little expenditure. That can be done as a matter of course by professionals already in the system.

A more difficult type of service to provide is a direct support service for victims, victim-witnesses. We have to eventually aim for a support service that is specifically geared to the high risk, highly traumatized victims and witnesses. I am not one to argue for a whole new level of services to be laid on existing systems. We need victim support workers for every victim of every crime.

We do need victim support workers in the system for victims of wife assault and child abuse. That is where we will spend any incoming funds. The resources are so scarce that we focus on these two areas of crime.

While there are others who have arrived at policy development from another angle and have started with the services right at the beginning, we have come to this stage over the last couple of years. In policy development you have to face the issues of planning how you are going to provide these services and deal with the question of specialist versus generalists services. In British Columbia we decided in our policy development stage to go with a generalist model for justice system professionals. For wife assault, we felt everybody needed to be able to deal with it. All police officers should be trained in responding to these cases, and all Crown should have some knowledge of the nature and dynamics of wife assault in order to deal with it.

We made a different decision on the child abuse policy. We felt that this area required a specialist. I am sure there will be people who have adopted different models. We felt in most cases that if we had a specialist approach, which we do, it should be in addition to a generalist approach for wife assault.

Regardless of which model you choose, there are two things that stand out as necessary to change the system and its response to wife assault or child abuse. One is use of community agencies and a developed integrated referral network in which not one part of the system can serve victims by itself. We need to use every single resource we have in the community, and we need to have very active referral and follow-up systems. We need developed training both for justice system professionals and for specialists. That is where we can use tight money in a very effective way. We can design training packages that can be used for the specialist workers, self-help modules for people working in the system. We need to maximize these kinds of resources because of the constant problem of funding. We have to also look at changing attitudes.

Let us not throw out the baby with the bath water and make premature decisions that the justice system is not the answer. After two or three years in the field, we are looking at proactive prosecution policies which still face the very big issue of reluctant witnesses. We cannot say this will not work until we make the system a helpful one. We really try to get victim support workers in to help these victims with what we know is a very difficult situation. None of us ever thought it would be easy for wives to testify against their husbands or to go through this kind of a process in the justice system. Until we can focus the energy of the system on helping these victims, we cannot say that the justice system has succeeded in reducing incidents of family violence.

FAMILY VIOLENCE

Sue Johnson
University of Ottawa

My subject deals with the present status of the treatment of assault in Canada, and I plan to profile the man who batters his wife.

In 1984 there were 30 treatment programs in Canada for assaultive men which is a fairly conservative figure. These programs represented a relatively homogeneous philosophy of treatment which included a combination of education and skill training. The goals of treatment were to stop the recurring violent behavior and to help abusers build a self-image without violence.

Movement towards the treatment of the offender is a logical step because many of the victim's basic needs must be addressed. As the seriousness of this problem has been recognized, and as the justice system has responded to this issue more and more, offenders are being charged. This highlights the need for viable sentencing options.

If you ask women why they stay with men who hurt them, they tell you they love them. We cannot underestimate the fact that women will protect their bond.

We also now have model programs from the United States which is encouragement for us here in Canada. For example, the classic one emerged which had been established in Boston during the early 1970s. We have treatment formats. We begin to know what we are doing here. And most importantly, the treatment of the offender addresses the issue of recidivism. Men abuse continually if they are not treated, and they abuse in more than one relationship. Women often choose to return to an abusive spouse. The most salient target for intervention therefore appears to be the abuser himself.

The first Canadian program for abusers began in Toronto in 1980. The most common setting for this kind of program is a family service agency. There are variations on that, pastoral, correction and hospital settings. Most programs have not been the result of government policy or agency initiative.

The typical client in this kind of program would be somebody who is in his early 30s with a high school education and who is employed as a skilled or unskilled laborer. Clients can either be mandated by court or be voluntary. That is one of the issues in this area. Coming voluntarily is often suggested by the spouse. Since most of the men attending treatment groups are separated, pressure from the spouse is the key motivation for treatment. One of the problems with voluntary clients is that when the wife returns, they stop attending the groups.

The violent behavior in such a group of men ranges from an isolated slap to repeated life endangering abuse. Even with slight physical abuse, there is often psychological and sexual abuse which may be even more damaging than the physical violence. You might get a man for example who says, "I don't know what I'm doing here. I'm not an abuser. I'm not like these other men. I've never actually hit my wife." Then, six weeks later when he really begins to talk about his relationship, you find that he did not actually hit his wife, but rather he threatened. He would, for instance, lock her in the basement for endless hours.

Only about 20% of the men involved in treatment in Canada also tend to be violent outside the home. What the groups focus on is violence inside intimate relationships. Most treatment programs exclude clients who exhibit extreme drug or alcohol abuse, psychopathology, apparent neurological impairment, suicidal risk or extreme denial or resistance. If a man takes no responsibility for his abuse, it is very difficult to see how useful it would be to put him into a treatment group.

Assessment, including consultation with the battered spouse, is a key element in treatment. Such assessments include details of current and past violence, a relationship history, current stresses and an assessment of how lethal the act is. That is very difficult to do. It includes things like the frequency and the severity of the violence, the use of weapons, drug use and factors like that.

Referrals come from women shelters, courts, social agencies, client self-referral and occasionally the police. This seems to be an underdeveloped source of referral.

The basic principles of treatment which seem to run across all the programs in Canada are first of all that the batterer is responsible for his violence. Neither provocation nor justification are accepted. I think there is a useful differentiation here which is that the battered spouse may contribute to the conflict, may contribute to the escalation, may contribute to the distress in the relationship, but it is the one who hits who is responsible for violence.

Violence is also considered on a personal level as a response to conflict, anxiety or frustration and is condoned as part of the male role. It is viewed primarily as an attempt to control the spouse. I think one of the important things to remember in this kind of context is that the immediate effect of such violence can be very rewarding, even addicting, because it is the batterer who wins the argument. It is rewarding for the man to hit his wife in the immediate context. It is not rewarding in the long-term. The long-term affects both the spouse and the relationship.

Most of the treatment groups contain approximately eight to 13 men and two male leaders. Sometimes there will be a male and female team. They are structured in a closed format for approximately nine to 19 sessions. This is shorter than is recommended by recent authors. Most of the treatment programs in Canada are relatively short-term.

The most common clinical problem is resistance, denial and minimization of their behavior. The key factors in the change process are considered to be the use of peers to confront denial. Group support helps facilitate self-awareness, emotional exploration, learning and isolation. Most of these men are totally dependent on their wives.

There is modelling and teaching of structured skills such as anger control, communication and assertiveness skills. This might include the teaching of anger discrimination clues so that men can recognize when they are becoming angry and the use of time out procedures to prevent loss of control. Many programs will use things like anger diaries, for example.

In such a diary, batterers will use actual incidents in their everyday life to identify triggers and cues preceding anger. A group will focus on a type of violence that occurred in a relationship and ask what particular incidents and stresses came up that week.

The second part of the group would concern coping strategy. For example, one deals with extreme jealousy. The typical client begins by stating that he does not have a problem, and the reason he is there is because his wife is impossible, or the system is unfair. The group does not respond to that. The man stops presenting that view, stops denying so much and is likely to become uncommunicative for a little while.

Most groups require new participants to share their most recent and worst violent episodes immediately. Gradually the man discusses his response to his violence, his fears of losing his wife and begins to take some responsibility for his behavior.

If the group is a safe therapeutic milieu, he receives support. The man then begins to re-evaluate his attitudes towards his spouse, his role as a male and his own behavior. He begins to view his own responses critically and to see the triggers to his anger.

With each stage of treatment, predictable issues arise. For example, in the middle stage of treatment one of the big issues is that the man will say things like, "I'm trying. I'm doing my best. I am changing. There's really no point, because she doesn't trust me anymore." It is very difficult for them to accept the fact that there is no immediate reward.

The other thing the group deals with is crisis management. As men become senior members, they begin to take more of a leadership role in confronting and supporting others. Group leaders have to be able to facilitate group process and respond sensitively to new emotional responses, confront denial and dysfunctional attitude and teach structured skills. One of the main difficulties for group leaders is burn-out.

There is a need for treatment outcome data to establish effectiveness and accountability. Secondly, there is a lack of funding and a need for an integrated response to wife assault. Third, there is the question of enforced treatment versus voluntary treatment and treatment dropouts. Fourth, there are clinical issues such as optimum length of treatment.

Outcome research requires resources that are difficult to muster when programs are just struggling to stay alive and maintain service. The majority of men seem to be non-violent when they are attending the group. However, in the survey that Dr. Browning from British Columbia did for the National Clearing House on family violence, he estimated that after four months only 60% maintain the lack of violence in their relationship. The violence can be reduced in severity and frequency. Alcoholics and violent and highly resistant batterers do poorly in these programs. That estimated success rate is consistent with general rates of success in psychotherapy.

Lack of funding is the most serious pragmatic issue in this field. Only a few programs receive direct government funding. To run programs like this as adjuncts to larger agency programs often leads to poor support and leader burn-out. One of the answers is to have programs with a mandate for voluntary clients to reach some of the more resistant clients. It has been estimated that presently there are approximately 750 men in treatment in Canada. That is a small number considering the pervasiveness of this problem.

FAMILY VIOLENCE

Linda MacLeod
Consultant, Ottawa

We are currently not only at a crossroads concerning crime, but we are also at a significant crossroads with respect to our knowledge of, and responses to, wife battering.

My first general theme deals with wife battering as a political issue. What is the possible benefit to the state of maintaining a public interest in wife battering? Why has wife battering remained fashionable? The political interest in wife battering could be a way of containing and controlling wife battering by fashioning services to make wife battering less troublesome, by further isolating battered women in shelters and on welfare roles, by placing them in ghettos, by forcing them into poverty and by persuading them to return to their husbands and to accept their fate. Is the current state response to wife battering in fact an example of what is being called state violence? A road paved with apparently good intentions is subverted by the government will to preserve control over the private lives of individuals.

My second theme deals with definitions of violence. How does definition influence our policies concerning wife battering? Definition problems have plagued the wife battering debate, and definition debates are inherent in the battered woman.

Families teach children that those who love you are also those who hit you, that those who love you are also those you can hit. The paradox muddles the understood definitions of both love and violence. On the policy front, advocates have fought long and hard to extricate wife battering from the suffocation of family violence. We are also witnessing new terminology over whether to use wife battering or the term wife assault to punctuate the illegal nature of wife battering. There is also the term violence against women in the home to emphasize the multidimensional nature of such violence. If we choose wife assault, we will go in the criminal justice direction. There is some concern being raised as to whether state intervention is slowly eroding our underlying understanding of what services and other responses to battered wives is about.

The third overall theme is that violence, and particularly violence that occurs in the family, is extremely complex. There is not one causal factor which can adequately explain violence and give easy solutions.

In addition to these general themes, two major sub-themes have been continually repeated with respect to wife battering. The most contentious is that although the general agreement seems to be that wife battering should be seen as a crime, there is also growing speculation that the criminal justice system should not be seen as a panacea in wife battering cases. This form of violence is significant not only because it is widespread, but also because concern with this issue may signify an expression of emerging values concerning the human condition.

My third theme deals with this complexity of wife battering. How can we make sense of the complexity of wife battering? Definition problems naturally enter into our debates about solutions. My one general response to the question of dealing with complexity is that while we must consider theoretical positions and distance ourselves from the horror of wife battering periodically, we must also return to the victim's wants and needs. Only in this way will we be able to make sense of the complexity in a way which will preserve our goals of justice, truth and love. To elaborate on this slightly, we can distance ourselves from the empirical reality and categorize solutions into long-term as well as short-term solutions. We can stress the difference between wife battering and child abuse. We can stress the separation between the man's responsibility and the woman's victimization. But unfortunately, battered women do not always want to make these clear distinctions. Battered women find it just as hard as any of us who are not currently battered to give up all hope of things getting better. Their anguish is long-term. Most battered women reject short-term solutions which dash, or appear to dash, this long-term hope.

The fourth theme deals with the criminal justice system as an appropriate vehicle in reducing or even preventing wife battering. Reliance on the criminal justice system is, to many women, a very unpalpable solution because they perceive that legal intervention will increase the chances of splitting. The law also gives them no assurances that the violence will end. The criminal justice system is generally an appropriate vehicle to use. The criminalization of a phenomenon traditionally has been a way for the government to expand its control. A criminal justice approach to a problem inevitably takes on the characteristics and underlying assumptions of the criminal justice system. The criminal justice system is rooted in punishment, elitism and dependency. It is a system based on the logic of detail, discrete events and narrowly defined acts. It is a system in which the individual victim is not inherently a partner in the system and in which the victim's comprehensive problems frequently have no place. It is a system in which crimes are technically against the government.

Traditionally, the law has been used to subordinate women. An increase in influential women could have an effect on the laws of our land. The criminal justice system simply does not provide one-stop shopping for the battered woman in her search for services and tends to fragment her problems. Currently across Canada it is common for the police to remove a woman who is being battered and place her with a relative or friend or in a shelter. Removal from the home is in itself frequently a form of punishment. Women and children must live in communal settings and transition houses which rob them of privacy. Many women feel they cannot subject their children to the reduced standard of living.

There are other solutions to wife battering. One is to remove the man from the home. Another is to reduce stress.

PART VIII

ABUSE OF THE ELDERLY

ABUSE OF THE ELDERLY

Eleanor Cooper
Co-Ordinator/Researcher,
Mayor Lastman's Task Force on the Abuse of the Elderly

Many individuals and groups have been working in the area of elder abuse for many years, but because of lack of information on the topic and a lack of coordination of the various programs, it has been very difficult to get good statistics and a clear picture as to the extent of the problem.

The first and only widely publicized definitive study on the subject of elder abuse in Canada entitled "Protection of the Elderly - A Study of Elder Abuse" was published in 1982 by Donna J. Shell under the auspices of the Manitoba Council on Aging. Four hundred and two cases of elder abuse were studied. The Manitoba Study estimates that 2.2% of the elderly are subject to abuse; therefore, the number of abused elderly in Toronto alone would exceed 1,600 people. Province-wide, the number would be approximately 22,000. However, it is likely that this is an underestimation because of the victims' reluctance to report and the inability of many professionals to recognize when abuse has occurred.

Available statistics show that close to 70% of abused elderly people live with the abusing caregiver who is likely to be a family member. Most abused elders are females (67.7%), and most abusers are male (60%). The most likely abuser is a son, followed by a daughter and by a spouse.

The areas that the task force looked into which we felt were the three main areas of abuse are neglect, financial and physical. The question is often asked, "Why, if these people are being abused, do they not report?" The answer is manyfold. They do not wish further abuse. They are fearful that they will be removed from their homes and placed in an institution. If the abuser is a child, there is the double shame of the abuse as well as admitting that you brought up such a terrible child.

The abuse is not always recognized by a professional because elderly people tend to bruise easily and have bones break frequently. The professional cannot always recognize the signs of abuse.

With this in mind, the task force, Mayor Lastman's Task Force on Abuse of the Elderly, was formed in mid-January 1985. Its membership represents people from various professions as well as interested laypeople. The chairperson is Dr. Jerry Cooper who is Chief of Psychiatry at York-Finch General Hospital, and everyone who is part of the task force represents the different facets of the community involved in the area of abuse. We have a social worker, the executive director from the hospital, a geriatric psychiatrist, a forensic psychologist, a lawyer in private practice, a chief of family practice, people from York University, people from Metro Housing, the Director of Public Health Nurses of North York, people from the police department, university students, the chief of radiology from the hospital, and the director from the hospital services. We really have tried to put in as many people as possible on the task force so that we would have a clear picture of the problem.

On February 27, 1985, the task force, in conjunction with the Canadian Mental Health Association, North York and the National Council of Jewish Women, Toronto Section, held a panel discussion on the problems of the abuse of the elderly. The discussion took place in the council chambers of the North York Civic Centre. The discussion was well attended by elderly people, interested laypeople, students of geriatrics and professionals in the field. Many issues were discussed, and some interesting facts were brought to light. For example, one member of the audience told the panel that she had been successful in her bid to gain access to her grandchildren. She had gone to court and had been granted visitation rights to see her grandchildren. This was an abuse that we had not been aware of, the abuse of taking grandchildren away from grandparents in order to gain money from them, in order to put leverage or pressure on them. Various members of the task force have met with representatives from the United States and have discussed their programs with them. Many of our members travelled at their own cost to various centres. They met with Terry Fulmer from the Beth Israel Hospital in Boston, Massachusetts, John Stokesberry who is with the Department of Health and Rehabilitative Services in Fort Lauderdale, Florida and a Congressman and his aides who have expressed an interest in our project.

The task force is reviewing all the literature that is available on the topic of elder abuse, and it is hoped that some Canadian statistics will be arrived at. At the moment, very little Canadian information is available. Most of the statistics are American, and we will have to extrapolate from these statistics. It should be noted that even the American statistics are not specific and are not broken down into regions. When we visited people in London, England, they were using the same American statistics. They did not have their own. The statistics are general. There are some Canadian statistics available from some provinces, but the results reflect those of the American statistics. According to a recent Ontario study which only had a 7.6% response to its questionnaire, the results suggest that abuse and neglect of the elderly are problems in Ontario. These problems most often take the form of neglect and/or material abuse. Physical abuse of the elderly seems to be less prevalent, and the findings also indicate that the problem seems to be observed more frequently in large urban areas. I have questioned that final result. The small percentage responding generally came from urban areas. They just said that there probably is not a problem in rural areas. I do not believe that. Maybe that is just something that they just did not bother to answer.

The task force became involved in four major areas of concern. A survey of hospitals and social service agencies who care for the elderly was put in place to discover the type of service for the elderly, the name of the contact person, objectives of the service, description of the service, the staffing of the service and if such a service exists.

The survey was done by Richard Cooper, a York University student. It was undertaken to enable the task force to pinpoint those hospitals as social service agencies which specifically provide services for the elderly. The survey showed that most hospitals do not have anything specifically set up to deal with the problems of abuse of the elderly, but many showed interest in our proposed elder assessment program. The survey did pinpoint a big problem that elderly people have. If they go to an emergency department, there is nothing specifically set up for them, and if they do call a hospital, they really are just put onto a social worker who may or may not be able to help them. That was something that we were quite concerned about, and that was one of the reasons why we set up this pilot project at York Finch General Hospital.

This pilot project was set up in the emergency department of the York-Finch General Hospital. It is based on the model of the Beth Israel Hospital in Boston, Massachusetts. Persons involved in this project went to Boston to observe the program there. The team consists of a social worker, hospital administrator, the head nurse, public health supervisor as well as a general practitioner. Psychiatrists and radiologists act as consultants to the assessment team.

A screening process is used to identify needs for the elderly. The project began November 1, 1985, and is continually assessed and revised. This kind of project will heighten the awareness of personnel in the emergency department to the needs of the elderly. The program was set up to determine whether or not abuse was present in persons 65 years of age and over who presented themselves to the emergency department.

The team was set up, and through examples in information found in literature, they developed an Elder Assessment Form. It was decided that the survey should include all patients coming to York-Finch General Hospital emergency department who were 65 years of age and older. A form should be completed on every patient who presented himself to this department. Through this means there would be an attempt to identify concerns of the elderly population utilizing York-Finch General Hospital. The survey was to last for a three month period, November 1, 1985, to January 31, 1986.

The number of forms returned from the emergency department in November were 101. There were 94 in December and 73 in January for a total of 268. They discovered that not all of them were completed.

What they looked at was a breakdown of the age of the patients, male or female, their marital status, their living arrangements, how the patient was brought to the emergency department, the general assessment of the patients as to their clothing, their hygiene, their grooming, their mobility.

Concerns were found in 32 cases, 6 male, 26 female. The average age for the male was 74.83 years; for the female, 82.44 years. Again, the breakdown was according to marital status, the living arrangements, how the patient was brought into the hospital, the general assessment and the physical assessment. And the cases regarding concerns for medication were three for the male and 17 for the female.

The number of Elder Assessment Forms returned without being completed was high. It was 32.46%. This was due to the extremely busy emergency department of the York-Finch General Hospital. Even in view of this fact, there was sufficient evidence that there should be concern for the care of senior citizens. In 20 cases there were concerns over the amount of medication being taken by the elderly person. In three of these cases, concern was expressed over the ability of the person to administer the medication.

In the area of physical assessment, there were also areas which bring into concern the care of the elderly person. The information obtained from this form does not allow a definite conclusion that the condition is due to poor care by the caregiver, but it does indicate that further investigation would be merited. The research technique of randomized sampling was not utilized. As the form was completed, the evidence found indicated that concerns do exist.

The elder assessment team recommends that nurses in the emergency department be educated to the existence of this problem. Hospital emergency departments should be staffed sufficiently to be able to interview the patient regarding concerns. The form utilized for this survey should provide information based on observations by the nurses. Where indicated, investigations should be delegated to some authority for further investigation. Ideally, there would be a government agency as in the United States with the responsibility of ensuring that the elderly person's rights and his personal needs are met. A provincewide crisis telephone line would be operated by the provincial government. This should be operated by professional personnel and would be able to address not only the concerns of the elderly but also child welfare concerns and all other areas of social services. The British Columbia government has operated such a line since 1978. The provincial government should engage in a campaign to inform the public regarding concerns in caring for the elderly and should become more active in this area as the percentage of the total population, which is in the senior citizen category, steadily increases.

We are now in the process of doing the second step to this elder assessment team. We are looking to gain further funds to hire a student for the summer who would be specifically trained in using this form and staying in the emergency department and actually doing the form in a specific manner. We want to compare the two to see if someone specifically trained in this area, not a busy nurse, would get a different result or would get a more intensive reading. That is what we are in the process of doing right now.

Another one of our projects was an information hotline which was established at York University. Laurie Peasley, a former emergency nurse, and presently an undergraduate student in psychology at York University, was in charge of the hotline.

The hotline began in 1985 and continued until May 1986. The results are now being reviewed. The calls were anonymous and not taped. The log of calls received was kept, and the phone was funded by the LaMarsh Research Program on Violence. The volunteers manning the telephone were undergraduate students doing a practicum in social work or taking a counselling course as well as other undergraduate students. A directory was compiled specifically for the elderly, listing the name of agencies, the type of services and the given name of the contact person.

The purpose of this hotline was to give out information to elderly people who would not necessarily know whom to call. It is very frustrating when you call a hospital, as was done in our survey, and then are given another number. Sometimes five or six telephone calls were needed, and then you would discover that there was no service available. What this information hotline attempted to do was to reduce the number of calls and to give people information as to where they could call to get help. We are now assessing the effectiveness of this kind of a hotline.

One of the other projects that our task force did after only a year was to hold a forum at York University which was co- sponsored by the LaMarsh Research Program on Violence, the York- Finch General Hospital and the Canadian Mental Health Association, North York. This forum was held on Saturday, October 19, 1985, at Osgoode Hall and was open to the community. Various organizations could present briefs to the task force at this time.

Each group was given 10 to 15 minutes for a presentation. A written brief was also presented. Questions were taken from the floor. All these briefs will form the heart of the final report of the task force. Various experts from the task force were present during the day to answer any questions. The day was chaired by myself. A Congressman sent a video which was shown at the beginning of the day congratulating our task force on its efforts. He is a Florida congressman who initiated the concern about elder abuse and has been active in promoting education interest in the plight of the elderly. Municipal, provincial and federal politicians were in attendance at the forum. The forum at York University could not have been realized without the help of all the three sponsoring organizations, especially the York Finch General Hospital.

Presently, all the proceedings from that forum are being edited, and the final published report with an update on the task force activities will be available shortly. Since the conclusion of the forum, the task force has put into practice a number of the recommended programs.

For older Americans, according to a Federal Drug Administration (FDA) report, an assortment of drugs is the rule rather than the exception. A University of Florida College of Pharmacy survey found that elderly patients take an average of 3.2 drugs per month. Other studies have shown that older patients may be getting as many as 10 to 18 different drugs in the course of a year. The same FDA report states that nursing home patients may take as many as 20 drugs a month.

To physicians specializing in geriatric medicine, these figures are particularly shocking because drugs and their undesirable side effects may affect an older person much more than a younger one. According to the FDA, age makes a difference in the way the drug is distributed in the body. We were concerned about the number of people arriving in the emergency departments of hospitals completely disoriented and showing certain signs of senility and depression. When taken off all of their medication, many of their symptoms disappeared. That concerned the physicians in attendance. Elderly people do not tell their doctors that they are seeing more than one doctor. They forget that they are taking other drugs. They take a lot of over the counter medication.

To counteract this program, we introduced what we called our brown bag program. It is a unique outreach program of the task force and it has successfully been in operation for several months. It is coordinated by myself, the researcher and co- ordinator for the task force, Barry Phillips, who is past president of the Ontario College of Pharmacists and Bobby Cates, past president of the Metropolitan Toronto Pharmacists Association, as well as Sheila White from Mayor Lastman's office.

The purpose of the program is to promote the wise use of medication, both prescription and non-prescription. The co- ordinators have visited numerous community centres, seniors residences and church groups. The participants are asked to bring all their medication prescriptions and non-prescription drugs in a brown paper bag. They are then told about the proper use of medication. After a short question and answer period, the pharmacists speak to each participant individually answering any of their questions regarding their drugs. They also examine everything in their brown paper bags.

Numerous abuses have been detected, and the individuals have been urged to speak to their physicians. We discovered that people who use nitroglycerin do not know how to use it at all, and many of them do not store it properly. It becomes either too effective or not effective enough. We found that safety caps on medicine bottles are not easily opened by people with arthritic hands so people do not take their medication. We inform them that they can get flip-top bottles. People keep their drugs for many years, and if taken in combination with their present drugs, they would have some fatal results. Many of these glaring things have been picked up, and it is very important that they have done so. We really feel we have been providing a service to the community.

This project has become so successful that there have been requests from outside North York, and coordinators have started to visit some of these outside centres. Florida, as well, has shown a great deal of interest in this project, and they are going to set up their own program based on our model. We have discovered that many of our programs can be emulated anywhere. We are trying to set an example for other communities and for other parts of the country showing them what a community can do in a preventive way. All the things that I have discussed have been preventive measures that we have instituted.

Finally, one of the biggest problems facing the elderly is loneliness. To combat this problem, the task force is proposing to set up a project whereby some of these people can have a pen pal from Florida. A questionnaire will be sent out to those individuals interested in taking part in this program. They will be matched up with a compatable individual from Florida. If some of these individuals have difficulty writing, volunteers will help them with their letters. We are quite optimistic about this project since we feel it would be a good outlet. We have already collated a large number of names. I have been in contact with our person in Florida who has done the same, and this project will be initiated very shortly. We hope, if it is successful, that we can introduce other countries using other languages besides English and using volunteers as well.

ABUSE OF THE ELDERLY

Suzanne Steinmetz
University of Delaware

A major concern is what is the relevance to the study done in the United States to Canadians. Canadian and American families are becoming smaller. There are fewer children. Therefore,there are fewer children to care for the elderly. Singlehood, the single parent family and childlessness are increasing. Many elders will have no children to care for them. Also, you have the single parent families growing, and divorce and remarriage increasing. Thus many families will not only have to deal with caring for an elderly parent but also for an elderly step-parent. They may be caring for in-laws, and they may be caring for ex in-laws, those in-laws and relatives from an earlier marriage who have maintained close ties with the children and now are looking for reciprocation in terms of help as they grow older.

Life expectancy and median age are increasing. This means that the elderly population is growing. It is in both Canada and the United States according to the data that I was able to access, the fastest growing population. What this means is contrary to the stereotype we have in the States that it is the 40-year-old who is abusing the 60-year-old. What we have really is the 60- year-old who is taking care of the 80-year-old.

Many women are employed in occupations in which mandatory retirement is not enforced. Because women tend to have smaller incomes, they have fewer resources built up in their pensions. Their husbands die early, and they are less likely to remarry, or they are divorced and are less likely to remarry. It means that they find they have to work. They do not have enough money. When you first marry, you have brand new things. Ten years later everything is broken. When you retire, it is the same thing. People tend to buy new things so that they are all set for retirement. Ten or 15 years later the stove goes; the car goes; the washing machine goes; the refrigerator goes. The car probably goes in seven years, but the other things hang in a little bit longer. All of a sudden, these people find themselves with extremely limited resources. Savings dwindle. Retirement and pension plans dwindle. The cost of living, of course, has increased, and it becomes very difficult to deal with.

The study that I am reporting on was gathered by what is called a snowball technique. What I did is put advertisements in papers. We got families. And at the end of the interview, we said to them, "Do you know anyone else?" This is, to my knowledge, the only study in the

United States, in Canada and in Europe which interviewed families that were caring for the elderly as opposed to service populations or police surveys and things of that sort. We are specifically looking at the abuse that adult children or surrogate children perpetrate on the elderly.

We did interview the adult children for many reasons. One was to ascertain age. We would have to have the interviewers go in and run cognitive functioning tests and assessment tests to see if it were indeed reliable information.

The study was designed in 1979 and 1980. The data was collected at that point in time. That was before there was widespread advertisement and knowledge about the term elder abuse. It certainly was going on, but we did not have a term. In that respect, I feel quite lucky because indeed it is a virgin sample. It was not contaminated by knowing what was going on was labelled bad. And the other thing is, because at that time there were no support groups. People were in many cases provided with the first opportunity to talk about things that they found stressful.

We have 13 state wide support groups now. We had none then. What we found is that it is not socially acceptable to say to your neighbor, "My mother is driving me up a tree!" It is alright to say that your kid is driving you crazy, but somehow when these people reached out to tell someone how stressful this is, they were told that this is not appropriate. This is not the way you are supposed to behave.

With some demographic data, the sample is predominantly white. It is predominantly middle class. Although we made a conscious effort to get working class and low-class families, it is still predominantly middle class. Caregivers were predominantly women, and in cases when we interviewed males, they often told us that indeed their wives provided most of the care.

We did have one Canadian family in which the husband commuted to Delaware where his parents had a business and were quite old and could no longer take care of it. There were lots of other sisters and a brother in the area to carry on the business, but this was the oldest son, and he felt that this was his responsibility. He, for four years, had been commuting back and forth to Canada which is a bit of a commute.

The average age of the caregiver is fairly old; 44% were 50-59. Nineteen per cent were 60 and older. Likewise, the age of the elders was fairly old. We are not talking about middle-aged people. It is the demographic and family stress characteristics that in some ways influence the dependency tasks that have to be performed, perception of burden and the elders control maintenance techniques. The things that the elder does to try and maintain control are crying, pouting, yelling, etc. All of these things then lead to the dependency task stress. What we have found is that it is not how many tasks you have to perform but the perception of how stressful it is. Indeed we had families who talked about the terrible things going on, and I go back to the transcript and these people are ready to commit suicide. It is a perceptual thing.

Only 23% of my sample had any kind of elder abuse, and that included the abuse of forcing food and medicine which in many cases is benign in intent, restraining in some way as well as hitting, slapping and threatening with those things. While everybody is equally performing these tasks it did not differentiate who was abusive. The perception, how you define the situation, seemed most critical.

Being caught in the middle is when you have small children needing your time and attention and a home to manage, and you are working five days a week, and you have an older person whose needs are even in excess of those of the children. It is almost next to impossible to handle it all and do it to any degree of satisfaction. You always feel like you are just not cutting the mustard. What you do is just handle the priorities and emergency situations and just take one situation at a time. You are constantly pressured. You feel like there is someone behind you ramming you with a ramrod. You push as hard and as much as you can, but you can not do it all. It leaves its mark. A 57- year old daughter who has been caring for her 81-year-old mother-in-law for 14 years brings constant demands. "Towards the end, she really got bad. She would not let me sleep 10 to 15 minutes, and then she would call me again. All night she would do this. All day and night. Demands do not bother me, but excessive demands do. She was running me down into the ground. She was always demanding, and I met her demands. That is the kind of person I am. I figured if she wants a drink, she wants a drink, and she wanted a drink of water every 20 minutes. She was constantly drinking and constantly going to the bathroom."

The 62-year-old daughter caring for her 83-year-old mother for one year and her 90-year-old mother-in-law for 18 years brings on sleep deprivation as is obvious in this quotation. "He has his own bedroom; I have a bedroom too, but I never get to sleep in it. If I sleep upstairs in my room, I am afraid that he will fall, and I will not hear him so therefore I always sleep down on the couch. I have ever since he has been here. I do not think I have slept on a bed a dozen times since he has been here which is four years. He does prowl a lot at night. He is getting up to get a drink of water, going to the bathroom, back and forth, getting a little cereal, back and forth. I have had to try and learn to block out the noise at night because it is just a constant thing. Up and down. He must get a drink a half a dozen times and then go to the bathroom. He sleeps so much during the day. I guess this is what old people do as a result of sleeping all day. I guess I have not really had a good night's sleep since he has been here."

The 66-year-old daughter caring for her 86-year-old father for four years has lack of services. The person taking care of a parent in their home gets no help whatsoever.

With the 51-year-old daughter caring for an 86-year-old mother for seven years, it was hard starting to care for someone at eight or nine o'clock in the morning. It takes hours and hours. "She would be up for a few hours, and I would put her back to bed for a nap. I found myself not doing what I should do such as cleaning the house. I would run out and shop. During that time, had I been able to afford it, I would have had someone do those things. It would have been great."

Some of these people find the situation so stressful that they say things like, "There are times when it crops up when I feel so guilty about things; I just think I must be no good to someone. There are times when I think if I could just die to get out of this whole stinking mess without having to live with it another day, day in and day out. The thing goes on. There is no end." When this respondent was asked how she coped with the stress (a 66-year-old daughter who had been caring for her 86-year-old father for four years), she replied, "I have left here sometimes at 8:00 a.m. and walked the street until 3:00 or 4:00 p.m. just to let off steam. That is the only way I can explain it."

Another caregiver reported, "I was so tired as a result of not being able to sleep that when I thought about sleep, I had the most peaceful feeling come over me, and I wished that I would never have to wake up again. When I thought about this, it frightened me. This came to me one time. Getting away from it all comes to me a lot of times. I wish I could get away. This has created a lot of stress." This is a 56-year-old daughter caring for her 79-year-old mother for eight months.

They can do instrumental tasks such as providing special diets, providing financial help which does not always mean money. Sometimes it means paying the bills for the elder or dealing with the fact that the elder will not eat, but what really gets to them is the loneliness, privacy, dealing with the fact the person has no friends because everyone has died or their own children have all died off. They have outlived most of their children. This is very sad and demanding. These are the things in most cases that really are very stressful. As a result of this stress, we find that there is a tremendous amount of elder abuse. It goes both ways; it should not be surprising that elders are quite violent themselves.

If you look at elder abuse, you will find that 41% of the caregivers resort to verbal abuse. You realize they are screaming and yelling at 80 and 90 and 95 and 103-year-old people. Total abuse is a combination of the medical abuse, the physical abuse and the severe physical abuse. Severe physical abuse is actual hitting and restraining. Physical abuse has the threat of that as well as the actual abuse, and then the total abuse has the medical abuse component in it which is forcing food and medicine. You can see that very often those things as well as tying the person in bed are done for benign reasons; they are not necessarily done as a harmful thing.

What is likely to predict elder abuse is an elder who has been abusive when he was rearing the child. "I can count on one hand when I saw my mother cry. She would just as soon pick something up and throw it. During the last six weeks, generally towards the end of her life, she only made a swipe at me once. She really never threw anything in those last six weeks. She was always a very physical person when I was younger. My father never spanked me; she did. When she was mad at me, she would let me know I am just like her." A 50-year-old daughter caring for her 87-year-old mother for 15 years said, "I would say that if a parent has been a very loving parent and a caring parent, then a child could handle that, but when you know that they have not been, it is very difficult to handle. It has been said that you do not forget what is in the past. You do not forget these things. Even an old dog, if you have beaten him, will cringe when he sees you. Even he does not forget. He either cringes, or he bites you." This is the 66-year-old daughter who had been caring for her 86-year-old father for four years.

It was clear that the families that worked the best had set guidelines. This is a utopian situation where you can plan. We generally take these people in at the last point, when the hospital calls you and says "Your mother is in here. She has broken her hip, etc." But if it is at all possible, if the person is positively able, you really do need to sit down and do some of these things even if you do not do them with the person. Perhaps the adult children are not the best people to care. Maybe another adult child can care much better for your parent than you can. Maybe you should switch. It is difficult.

In our society, and I suspect in Canada, we want to maintain our independence. We train people for a lifetime of being independent, and then all of a sudden we deny them that because we want to keep them safe. We do not want them to get hurt. We know what is best for them to eat. We know how important it is for them to take their medicine at a particular time. No wonder these people strike out. They want to maintain some sense of independence. If they are cared for by someone else, they are not dependent on their children. They do maintain that feeling of independence.

Local communities can establish support groups which are critical. People need to talk to other people. What we have found in our support groups is even when either the parent has died or a decision to put them in the hospital arises, people still come to the support group so they can share their information with others get support. At least of the books I am aware of, there is no Dr. Spock for caring for your elderly parent. You have to learn from other people. We do not have education. We do not have courses in our school system that teach you how to be old gracefully. We teach you how to prepare for a job, how to prepare for parenthood, how to prepare for a marriage. We do not do those last two things so terribly well, but we try. We also have no role models. When we do see elderly people, we see them in two categories, the young vibrant 50-year-old grandmother who goes dancing or the very, very sick older person in an institution or in a show on television. In our own homes, most of us have not had the opportunity to grow up seeing an older person age and need that kind of care. Many of us have played with dolls. We have all babysat. We have taken care of older cousins. We have experience with that. We do not have experience in caring for older people.

Short-term respite and household chores are very important. If you could just get someone to come in for a couple of hours a day so I could get away. If someone could just come in and take over so I could go to a hotel for the night and get a good nights sleep. It was amazing how very simple and relatively inexpensive the remedies were. Yet, for a woman who is 68 who has dwindled down all her resources, cannot really hold a job because who is going to care for her mother, she may not have $10 to have somebody come in and take over for four hours. These are very simple things that could have made a difference in the quality of life.

The final thing is increased education and awareness. We are starting to do that, but we have to start really in the younger grades. We have to tell people what it is like to grow old. We have to prepare them for aging. We have to prepare them for what our society is. The one thing that truly worries me is you can make a case on an economic basis for providing support and services to battered children and battered women because you will return them to being an economic and productive component of society. There is a cost benefit. Unfortunately, we have not recognized we owe these people something, and it is a quality of life and dignity and services which reward children who take care of their elders and not penalize them which is what our services do right now. I think we have to start making people aware.

Awareness of elder abuse is a very narrow part of it. It is broader than that. Most of my family members were warm, wonderful, loving people. They in no way thought of themselves as abusive. Yet they did a lot of abusive things because of lack of alternatives, lack of awareness of the appropriate way to care for the elderly. So we have to start providing resources for these people. We have to start young. If you are not getting along with your mother when you are 40 and she is 60, why when you are 60 and she is 80 do you think you are going to be able to care for her? How are all the mother daughter conflicts going to be resolved? They are not. You have to start earlier.

ABUSE OF THE ELDERLY

Birthe Jorgensen
Carleton University

Through my involvement with a voluntary consumer organization that supports elderly residents of institutional care and through the generous financial support of an independent research grant from the Ministry of Solicitor General of Canada, I was able to conduct research on institutionalization of the elderly in Canada.

First of all, it is a fact that the population of Canada is aging. The figures show that at the present time one in 10 Canadians are over the age of 65. As a result of this increased longevity and a decreasing birth rate, the proportion of our population over the age of 65 is going to be increasing over the next several decades.

Since this is a relatively recent historical phenomenon, we have not responded to the particular special needs which we as a society may be confronted with by this aging population. The response which has taken place has been largely in the health care field when it takes place at all. The thrust of our health care response has been institutionalization, particularly in the province of Ontario. Our financial resources and our planning in Ontario has been in the institutionalization area.

In Ontario at the present time, there are about 600 facilities for the elderly providing some form of medical care. These are varying in size. Some are small converted houses in the countryside, and some are very large institutions. The total composite of the 600 nursing facilities include among them 331 nursing homes.

Nursing homes are privately owned residences for elderly persons. These are licensed and regulated by the Ministry of Health, and they are largely financed on a per diem basis by the Ministry of Health. Most of the nursing homes in Ontario are run for profit and are owned by private individuals or private corporations. We also have in Ontario homes for the aged which are administered municipally and monitored by the Ministry of Community and Social Services.

There are also in Ontario an increasing number of retirement homes. It is estimated that there are as many retirement beds in this province as there are licensed or regulated nursing homes and homes for the aged. These retirement homes are not regulated nor controlled. While they are called retirement homes, we have no legal category of something called a retirement home. It is a boarding house where elderly people or the handicapped go to live.

In total, these facilities constitute thousands and thousands of beds in Ontario for elderly residents and for handicapped individuals not placed in the hospital setting. Ontario has the distinction of being cited in the United States 1974 Senate Committee hearing reports on aging and also in Joan Watson's Ontario task force funded by the Ontario Medical Association. It has the highest institutional rate of any jurisdiction in comparison to Europe, the United States or Japan. The estimate for Ontario is that between 8% and 10% of our elderly people over the age of 65 are now residents of these nursing facilities, and they receive some form of nursing care on a guaranteed fee basis.

While this represents a very large number of persons and a large number of facilities, the demand for more placement exceeds the actual supply of institutional care available. There are very long waiting lists, and it is very difficult to transfer from one institution to another in the province.

What are the conditions like in nursing homes? They have been described as understaffed. They have been called warehouses for death and have been described in one eloquent book title as the focus for tender loving greed on the part of certain entrepreneurs. Some writers on elderly abuse in domestic situations have said that the threat of placing an elderly person into a nursing home should be considered to be tantamount to abuse of that elderly person. That gives some idea of how people fear these places. There is a growing consensus that they are not desirable places to live, but I think many people lack information and experience to make such a judgment.

There is a group in Ontario called Concerned Friends of Ontario Citizens in Care Facilities which is a voluntary non-profit and fiercely independent group of mainly female relatives of residents of nursing homes. These individuals visit residents of nursing homes, and then they advocate on behalf of these residents. They also write to, and tend to advise, the government on behalf of consumers about the direction they think should be taken in regard to institutional care and also in regard generally to policy on the elderly in Ontario. This organization has gained considerable credibility through public speaking. As a result it receives confidential individual complaints from residents of nursing homes, from relatives of residents of nursing homes and from staff of nursing homes and from other institutional care facilities for the elderly. The tradition in Concerned Friends has been to approach administrators of these facilities, approach the Ministry of Health, the Inspection Services Branch of the Ontario Ministry of Health in regard to nursing homes or the other policing agencies within the Ministry of Community and Social Services to get them to look into an inspection in regard to a particular complaint.

The record with these inspection and policing services has been very good. The process is, of course, very slow. The inspection will result in citation for breach of regulation followed by a long, dreary and highly unsuccessful prosecution process. The Ministry also receives independent complaints from people who write directly.

I was able to look at the files of complaints of Concerned Friends of Ontario Citizens in Care Facilities through an agreement of confidentiality. At that time, there were 250 complaints about nursing homes and homes for the aged in the province of Ontario. I read over the files to get a feel for the situation. Then I did a more indepth analysis of 56 of these complaints because they were complaints where I had not only the original complaint from the person contacting Concerned Friends and copies of letters which they had sent to other people about the situation, but also I had evidence and records of follow-up proceedings and responses from the government.

The complaints received by Concerned Friends concerned the taking of administrative decisions without consultation with the resident or relatives. This included decisions to transfer people, to charge them more money, to deal with their personal belongings in a particular way and to take medical decisions without informed consent which is a persistent problem in institutional health facilities.

I concluded from my examination of these 56 cases that 46% of the complaints involved an allegation of a serious criminal law breach which could warrant criminal investigation and perhaps criminal prosecution under the criminal law. There are some very grave conceptual problems which we all experience. I think abuse of the elderly in institutions shares some of the same conceptual difficulties of recognition with domestic abuse situations such as spouse abuse and child abuse situations and abuse of elderly relatives in their own homes. There is an additional conceptual problem regarding institutional abuse because we think that we have already taken care of these people. These people are in care by simply being in an institution. They are already under someone's care, and we hope that these are nursing care facilities. There is also a problem in alleging that these are criminal violations because these are institutions which are already policed and inspected. We have already taken care of that by creating regulations. We have set up an outside independent inspection service whose work it is to protect these people and to protect their interests.

The additional conceptual problem is that criminal offenses are considered by the commission to be the most serious breaches of social values in our society. The criminal law is a blunt instrument, and it is used for the most heinous offenses where other social and mediative types of remedies have not been available nor successful. It is very difficult to think that criminal offenses are occurring in these institutions for these reasons and for our respect for criminal offenses and the power of the criminal law.

Unfortunately I am able to provide in my report several examples of incidents involving elderly people which do fall into these criminal conditions. In my sample of 56 cases, seven cases contain allegations which specifically provide grounds for laying charges, and 10 cases describe situations where there had been an inadequate and improper provision of medical care resulting in permanent danger to the health of the elderly resident. These are the most serious and severe cases in which I am involved. Two of the 56 cases involved theft from the residents of personal property. I think theft is a recognizable concept in law, recognizable for the purposes of criminal prosecution. Two cases involved physical assault on a resident involving very real personal injury. Five cases involved some elements of all of these. Someone wrote and said things had been stolen from a sister. She woke in the morning with bruises, or I found her in her bed with bruises which she says were the result of someone striking her. She is malnourished and dehydrated.

Seventeen of the 56 cases had evidence that prosecution would be successful. There were 16 cases which described conditions which would create criminally negligent conditions in these institutional facilities. An example of such a condition which might warrant criminal prosecution was an inquest into deaths of residents from a particular nursing home. The home itself had been purchasing 18% less milk than would meet the daily minimum food requirement of the residents. It had been purchasing 24% fewer vegetables than would meet the daily food requirements of the residents. It had been purchasing 32% less meat than would meet the daily food requirements of the residents alone, not to mention the staff who are in and out of these institutions. In the case of that particular nursing home, it had been cited repeatedly for violations of regulations under the Ministry of Health Nursing Homes Act, and over a number of years there had been these citations. It was additionally cited for being understaffed and for providing inadequate bed care to residents and providing inadequate ventilation and for over-medication which is often the product of understaffing.

Unfortunately however, it was that example which did not meet with criminal prosecution and which successfully was not corrected by citation of these breaches of the regulations. The process of regulation is a very slow one and seems to be very unsuccessful in correcting these conditions. If you view them from the perspective of criminal negligence where there is a legal duty to provide necessities of life to these residents, you see them for the severe conditions for which they are. That is the same with the medical cases where, for one reason or another, medical care is not forthcoming.

My paper is a product of repeated frustration with the inadequacy of enforcement of regulation mechanisms which exist in Ontario in regard to institutional care of the elderly. Consumer complaints simply have not been enough to improve the service product which is available in this area. The lack of alternate facilities and alternate arrangements which could be made on behalf of people who complain means that some victim services would have to be provided to elderly residents in order for them to complain. It is their vulnerability to retaliation which really would stand in the way of the usefulness of criminal prosecution.

In terms of the benefits, I think these could be considerable. I think that such prosecutions bear with them the recognition that residents of the institutional care facilities are members of society who share equal protection under the law. Other legal remedies available to these people actually are failing them and are not necessarily available to them. Things like coroner's inquests are not very useful in some circumstances if the recommendations of the jury are not implemented. There is no court order demanding that conditions be improved for other people.

The administrative and regulatory mechanisms are because the demand exceeds the supply in this area, bound into a process of trying to keep and improve the facilities that exist. As long as we lack a policy on the elderly which involves viable community alternatives to institutional care, the Ministry of Health and the Ministry of Community and Social Services will be in a position of trying to keep the facilities they have going because there is a demand for them. The nursing home industry has considerable motivation to remain in the marketplace particularly because it is one of the most popular investment areas for people who have some dollars to invest. It is a growth area because of the isolation which has existed in regard to those in institutions and the helplessness of people to do what they would like to do for those placed in these nursing homes and facilities.

The causes of these conditions, really crimes against the elderly in institutional care, are taking place because of understaffing and improper training. That is very clearly tied to existence of a profit motive in the provision of human services. Because of this isolation and separation, the elderly are treated in institutional care as being outside of the normal and ordinary protection. I am pleased that this issue has been raised at a Conference on Violence in Contemporary Canadian Society, and I hope we will come to realize that institutionalization as it presently exists is not the answer for domestic abuse. What needs to be done in the area of the elderly is to correct some of these crimes against them and to develop a better and certainly a more multifaceted approach to aging and to the aging population in Ontario and throughout Canada.

Perhaps it is a luxury of relatively non-violent societies that we can talk about this issue at all.

PART IX

ALCOHOL / DRUGS AND VIOLENCE

ALCOHOL/DRUGS AND VIOLENCE

Howard Barbary
Queen's University

There are a number of factors which make us think that alcohol intoxication plays some kind of role in sexual violence. The first deals with a number of surveys which asked inmates to report their degree of intoxication on the day of their offenses. These surveys sometimes used cooperative evidence from police reports and other clinical reports. The surveys taken together show that 30% to 50% of the men had been intoxicated on the day of the offenses.

The second factor is that those of us who see sex offenders clinically and talk to them in detail about the events that lead up to their offenses are often struck by the number of men who report being quite intoxicated on the day of the offence. This data encourages us to think that alcohol intoxication plays a role in sexual crime. It is not very strong data if you step back and look. The data is more coincidental. All that we really know is that men who commit sexual crimes are often intoxicated. We need to increase our understanding of the role of alcohol in sexual crimes.

I would like to begin by describing a laboratory analogue to sexual violence. What we are accustomed to doing in these experiments is having a man sit in a private room which is sometimes just closed with a curtain. He sits in a comfortable chair, and we ask him to put a device on his penis which allows us to monitor erectile responses. This device is a small almost elastic-like band that goes around the penis and is filled with a column of mercury. As the erectile response occurs, the column of mercury changes in its ability to conduct electric current, and we can monitor the circumference of the penis. You can write out the output of this device on a polygraph. The onset of the stimulus produces an increase in erectile circumference, and then there is a slow increase to the peak which is about three-quarters of the way through the stimulus.

We have next door to this room a computer which monitors the device so we can calculate the peak circumference through a stimulus on each patient. We then usually express that peak circumference as a proportion of the circumference for erection. The response when you give a stimulus is given as 0% of full erection when there is no erectile response at all up to 100% for full erection. This is a sexual stimulus. We define a sexual stimulus as such when it has some influence on the erectile response. It is defined functionally.

Sexual stimuli can have one of two effects on sexual level. They can excite in which case the onset of stimulus causes an increase in erectile response, or they can be inhibitory in which case given that there is already an erectile response ongoing, the stimulus change has the effect of decreasing the erectile response.

This is the result from an experiment in which we tested college undergraduates as well as inmates at Kingston Penitentiary. There was a large number of men in each group. I think there were 60 rapists and 41 university undergraduates. I will have to describe here the way that we constructed our stimuli.

There are six different two-minute verbal descriptions of sexual interaction. Number two is the benchmark episode. It describes interaction between a man and a woman who meet at a party, go back to his apartment and engage in sexual interaction. The sexual behaviors described are foreplay which includes undressing, intermission or intercourse. The interaction ends with the orgasm or ejaculation of the male. It is described in fairly graphic detail.

The other episodes are similar to the benchmark. They are similar to the second episode in that they all describe the same sexual behavior, and the sexual behavior is described at roughly the same tempo and focus in that two-minute period. They are all describing a similar context, a man and woman meeting at a party and going home to his apartment. All six episodes are roughly similar in these respects. The episodes do differ in a number of respects which I will describe now.

In the first episode, the female is described as being enthusiastic in her sexual interaction with the man. She initiates many of the sexual behaviors, and there is quite a vivid description of her interacting in this sexual episode. In the third episode, the woman is described as being reluctant. She is described as saying in the beginning that she does not want to go ahead with the sexual interaction, but she relents eventually, and intercourse occurs. These three episodes then are similar in the sexual behaviors described and in the context in which they occur. They are different in the degree of consent that the woman offers the man.

In the remaining episodes, a rape is described. They are similar to the first three in the sense that the same sexual behavior is described. They are different in that in all three of these episodes the female clearly does not give consent. She says quite clearly that she does not want to engage in these behaviors and is quite vociferous in her objections to the behavior. In the fourth, fifth and sixth, what we varied was the behavior of the man.

In the fourth episode he is described as verbally threatening. In the fifth he is threatening to her, and he physically restrains her. In the sixth episode the man threatens, and he is violent. He slaps and punches her. The data from these two groups of men show that the mutually consenting episodes evoke quite strong arousal with average erectile responses. On average, men respond between 45% and 65% of full erection to the mutually consenting episodes. With the men in the university sample, there appears to be control over arousal by the woman's consent. When she is enthusiastic, the response is stronger than when she is passive. When she is passive, the response is stronger than when she is reluctant. In both groups we see quite a distinct break in the levels of response. In response to the rape episodes when she clearly does not consent, the response is considerably less. Most of that response occurs in the first few moments of the episode.

The two groups are significantly different in the extent to which they discriminate in free consenting to rape arousal. There really is quite a strong difference between the consenting and the rape episodes with the non-rapists. With the rapists, there is a difference which is significant. They show similar patterns in the arousal, but the difference is not as strong as it is with university students.

We interpreted the data using a inhibitory hypothesis. What we said was that since the same sexual behavior occurred in all six of the episodes, we can assume that the same views are presented to the man on each page. Since we describe fondling, intercourse and ejaculation in the same sequence of events and using similar language, then all six episodes present the man with similarly exciting sexual cues. What is different are the cues which serve to inhibit or suppress the arousal which occurs. In other words, when the woman clearly does not consent to the episode, the arousal to those cues is suppressed. As the man's behavior becomes more severe, it adds an inhibitory effect. We have computed this difference between mutually consenting and rape episodes using inhibitory hypotheses.

If we use an inhibitory hypothesis to explain the data, then one way we can explain the occurrence of rape or sexual assault would be that if the inhibitions of a man who would normally show inhibition to a woman's non-consent and to violent sexual behavior are somehow disrupted, we might have a rape ensue. One of the confusing and unexpected things about the data is the inhibitory process present in these men who committed rape. The men who committed rape here are incarcerated in a federal penitentiary. That means they were sentenced to more than two years. The average length of sentence is seven years. There is a murderer included in this sample, and for the most part the rapes that have been committed have been quite violent. Yet when you test them using this procedure, they show the same inhibitory effect of normalcy. So you have to explain somehow if sexual arousal has anything whatever to do with sexual assault. If you want to use some account which includes sexual arousal, you have to use some kind of a disinhibition or disruption of the normal inhibitory process that we see here.

There are a number of things that are common features to the stories men tell you when they describe the events leading up to a sexual assault that could serve to disinhibit arousal. One of them is alcohol intoxication; the other, anger provocations. Very often men will describe at some point before the sexual assault some incident which made them very angry, and that anger lingered until the occurrence of the offence.

The obvious experiment to do here is to have men come to the laboratory and test alcohol intoxication as a disinhibitor, to present them with the same cues I have mentioned and compare men who are sober with men who are intoxicated. When we set out to do this experiment, the balanced placebo design was just being developed.

Terry Wilson and Allan Marlak, two prominent researchers in the alcohol field, were arguing about eight years ago that many of the effects we see in alcohol, in laboratory tests and elsewhere are not due necessarily to the pharmacological impact of the drug. They are due to the subject's expectations in getting the alcohol and drugs and in what alcohol's effect should be. They argue that you cannot simply take alcohol and give it to one group and compare it with another because if you find the difference between those two groups, you cannot say whether it is the expectation effect of alcohol or the pharmacological impact of alcohol. What was ingeniously proposed is the balanced placebo design.

In the balanced placebo design, subjects come to the laboratory, and you randomly divide them into two groups. One group gets alcohol as a beverage to drink before whatever test you give them. The other group comes and is told they do not get alcohol. In each of those two groups, you randomly split them in half. One is whether or not they actually get alcohol and then whether or not they are instructed about it. When they arrive at the laboratory you tell one group of subjects that they are going to get alcohol, and the other group is told they are not going to get alcohol. Then those two groups are further subdivided; half get alcohol and half do not.

When you look through the literature on balanced placebo design, it really tells a very nice story. One of the things that people find hard to believe is that the subjects are not aware as to who gets the alcohol and who does not.

Many things are done to deceive subjects even further. One is for those subjects who receive a simple tonic beverage to have a drop of alcohol floating in the beverage to give it a bit of a smell of alcohol. Another thing to do is to have subjects believe that they cannot do a proper breathalyzer reading unless they rinse with mouthwash. So they rinse their mouth with Listerine before they drink their beverage. Another thing is to give them false breathalyzer feedback. In subjects who have been given a simple tonic beverage, you give them breathalyzer feedback. You give them a breathalyzer test and then show them the front face of the breathalyzer equipment showing that they had it lit up at a concentration of 0.055. With subjects who have been given alcohol, you show them the breathalyzer test is .000.

These things are done to help deceive subjects or to help the experimenter to deceive the subjects into thinking that the beverage they consumed is in accordance with the instructions that they have been given. One of the things that experimenters in this area are encouraged to do is after the subject has consumed the beverage and done the test, they are asked to fill out a questionnaire, or they are asked verbally a number of questions. The questions will concern the amount of alcohol contained in the beverage and the level of intoxication during the test.

In order for the study to qualify as a real balanced placebo design study, it is important that the subjects who were instructed that they got alcohol report that alcohol was in their drink and that they were intoxicated during the test. It is important that subjects who were instructed that they were not given alcohol report that their beverage contained no alcohol, and they were not intoxicated during the test.

By now there is a large amount of literature on the balanced placebo design. What you find is that for a fairly wide variety of antisocial behaviors and sexual behaviors, the belief that you have drunk alcohol is an important controlling variable in the occurrence of antisocial behavior. Two studies have shown that this simple belief causes an increase in arousal to various kinds of erotica.

Two studies have shown, and this is quite rare to see, male university undergraduates feel sexual arousal to male homosexual videotaped activity. Two studies have shown that men who believe that they have drunk alcohol showed increased arousal to homosexual interaction. One study has shown that when you believe you had alcohol, the sexual content in your thoughts increases. One study has shown that when you give subjects the opportunity to present themselves with erotica on a slide projector and to control viewing time, men who believe they have drunk alcohol spend more time viewing violent erotica compared with men who believe they have not drunk alcohol. It is important to note here that in these studies with men who have actually drunk alcohol, there is actually no difference between men who have drunk alcohol and men who have not drunk alcohol.

Verdell and a number of his colleagues, at about the time we were doing our balanced placebo design situation, did a study that was almost identical to ours. In that balanced placebo design, half the subjects got alcohol, half were told they got alcohol and half were told they got tonic. The important result was that men who are told they get alcohol in contrast to men who are told they get tonic show an increase in their arousal to violent sexual cues. They used audio-taped stimuli and measured erectile responses in exactly this situation.

This is exactly the effect that we were looking for, and it matches the effect that we found with anger. Men who were intoxicated show less of a discrimination between mutual consent and rape, and we have shown the same thing with anger. Our results from the balanced placebo design with alcohol did not yield the same results. There were a number of things in the responses of our subjects that led us to believe that the expectation effects did not work very well. Initially, we thought that there was something wrong with the procedure that we used. Perhaps we had done something that did not convince subjects. Very often the subjects' estimates of how much alcohol was in the beverage was in accordance with the instructions that were given, but they said things informally after the experiment was over that indicated that they thought they either got alcohol or were in the instructed no-alcohol condition. We thought initially we had done something wrong and had failed to do a proper balanced placebo design experiment.

It is important to note that the total results of the balanced placebo design literature are to encourage us to believe that the anti-social effects of alcohol intoxication are effects of the expectations that we have about alcohol's effect and has nothing whatsoever to do with the pharmacological effects of alcohol.

What we tried to set up was an experiment which relieved the experimental subjects entirely of all demands placed on them. We put them in a situation where they can respond with what they really feel they had in the beverage, and they are asked what the alcohol content was without any fear of reprisal or cursing or without feeling that they might ruin the experiment by responding with what they really think.

The subjects are run in two sessions. They come to the first session, and the experimenter and researchers assist them and tell them that this is a study of the effects of alcohol intoxication and sexual arousal. They are told that they are going to come back to a second session in which they will be given a beverage to drink. After they drink the beverage and wait for a suitable period of time, they will be put in a situation where they will be presented to sexual stimuli. They will be asked to rate the sexual stimuli in a number of dimensions. They will be asked to rate the attractiveness of the subjects in the stimuli. They will be asked to rate how aroused they were by the stimuli. They are told that there are going to be two groups in the experiment, an experimental group and the control group. They are also told that since this study is of a sensitive nature, and they are rating their own sexual arousal, it will be anonymous. They are given a card with a code number on it and are told that when they come back to the second session to just simply give the research assistant their code numbers.

They are met for the second session by the research assistant who uses a computer with their code numbers. The computer screen shows clearly what group each subject has been assigned to. Then they enter another room. They return with their numbers. They then drink the determined liquid and subsequently go through the rating of the sexual stimuli.

The experimenter then asks the questions. They then fool the subject by pretending the computer is broken. The questioner returns with the person running the study. After their conversation, they explain the balanced placebo design. They say that half of the people who were given that instruction on the screen got alcohol and half did not. He asks whether they mixed the drinks for him, and the research assistant describes the double blind study. After the apparent experimenter leaves, the research assistant says, "I hate loosing data. Let us see if we can figure something out." So she grabs a pad of paper and a pen, and she then begins asking in her own words the questions that had been asked on the computer earlier. Embedded in those questions are questions as to how much alcohol they thought was in their beverage and how intoxicated they thought they were during the test.

We did a study using the balanced placebo design, and we got results that were not quite like the results that are usually found in balanced placebo design. One of the phenomena that I eluded to earlier in these studies is that when you test subjects from a first or second session, college undergraduates anyway, they tend from session 1 to session 2 to show a big increase in the magnitude of the discrimination between rape and the mutually consenting cues. In session 1 you cannot really point to much of a difference in response between the two groups. In the second session, what happens is subjects, particularly the university students, decide that there are appropriate and inappropriate cues being presented. They decide that what is most appropriate here is the maximum response to the appropriate cues, minimum response to the inappropriate cues. They come back on the second day having decided that and produce that result as much as possible. On the second day they have really increased their arousal to the mutually consenting cues and have increased the discrimination.

The results of the alcohol study show the difference between the mutually consenting and the rape episodes for each of the stimulus pairs in session 1 and session 2. In session 1, the first two cues presented would be one mutually consenting cue and one rape cue. We calculate the percentage of full erection in response to the rape cue, and in response to the mutually consenting cue and then calculate the difference between them. From the first session, all 32 subjects in the experiment showed that roughly 20% of full erection differentiates the mutually consenting and rape arousal. The mutually consenting arousal was greater.

In the second session, there are two groups. One group of subjects is run in the second session in exactly the same way as they were run in the first. They are run sober after drinking a quantity of tonic water. That group of subjects is the group of subjects in the closed circles that increase the magnitude of the difference between mutually consenting and rape arousal. The group of subjects that shows an upward curve have increased the magnitude of the discrimination between appropriate and inappropriate cues. They have come back after an evening away from the lab and have been able to show more appropriate response in the second session. The subjects in the group who received a dose of alcohol in their tonic, showed no such increase between appropriate and inappropriate cues. As I said, that was the balanced placebo design, and we really had four groups of subjects. The subjects who did not receive alcohol showed an increase in the discrimination. Mutually consenting arousal goes up; rape arousal goes down. The subjects who received alcohol showed no such change over the session. With the subjects who expected alcohol, there is no difference between them and the people who did not expect alcohol. There was no expectation effect.

ALCOHOL/DRUGS AND VIOLENCE

Helen Annis
Addiction Research Foundation

I have drawn five conclusions that I think we can make in the area of the treatment of alcoholics. These have to do with comparative cost effectiveness of approaches to delivering service.

The first substantiated conclusion is that the length of our residential programming does not seem to be a critical variable in terms of outcome. There are now a number of randomly controlled trials where you look at periods from a few days to a month or a few weeks to several months which show that a longer program does not relate to greater effectiveness. It does not relate to more success stories in follow-up. The questioning of this intensity is in terms of offering more of the same.

The second conclusion which is well supported is that we need not offer detoxification services on an inpatient basis. There are cheaper alternatives to that. Many alternatives are in Ontario which the Addiction Research Foundation has been looking at for many years now. The results for the majority of alcoholics show that they can be safely detoxified in such settings. There are, of course, a minority who will require acute care, but overall we can service a large population requiring these services through alternatives. Also very promising is the literature on the use of pharmaceutical therapy in detoxification, and these programs are typically on an outpatient basis. These are cheaper alternatives than the former notion of hospitalization for detoxification.

The third conclusion is that offering day treatment programs can have a good result with offering inpatient programs. The first trial, by John McLaughlin of the Donwood Institute in Toronto, randomly assigned the patients to a new day treatment program. Formally these patients would have received hospital treatment. Those requiring acute medical care were excluded from the trial, but the great majority approaching Donwood during this period of the study were randomly assigned to this cheaper alternative. The results were very similar in the two groups. The results that did show trends tended to favor the day treatment alternative.

Since then we have had another study very similar to John McLaughlin's study at the Butler Hospital in Providence, Rhode Island. Again, the results showed there is no significant difference.

Offering a nine-to-five program on an outpatient basis to alcoholics can be as effective as a more costly hospital stay.

These studies are all done on heterogeneous groups of alcoholics approaching us for treatment. The question is not yet resolved as to whether a subsection of this population require the more intensive hospital treatment regime. For the great majority approaching us, we have tended to give the more expensive alternatives with no particular reasons for it.

A fourth conclusion is that outpatient programs have produced comparable results to inpatient programs. These programs typically see the alcoholic for an hour a week or an hour every other week. The randomized control trials done in this area also support the fact that this type of treatment delivery can be as effective as in-hospital treatment. Again, these are unselected groups that normally would have been given the hospital treatment. There may well be sub-populations that will do better, but we need more research data on that.

The fifth conclusion that I would like to draw is perhaps the one that would receive the least controversy of all. It is a comment on what we are dealing with when we are dealing with an alcoholic in treatment. It is the nature of the behavior disorder of alcoholism itself. Some progress has been made in looking at a definition of the behavior that we are trying to change. That is a question of looking at alcoholism as a chronic disorder with a very high risk of relapse. It implies that we are not dealing primarily with the problem in the initiation of the behavior change but rather with a problem in the maintenance of a change over time.

We speak of an alcoholic relapsing from a period of abstinence. This period of abstinence is successfully embarked upon, and often alcoholics in the community do this on their own without any professional intervention. The problem is not primarily getting an alcoholic to stop drinking. The problem facing us is getting that behavior maintained over time. This has implications for how we would approach this therapeutic service.

A study was done on married males who were being treated at the Mosley Hospital. There were 100 male alcoholics who should have been very good prognostic risks. They were all accompanied by their wives who consented to being involved in the treatment. What we saw was a relapse curve for these men. The curve was very steep at the beginning. By the second month after discharge from treatment, of all

100 men who were successfully abstinent at discharge, 80% had taken a drink. After the two- year period, the last man had had a drink. These were men who were in an abstinence-oriented program.

The problem we are facing is not getting everyone to abstain, but it is getting them to maintain abstinence or moderation depending on what goal they have. This is a very severe look at the magnitude of the problem. Nevertheless, it helps focus our attention on exactly what does go on after discharge of treatment. Many of these men, of course, were much improved even though they had taken a drink.

In order to get a handle therapeutically on how to maintain the behavior change, we need the individual at risk in the community. Violence in our institutions is not a good predictor of whether or not that offender will be violent in the community after discharge. The same is true in the alcohol field. If you put an individual in a highly artificial, restricted environment, be it in a hospital or in a correctional institution, the behavior of that person where alcohol is highly restricted or unavailable will not be a prediction of how that individual will cope in the community. We need to look at putting that individual in therapy within the situation in which he will be at risk while within a supportive counselling arrangement.

There are other advantages in treating an alcoholic on an outpatient basis. You get a much better baseline assessment of the cognitive, emotional or environmental triggers to drinking episodes or drinking urges if the client is at risk during the period that you were working with him. You also have the opportunity of looking at new coping responses while you are still in the counselling part of the arrangement together.

Those are the five conclusions that I wanted to bring out of the alcohol treatment outcome field. Intensive programming in terms of length of programming may not be a critical variable in the success that we obtain. We can be taught safely on an outpatient basis with or without pharmacotherapy. We know that day treatment programming can be as successful as residential programming with the same being true of outpatient programming. We are dealing with a problem in maintenance of behavior change and what we might want to draw on in terms of the individual being at risk in the community while we are working with them.

What then might be the implications of this? I do not think we should pull out of institutional-based programming. We have to take a sober look at what we are doing in terms of intensity and perhaps focus less on wanting to work out programs of great intensity while the individual is completely incarcerated. We might want to look at programs of a briefer nature and at programs that would make therapeutic use of temporary absence passes. We could have our alcoholic clients exposed to risk situations in the community while working with them in places such as detention centres.

What is gaining popularity is intermittent sentencing. Certainly in the drunk driving area in Toronto we have many of our offenders receiving weekend passes. I am not sure what is going on in Ottawa. This exposes the client to risks during the week and alcoholism programs during the weekend.

Probation and parole are important when working with the individual in the life situation that they will be returning to. This is ideal for working through what will be necessary for maintenance of change in behavior. In the area of sentencing, we have not gotten very far in looking at community service orders that would involve therapeutic use of referral as part of the order for alcoholism treatment.

The final part of my paper is a description of a particular cost effective treatment strategy that we feel could be used in any one of these types of correctional programming. What we try to do through questionnaires is isolate the situation when the individual is at risk for drinking. This questionnaire stems from a number of studies looking at alcoholic relapse. What we do then is begin our treatment with a situational assessment of this particular client's drinking problem.

There are eight categories in this work. The first three are negative emotional space, interpersonal conflict and social pressure to drink. They are the antecedent events that have been found to account for roughly three-quarters of the relapses of alcoholic clients. Interestingly enough, these are the same situations that also account for about three-quarters of the relapses in heroine addicts and in smokers who return to cigarette use.

Reacting to a negative emotional state could be taking a drink when you are feeling lonely, when you are feeling depressed, when you are feeling angry. That is the largest category and the one our clients have the most difficulty with. In interpersonal conflict, our clients tend to engage in the drinking episode following an argument with the spouse, following an argument with the boss or in the interpersonal area generally. With social pressure to drink, you might be offered a drink and feel under some social pressure to take it.

There are another five negative physical states. We had one client who was using alcohol primarily in reaction to pain. This is rare, but when you have such a client, you need to adequately have that diagnosed. Positive emotional states is a category which is endorsed by a substantial number. Personal control is tested. They believe they can control their attitude in this sort of cognitive process which is the immediate antecedent to trying a drink. There are urges and temptations which they can overcome.

Our own studies cover the situations that trigger drinking in our clients. They are substantiated by a fair number of studies on the follow-up of alcoholics in the community. What we try to do is simply take these eight categories and plot a profile for the client in terms of what is triggering this client's drinking. We will want to focus in on that.

In a profile typical of a young male alcoholic, we find elevation typically on pressure from others to drink. We get peaks and valleys which constitute well differentiated profiles with areas of little risk as well as substantial risk. What we do in our own therapy intervention work is develop a hierarchy of risk situations for our client and design homework assignments where they will actually go out and avoid this type of situation. The homework assignment will involve entering into that very risk situation with the objective of coping in a different way and coming back and reporting a successful experience in what normally would have led to excessive drinking.

Theoretically, what we are attempting to do is translate Vandura's work into the alcohol field. Vandura's work is the cognitive behavior therapy theory of change. The theoretical process looks extremely cognitive. It goes something like this. When a person enters the risk situation, here an alcoholic one, it sets up a cognitive appraisal process of how that individual has behaved in the past in that particular drinking risk situation. That in turn creates an expectancy of what will happen this time. If you can tap into the judgment of what the client feels he is able to do in terms of coping, this will be an excellent predictor of what he or she is about or about to do.

What we do is look for homework assignments and performance-based assignments, put the individual at risk, try to get him to behave differently in drinking situations and come back and report success. With the majority of cases, the cognitions will fall into place. The belief system that the individual carries, the judgment that they are now able to cope with drinking in that situation, will have been enhanced as a result of viewing themselves behaving differently in that situation.

There are some cases where this does not happen. Cognitions do not necessarily fall into place.

What we do in terms of monitoring these expectations during treatment is to use a questionnaire. On another questionnaire we ask whether they are now having an argument with the spouse and how confident they are that they could abstain. We see if they have made some progress through the homework assignment. Assessment and treatment are highly interrelated in this model.

By tapping into these cognitions, or judgments on the part of the client, we see they are now able to cope with alcohol in a particular situation. That will predict their probability of relapse. We are finding that that is holding up in our work as well. The client can tell us whether they can control their drinking or abstain across all of these situations. That is an excellent predictor. We have also found that we can predict their area of relapse by the area they tell us they are least confident in.

Our results are pretty good in terms of what is coming out in the field. These are six-month outcome results looking at people we have seen using these strategies of treatment. These were people seen in an employee assistance program at the Addiction Research Foundation. Very few of them were abstinent during the year prior to intake.

ALCOHOL/DRUGS AND VIOLENCE

Judith Groeneveld
Addiction Research Foundation

I have been investigating the role of alcohol and drug use in the dynamics of marital violence. It seems to be clear that one aspect of violence in contemporary Canadian society which we do not like to talk about is conjugal violence, but I feel the issue must be addressed if we hope to resolve this chronic problem.

Conjugal violence is not a new phenomenon. It has been part of our family dynamics since the beginning of our history. For decades it was seen as the husband's legal right to discipline his wife any way he saw fit. Not until 1867 was the husband's legal right to use physical punishment with his wife curtailed by the courts, and it took another hundred or so years before our socio-political system started to work towards the elimination of this social problem.

Current estimates place the prevalence of wife abuse at approximately 10%. One out of every 10 Canadian women living with a spouse is believed to be subjected to physical abuse (MacLeod, 1980).

What causes family violence and how it effects the victim is not fully understood. We also do not understand fully what role drugs and alcohol play in the dynamics of family violence. However, we are slowly gathering information on these topics. It is the purpose of this paper to provide an overview of the current state of research and to explain the relationship between violent marital interaction and the use of drugs and/or alcohol.

A number of definitions have been used to specify what conjugal violence is. For this overview, conjugal violence will be defined as covert, intentional (non-accidental) and physical aggression between spouses.

Conjugal violence in this context refers to three distinctly different aggressive interactions. These are wife abuse, husband abuse and mutually violent relationships. In the first two interaction patterns, violence is uni-directional. In these cases only one of the partners displays an overt and intentionally aggressive behavior while the other partner is a passive receiver of the violence. In the mutually violent interaction relationship, the violence is bi-directional; both partners display overt aggressive behavior towards each other.

Although there is growing evidence that violence in marital relationships is not restricted to wife abuse, data examining the relationship between alcohol and/or drug use and either husband abuse or the mutually violent couple is still non- existent. As a consequence, the present overview is focused on the relationship between drug/alcohol use and wife battering.

Research examining the relationship between wife abuse and alcohol/drug use is centred around two major issues. The first one is to what extent and in what ways does alcohol/drug consumption of the abuser directly, indirectly or in combination with other factors increase the likelihood of violence or the severity of violence. The second issue is to what extent does the exposure to conjugal violence affect the victim's use of alcohol and/or drugs.

There are a number of leading themes in the literature attempting to explain the relationship between the batterer's alcohol use and marital violence. The three most often cited approaches are the medical perspective, the excuse perspective and the social learning theory perspective.

The medical model attempts to explain conjugal violence, especially wife battering, as a symptom of a diagnosed disorder. According to Shainess (1981), the most common disorder linked to alcohol-induced violence is explosive rage. The followers of this school of thought argue that rage is an important component of personality and/or an important reaction to external stress. Individuals experiencing this rage tend to drink to anaesthetize their rage. Since alcohol acts as a depressant, it also impairs the ability to control rage. Consequently, the subjective feeling of rage increases. This in turn increases the likelihood of violent outbursts (Shainess, 1981).

Until the late 1970s, explosive rage was believed to be relatively rare. It has since been shown that explosive rage is a more common problem than originally believed. The still infrequent diagnoses result primarily from cultural taboos. In most cultures men are expected to be able to control their emotions. Failing to do so indicates inferiority. An admission of the inability to control rage in such a cultural context would mean the admission of inferiority. This understandably prevents patients with this syndrome from disclosing their inability to control rage (Elliot, 1976).

Although the medical perspective does not claim a causal relationship between alcohol and conjugal violence, it implicates alcohol as a crucial catalyst between certain psychiatric disorders and conjugal violence (Blant, 1986).

The excuse perspective gains its theoretical orientation from social anthropology. It draws on MacAndrew's and Edgerton's (1969) early research. They argued that behavior while drinking varies according to the situational context and is governed by social norms. They also argued that in most cultures the use of alcohol provides an excuse for individuals who wish to engage in actions generally proscribed under conditions of sobriety. Since the pattern of alcohol use in this context is believed to be a learned behavior and is governed by social norms, individuals planning to engage in socially unacceptable behavior will consume alcohol in order to claim clemency for their proscribed behaviors.

In the conjugal violence context, it can be argued that the abuser consumes alcohol to provide a socially acceptable excuse for the violent behavior. The excuse notion seems to be the most commonly held belief by women's groups, certain research groups and policymakers involved with domestic violence issues.

Steffen (1982) provides yet another perspective on the relationship between alcohol use and conjugal violence. Using the social learning theory as a conceptual framework, he argues that both behavior patterns, alcohol use and violence are established in early childhood and are patterned after the example provided by the abuser's family of origin.

The social learning theory has been used in both the alcohol and violence fields to explain behavior patterns. In the alcohol use area it has been argued that abusive consumption patterns are learned in the family of origin. This claim was substantiated by empirical evidence demonstrating abusive alcohol consumption patterns through different generations.

A very similar argument with empirical evidence was put forth by Gelles (1974) in the wife abuse context. He showed that men who battered their spouses were more likely, during their youth, to have been exposed to family violence at their home of origin.

Drawing on the two bodies of knowledge, Steffen argues that the behavior pattern regarding spouse abuse and alcohol consumption is learned, and the abusive behavior pattern is tied to alcohol consumption if the abuse pattern is dominant in the family of origin.

The 1970s was the golden era for empirical studies looking at the relationship between alcohol/drug use and conjugal violence. Most of the relevant research was conducted during this period. However, even during these years the popularity of the topic was minimal. Only about two dozen reports were published during this period, and even fewer have been published since. The reported research covered two major topic areas.

Empirical studies reporting on the relationship between alcohol consumption by the batterer and conjugal violence employed two research methods. A majority of the studies utilized the informant method. The major information source for the informant studies were the victims. The other studies used self-reporting designs. The main topic areas the majority of these studies examined were the relationship between the batterer's alcohol use pattern and conjugal violence and the violence triggering effect of alcohol use in conjugal violence.

A number of the studies attempted to identify the relationship between types of alcohol consumption, occasional, frequent, heavy and addictive, by the batterer and the frequency of battering incidents. The three most prevailing studies in this area are reported by Strauss, Bland and Byles.

Strauss (1980) collected information from close to 2000 households on the relationship between the level of violence in the home and the amount of alcohol consumed by the abuser during the 12-month period preceding the survey. His results indicated that the violence rate was the lowest (2.2%) for non drinkers, highest (30.8%) for the heavy drinkers and high (17.6%) for the alcohol abusing group.

Bland (1986) used a randomly selected sample of 1,200 people to collect data on the relationship between the batterer's alcohol consumption and his abusive behavior toward his spouse. He found strong associations between conjugal violence and personality disorder, recurrent depression and alcoholism. Each of these carried different risk factors for violence. Fifty per cent of those who had an antisocial personality or alcoholism were violent. One-third with recurrent depression also battered their wives. When alcoholism was combined with either of the other two conditions, the violent rate jumped close to ninety per cent.

Byles (1978) interviewed 139 clients of family court. Of these, 52% were wife or child abusers. He found that in 61% of the families, alcohol was consumed to the level of intoxication. Among the families with high alcohol intake, the likelihood of violence was 2.5 times higher than the non-alcohol abusing families.

The second theme getting attention from researchers is the violence triggering effect of alcohol consumption in conjugal violence. In the relevant studies, data was collected either through self-reporting or by using the informant method where the victims report their abuser's alcohol consumption pattern at the time of the violent incident. In this area, the research of Nisonoff and Gayford is quite informative.

Nisonoff and Bitman (1979) reported, on the basis of telephone interviewing of a randomly selected sample of 297 participants, that alcohol was responsible for 26.4% of the violent incidents.

Gayford's 1975 survey included 100 victims of conjugal violence. The information provided by the women showed that over 40% of the battering took place when the batterer was drunk.

A relatively large number of studies reporting on the relationship between alcohol use patterns of the batterer and his violent behavior toward his spouse used the victim/informant method to gather data. The majority of informant type studies examined both the pattern of alcohol consumption of the abuser and the violence triggering effect of alcohol consumption.

Hilberman (1977) studied 60 women who had been referred to a clinic for psychiatric assessment. All of the women were victims of domestic violence. Over 93% of the study participants felt that their husbands were alcoholics.

Rounsaville (1978) surveyed a sample of 30 battered women. Of those, 45% reported that the assailant was abusing alcohol, and in 29% of the cases the violence was linked to drinking.

Roy (1981) interviewed 150 victims admitted to a shelter. On the basis of information given by the women about their batterer's drinking patterns, Roy reported that 85% of the batterers had either alcoholic and/or drug problems but were not only violent when under the influence. Eighty per cent of the 15% who were not addicted to alcohol or drugs and who, according to their spouses, were only occasional drinkers were violent only when they were drinking.

Carlson (1977) reported on a study involving 101 battered women from a social service agency. Eighty per cent of the women reported that their assailant abused alcohol or drugs most of the time. In 60% of the cases, alcohol was involved in the violence which forced them to seek help at the agency.

Eberly (1980), using data collected from 100 victims, examined the abuser's alcohol use pattern prior to four different violent incidents. She found that only 16% of the batterers used alcohol excessively during all four incidents. Nineteen per cent did not use alcohol, and the others displayed various alcohol consumption patterns when violent. She also compared the alcoholic and abstaining abusers. She found that the abstaining abusers tended to be younger and belonged to a higher socio-economic strata and tended to inflict less severe injury on their victims.

Results of studies examining the triggering effect of alcohol consumption in violent incidents indicated that the behavior of batterers is not uniform. In some cases, violent incidents are always accompanied by alcohol consumption. The alcohol consumption of this group is reported to be moderate to high. Other abusers never consumed alcohol prior to the violent incident. Close to 60% do not have an established alcohol use- violence pattern. Here, abuse might take place with or without the consumption of alcohol.

The research on the relationship between the abuser's overall alcohol consumption pattern and abusive behavior indicates that heavy drinkers tend to batter their spouses more often than other types of drinkers. The incidence of battering is highest when alcoholism occurs in combination with certain other mental disorders.

As can be seen, empirical research does not support exclusively any one of the conceptual perspectives discussed previously. None of the suggested approaches to explain the dynamics of the relationship between alcohol use/abuse and conjugal violence is sufficiently broad to provide the needed conceptual framework. The difficulty in explaining the role of alcohol in conjugal violence probably stems from a number of factors.

The most critical factor is the assumption that one theoretical axiom could explain all the observed relationships between alcohol use and marital violence. When this axiom is dropped, and it is assumed that alcohol use influences conjugal violence in a number of different ways depending upon the psycho/social orientation of the batterer and/or the victim, the role of alcohol use in marital violence becomes much clearer. Within this conceptual context, batterers can be placed into three subgroups depending on their normative orientation towards conjugal violence. These are the behavior group, the normative group, and the excuse seeking group.

The behavior group, those who perceive conjugal violence as a legitimate way to resolve marital conflict, needs no excuse for beating spouses. These batterers use violence against their spouses to reduce frustration and stress, to increase self- esteem and/or to resolve marital conflicts. Very likely alcohol/drug use does not affect the frequency of the violence since these batterers do not see their violent behavior toward their spouses as abnormal. However, abuse committed during periods of intoxication might increase the risk of severe injury since drugs or alcohol may impair the abuser's judgment as to the extent of force being used. Therefore, alcohol use, while it does not have a causal relationship with violence, has a consequential aspect for this group.

The normative group includes those batterers who seem to have normative constraints against battering. This group contains abusers whose behavior is strictly controlled by cultural and moral norms which prohibit the use of physical violence against their spouses and probably against others as well. These batterers tend to have poor impulse control and experience extreme rage which is expressed as violence only while under the influence of alcohol. When they experience rage due to internal or external pressures, they consume alcohol in an attempt to lower their anxiety level. As described earlier, this consumption heightens the feelings of rage precipitating violent actions.

The frequency of alcohol consumption might vary, but the level of consumption on each of those occasions involving violence is high enough to produce the inhibition-rage-violence syndrome. The behavior of this group is best described by the inhibition approach where alcohol consumption plays a catalyst role in marital violence.

The excuse seeking group probably does not feel strong normative barriers or controls but would like others to believe they do (Groeneveld, Shain, 1980). The relationship between spousal battering and alcohol consumption for this group is probably best explained through the MacAndrew model described earlier.

Excuse seeking batterers pretend to be intoxicated thereby gaining social licence to be violent toward their spouses. The excuse group uses the cover of intoxication to camouflage their need for violent interaction. Batterers in this group do not need to reduce their inhibitions. They probably consume alcohol only in moderation since their final goal is not inebriation but an excuse for violent actions.

The deviance disavowal pattern of the excuse seeking group should not be minimized. Since the deviance disavowal pattern is a part of the marital violence dynamic, an understanding of this dynamic is important for effective intervention.

The second area of interest in the literature centres around the victim's reaction to violence and consequent drug use. Star (1982) is one of the few researchers who reported on the effect of abuse on the victims. She found that the three most common reactions to violence are depression, fear and impaired trust. Depression occurs when women feel powerless to take effective action to change their lives. In many cases failure to change their lives is closely linked to their economic dependence.

A large number of battered women are under 30, married, have been married longer than five years, do not have job skills, do not have a paying job, have not been in the labor force since their marriage, do not have economic resources of their own, have two or more children, have been beaten from the beginning of their relationship with the abuser and have attempted unsuccessfully to get help more than once.

After a number of unsuccessful attempts to alter the situation, battered women give up on changing their environment. At this stage they internalize their anger and turn it into a sense of futility and despair. According to Star, victims of family violence commonly function in a frozen fright state among captives. In these cases the victims' "fear is so overwhelming that it prevents them from hoping for escape, and they believe that their only survival depends on their ability to appease the assaulter."

The third common reaction of battered women to violence seems to be the loss of trust in their environment and their own abilities. Most of the victims attempt to solicit the support of their environment. The outside resources which these women most often try to reach are their physicians.

At some point, probably all battered women seek the help of their physicians. Since women tend not to voluntarily disclose the violent part of their marriages (Klechner, 1978) with the physicians not asking (Borkowski, 1983), the victims of family violence are often misdiagnosed and receive inappropriate medical care.

The Yale Domestic Violence Research Team (Stark, 1981) reported that only one in 25 battered women is diagnosed as a victim of conjugal violence, and even fewer are referred for appropriate treatment.

The low diagnosis rate was also confirmed by another study conducted at the University of North Carolina (Stark, 1981). It was found that over a 12-month period, 80% of the women referred to rural clinics for psychiatric help were victims of conjugal violence. Only 6.6% of these women's physicians recognized the violent marital situations.

Hilberman (1977) found that "after the abusive injury, battered women were four times more likely than non-battered women to be diagnosed as hysterical, hypochondriacs or females with vague medical complaints." The consequence of wrongful diagnosis is inappropriate treatment which most often involves drug therapy. Hilberman's research also indicated that a significantly larger proportion of battered women are placed on psychotropic drugs as opposed to their non-battered counterparts.

Chan (1973) reported that 47 of the 194 (24.2%) women involved in a study he conducted in collaboration with a crisis centre had a "history of use of psychotropic drugs." Furthermore, battered women were not likely to receive referrals to social or psychiatric services from their physicians.

From the literature review, it seems that a prevalent reaction of women to marital violence is the use of psychotropic drugs. The use of psychotropic drugs by women feeling trapped in violent marital relationships is quite understandable considering the mood-altering capacity of these drugs.

The unique feature which all of these drugs have in common is the "capacity to generate subjective pleasurable effects." All the types of users, pathological or not, describe the effect of psychotropic drugs as providing a sense of security and erasing anxieties while generating a sense of personal power (Bell, 1975).

The most commonly reported drug-induced sensation is confidence, providing relief from fear and insecurity. Without a drug effect, confidence is a pleasurable feeling which accompanies the success of effort. The confidence generated by the use of drugs does not require any effort. It can be experienced without achieving success.

A question which has been occupying drug researchers is why certain people select an illusionary confidence over reality. According to Bell, the drug induced illusion of confidence is most likely preferred by the drug user because the possibility of satisfaction from reality is so limited. This may explain the reported high drug use among battered women many of whom perceive their situations as unchangeable and permanent. Learning that psychotropic drugs can provide the confidence they desire by reducing fear, anxiety and depression, they probably choose to continue with the medication despite the negative long-term effect of this action. By so doing they achieve the sense of satisfaction apparently unattainable from their real environment.

The consequence of drug use is of course very serious. Victims who use drugs so they can tolerate their marital relationship subject themselves and their children to short and long-term consequences. Staying in a violent relationship means increased chances for severe injury since violent relationships tend to become more violent over time. The drug-using victim probably does not have the adequate defence reflexes. Long-term drug use can also create drug dependence with the usual nasty consequences. The children might also be affected by both the example of drug use and by the violence between parents.

A number of alternatives have been put forth to illuminate the role of alcohol and drug use in the dynamics of conjugal violence. The perception of the role of alcohol use by the batterer in the dynamics of conjugal violence is quite diverse as was shown by the various perspectives covered previously. These range from the medical perspective, which implicates alcohol as a crucial catalyst in certain psychiatric disorders, to conjugal violence through to the excuse perspective which argues that the abuser consumes alcohol to provide a socially acceptable excuse for the violent behavior.

It was also suggested that the role of alcohol use in the dynamics of conjugal violence is a complex interrelationship among a number of factors within the violent family, but it hinges mainly on the batterer's normative orientation toward wife abuse.

Empirical research focused on abuse and the main topic areas within the alcohol use context. It examined the extent to which the batterer's use of alcohol directly, indirectly or in combination with other factors increases the likelihood or the severity of conjugal violence.

Results indicated that the level and pattern of alcohol use by the batterer influences conjugal violence. Men who are heavy or abusive drinkers tend to batter their wives significantly more often and inflict more injury than those who drink very moderately or not at all.

Alcohol also alters the abusive behavior patterns of batterers who display anti-social personalities or who suffer from recurrent depression. Close to ninety per cent of alcoholic men who also suffer from either anti-social behavior or recurring depression batter their wives.

The triggering effect of alcohol use in family violence and data collected mainly from victims were also mentioned in previous reports. Data collected mainly from victims of wife abuse found that some of the abusers tended to abuse their partners only on occasions when they consumed alcohol.

The role of drug use in conjugal violence was examined in the context of psychotropic drug use by the victims. It is suggested by USA researchers that the prevalence of psychotropic drug use is higher among battered women than among their non- battered counterparts. Higher use is linked to two aspects of conjugal violence. The first is social taboo. It seems that the subject of wife abuse even in physician/ patient relationships is greatly avoided, and as a consequence the victim is often misdiagnosed and receives inappropriate treatment.

The second reason for the relatively high psychotropic drug use among battered women is attributed to the mood-altering effects of these drugs. Women who suffer extensive and prolonged victimization by their partner and perceive themselves to be entrapped in their marital relationships can get relief from the fear and anxiety which dominate their lives by using psychotropic drugs.

In conclusion, the literature review suggests that both alcohol and drug use have definite and distinct roles in conjugal violence. However, we need more extensive research to explain the scope of the influence that drugs and alcohol have in this interaction, to develop various intervention modalities to bring this knowledge forward to health care personnel and other professionals working in the field and to use this information to develop education for those most directly affected by the issue, the batterers and the victims of conjugal violence.

ALCOHOL/DRUGS AND VIOLENCE

Lynn Lightfoot
Addiction Research Foundation

My research has been in the area of alcohol and drug use and the expression of violence.

Although there is no universally accepted definition of aggression or violence, I have adopted a definition of expressive interpersonal violence as an actual or an attempted physical attack by one or more persons on another person for the purpose of inflicting physical injury or death. The attack is not related to an instrumental goal beyond the infliction of abuse, injury or death. Thus, violence associated with forceable rape and assault are included. Violence associated with armed robbery or homicide committed to prevent a witness from testifying are not included. It is important to point out that instrumental aggression is often described as a learned response which occurs in a particular situation because it has been reinforced in the past.

There is a long history of linking alcohol consumption with criminal behavior. Nineteenth century criminologist Lombroso believed that drinking was an important cause of assaultive crime. He preached that alcohol is a cause of crime. It is a cause because many commit crime in order to obtain drinks. Furthermore, men sometimes drink to gain courage to commit the crime or as an excuse for their misdeeds. He noted that it is also because of drinking that young men are drawn into crime. The bar is the meeting place where accomplices not only plan their crimes, but also squander their gains. He noticed that alcoholism occurred most often with those charged with assault, sexual offenses and insurrections. Next came assassinations and homicides. The last rank held those imprisoned for arson and theft, crime against property.

Lombroso is not very clear about how drinking exerts its criminal influence. I think it is fair to say that we in the 20th century are still unclear about how alcohol or drugs influence violent behavior in humans. It is also fair to say that we now recognize the influence of alcohol on violence as a complex phenomenon. It is not a simple or straightforward relationship.

In order to understand how complex this relationship is we need to briefly review the findings from a number of fields of inquiry. I begin with a description of the epidemiological literature. This literature on the alcohol-violence link has found a consistent positive correlation between violent crime and the use of alcohol or drugs. The crimes most frequently associated with alcohol abuse are homicide, rape and aggravated assault.

Some illustrious examples include the work of Wolfgang. He found, in reviewing 588 cases of homicide in Philadelphia over a four-year period, that alcohol was present in either the victim, the offender or both in 65% of the cases. In cases of rape, estimates range from 34% to 72%. In a review of 10 studies of homicide offenders, MacDonald found a range of between 19% and 83% of the cases where alcohol was involved. The frequency of alcohol involvement in these cases was between 50% and 60%. Mayfield, in his study of 307 convicted offenders of assault, found that 58% were not sober at the time of the crime.

It is often assumed that criminal behavior is part of the drug addict's lifestyle. The study by Ball and Associates found that in a random sample, 243 urban opium addicts reported committing crimes 248 days annually during periods of addiction and 41 days annually when not addicted. Eleven years elapsed between the onset of the addiction and the study. The authors estimate that this sample of addicts had committed about half a million crimes in this time interval. It is important to note that drug use and possession were not counted as crimes in this particular study. Theft was the most frequent offence, but others included drug sales, robbery, forgery, pimping, assault and murder.

Several theories have been proposed to account for the relationship between alcohol, drug use and violent crime. Pernanin pointed out that they are correlated phenomena. He does not provide evidence that alcohol is a direct cause of violence. He argues that there are more complex models in which both problem drinking or alcoholism and violence are caused by the same factors.

Pernanin also argued that the alcohol-violence relationship may be explained by interactive conditional, or what he calls conjunctive explanatory, models. The nature of the individual's socialization experiences, the characteristics of the drinking situation and the presence of alcoholism are all factors that might be included in a conjunctive explanatory model.

A fourth kind of model proposed by Pernanin is the spurious model. He argued that the association between alcohol and violence is not causal, but it is merely associated in a purely statistical sense. It may be that there are a disproportionate number of alcoholics in prison populations. This is true not because alcoholics actually commit more crimes, but because they are more likely to be arrested and incarcerated when they do.

Research in the field of alcohol, drug abuse and violence has usually been conducted in a large number of areas of specialization. These can be grouped into clusters where they share a particular perspective on the alcohol, drug and aggression link. I'm going to concentrate on the biological, socio-cultural and psychological perspectives.

Biologically speaking, it was generally assumed until quite recently that alcohol depresses the higher brain centres and affects moral reasoning and judgment. Inhibitions are released resulting in that spectrum of drunken behavior which characterizes the intoxicated individual. This is the so-called chemical disinhibition theory. Large individual variations in drunken behavior, however, occur in the moderately low-to moderately high-range blood alcohol concentrations, concentrations between .03% and .25%. Some individuals become extremely gregarious and euphoric; others, morose or withdrawn. Wide swings in moods and aggressive behavior may become evident. These individual differences appear to be related to a wide variety of factors including the drinker's mood, expectations, the setting in which drinking occurs, the extent of individual tolerance development, the behavior of others and past learning experiences. Thus, a purely biological or physiological theory of alcohol as a disinhibiter of aggressive behavior does not adequately account for the variability of aggressive and violent behavior observed following consumption of alcohol and drugs.

It is important to note that the extreme sociological-cultural perspective would lead us to the conclusion that assaultive behavior could just as well result from lemonade were it consumed in the same setting and embellished with the same beliefs, rituals and societal expectations.

Another category of empirical and conceptual work is represented by the socio-cultural perspective. The Laps in Northern Finland and the Irish engage in periodic binges and become aggressive. In contrast, the Camba of Bolivia who are also described as heavy drinkers do not become aggressive. The drinking binges act as an escape from tedious daily labor. Similarly, other researchers have found in comparing two central Mexican tribes that although both drank heavily, only one tribe engaged in violent behavior while drinking. These data and other cross- cultural studies suggest that the cultural meanings and the expected effects of drinking in turn affect the expression of violent behavior.

Social structure and social control influence drinking behavior. Drunken brawls are common in loosely organized societies with relatively powerless leaders, but they are uncommon in highly structured societies which emphasize authority and respect. It is clear that attitudes towards alcohol and drug use and abuse and the rules that govern behavior after ingestion are variable. According to socio-cultural theorists in predicting whether violent behavior will occur following drinking, the who, how, where and with whom are as important as the what and how much.

Although there are problems in this field caused by the lack of precise definitions for the terms aggression, violence and addiction, some generalizations are possible. Across most studies, cycliden amphetamine and alcohol at low to moderate doses do seem to increase certain attack and threat behavior in animals. At intermediate to higher doses, a sedating effect is usually seen. Cannabis or THC and the opiates are usually found to suppress aggressive behavior. These kinds of studies show that what and how much are important variables in predicting the occurrence of aggressive behavior.

From the psychological perspective, experimental studies with humans in the laboratory suggest that alcohol is a potent causal antecedent of aggressive behavior. It is neither a sufficient nor a necessary cause. For example, although subjects on average perform more aggressively with an alcohol increase, some intoxicated subjects do not inflict more pain on an opponent than non-intoxicated subjects. Even when provoked by having an opponent deliver high shock, intoxicated subjects are responsive to social pressure to reduce the severity of their aggressive behavior. These studies suggest that alcohol either increases preparedness to aggress or decreases the threshold for aggression. However, additional factors are required to elicit the expression of violent behavior. It also seems from these studies that alcohol increases the perception or attribution of threat. Intoxicated subjects expect more aggression than non- intoxicated subjects.

The effects of expectancy have been discussed in psychological literature. Taylor, for example, has found that intoxicated subjects consistently behave more aggressively than subjects with a placebo or a no-beverage. Higher doses resulted in higher levels of aggression. Other investigators have reported that subjects who received alcohol other than beer demonstrated more aggression despite comparable blood alcohol levels. Alcohol placebo was found to produce more aggressive behavior than beer placebo or beer.

It appears that who will be prone to aggression will be determined by a complex set of biological, psychological and social variables.

My co-author David Hodgens and I ran a study in the Ontario Region Federal Correctional Institution. To properly address the questions of alcohol and drug use and violent behavior in prisons, this survey of a representative sample of Canadian offenders was required.

In order to collect key social, demographic, cognitive and substance abuse data, a comprehensive assessment battery consisting of a structured interview format and six supplementary tests was developed. This structured interview was largely based on an instrument then currently being developed by the Addiction Assessment Interview. In general, questions in each section assess current levels of functioning, identify problems and ask respondents to assess the relationship between problems and substance use. An extensive determination of alcohol and drug patterns in the structured interview was supplemented by assessment of the degree of alcohol and drug dependence from two self-report inventories. The alcohol dependence scale, an instrument invented by Harvey, Skinner and Horne and the drug abuse screening test were used to assess the degree of drug dependence.

Use of alcohol and drugs and participation in criminal activity among family and friends of offenders was also addressed in the interview format. The legal status section of the structured interview elicited a description of the current offenses. A description of the degree of violence involved in that crime is included as well as the length of the current sentence, the amount of the sentence served to date, a criminal history and the institutional offence record.

The relationship between alcohol and drug use and the commission of the current offence was addressed in seven questions. They asked about use of alcohol and/or drugs on the day of the offence, the amount used, the perceived effects of the substance on judgment, the perceived relationship of use of the substance to the offence and the relationship of alcohol and drug use to previous convictions. Inmates were asked to respond to all questions relating to their functioning in the six-month interval prior to incarceration. This was retrospective information. In order to increase compliance and decrease suspicion, prison psychologists and previous researchers made no attempt to obtain information on current alcohol and drug use by inmates. All assessments were conducted by trained people and lasted two to three hours.

In order to get a representative sample of inmates from the Ontario region, a form letter was distributed to all inmates in the region. In the letter they were advised that the primary purpose of the study was to develop substance abuse treatment programs. They were also advised that there was no need for them to personally have a problem in order for them to volunteer to participate. Anonymity was guaranteed, and all inmates who volunteered were pre-screened. Inmates with obvious psychiatric disorders, brain damage, low IQ or security risks were screened out of the study.

In order to assess the representation of the obtained sample of 275 inmate volunteers, a comparison to Ontario region inmate population parameters was made. We looked at a number of variables including their age, marital status, language spoken, province of residence, length of sentence and time served. We found a difference with marital status and language spoken. For some reason we attracted more separated and divorced inmates. It was nonetheless a small difference. Overall, the data analysis indicated that the obtained sample was representative of Ontario and federal offenders.

The mean age of the sample was about 29 years. Ninety-eight per cent of our sample were males. Seventy-two per cent of the sample reported that they did not consider themselves to be part of a distinct cultural group. We had only 5% Natives or Metis. Seventeen per cent identified with another cultural group. The largest proportion of inmates, 54%, reported having completed some secondary education. Approximately 30% reported having completed secondary education. Most offenders reported unskilled occupations. Forty-four per cent were single. Forty- five per cent of the sample reported having been employed on a full-time basis prior to incarceration. About 13% indicated they were not in the labor force.

Inmates were asked to list all offenses for which they were presently serving time. The most frequently reported offence was robbery, 34%. Break-ins and theft followed at about 27%; murder, at 19%. Approximately 10% of the sample were serving time for a drug-related offence, 11% for possession of stolen goods, 9% for fraud and 5% for manslaughter.

As indicated earlier, the variety of measures relating to the nature and extent of alcohol abuse is obtained from inmates. These measures included subjective evaluations by inmates as well. The average age they began drinking was 15 years. The age of first problems associated with drinking was 18 years. The average number of drinks per day, standard drinks containing 17 milliliters of absolute alcohol, was 14 with an annual consumption of about 199 litres per inmate.

In the alcohol dependence data, approximately half the sample had low levels of dependence on alcohol while 20% were what we would describe as moderately dependent. Sixteen per cent demonstrated substantial dependence, and 11% were severely dependent on alcohol. A comparison of mean inmate ADD scores with samples of clients in treatment programs shows that approximately 26% of surveyed inmates in federal correctional institutions reported levels of alcohol dependence comparable to those observed in patients attending outpatient or in-patient treatment programs.

Inmates were asked to describe problems they had experienced prior to incarceration which they believed were related to their use of alcohol. Seventy-nine per cent reported experiencing at least one problem as a consequence of their alcohol use. In contrast, a national survey of Canadians showed only 12% of Canadian males experiencing a problem related to their use of alcohol. The most frequently reported problems, 67%, involved the law; 57% involved family and friends; 40% involved work or school. Only 25% of inmates reported health problems related to their use of alcohol. About 87% of inmates were drinking at levels associated with probable physical impairment.

When we combine the daily dosage and life problem information according to a procedure developed by Martha Craig of the ARF, about 63% of surveyed inmates could be described as heavy drinkers with problems and a further 15% as moderate drinkers with problems. Thus, about 78% of surveyed inmates were experiencing life problems related to their use of alcohol.

Approximately 80% of surveyed inmates reported having used at least one drug excluding caffeine and nicotine in the six months prior to incarceration. The most frequently used drugs were cannabis (71%), other hallucinogens (42%), amphetamines (40%), benzodiazapine (36%), cocaine (35%), analgesics (32%) and barbiturates and sleeping pills (29%). Few inmates reported using volatile nitrates (5%) or inhalant or solvents.

In addition, very few inmates reported using major tranquilizers or anti-depressants. When we look at scores on the drug abuse screening test, we can see that about 13% of inmates fell into the so-called severe range of drug abuse, 25% into the substantial range, 25% into the moderate range and a further 25% into the low range of Skinner's drug abuse categories. A comparison of inmates' scores to samples of drug abusers in treatment programs is provided.

Inmates were then asked if they had used alcohol and/or drugs on the day they committed the criminal offence. If they had, then how much. Seventy-nine per cent of surveyed inmates reported having used alcohol and/or other drugs on the day of the offence. Approximately 26% reported using alcohol alone; 13% said they used drugs alone; 40% reported they had used both. When asked how much they had used, 37% reported more than usual; 27% said about the same amount; only 10% said less than usual.

In order to more precisely examine the relationship between alcohol and drug use and violent crime, we asked how they would describe their drinking from toddler to alcoholic.

The degree of violence was measured on a 6 point scale from no contact with the victim to death of the victim. This alcoholism/crime variable was derived from factor analysis and consisted of four items. These items included use of alcohol or drugs on the day of the crime, the amount used, the perceived effect on judgment and the perceived effect of alcohol or drugs on the severity of the crime. The degree of violence in the crime was found to be positively associated with a self-definition of self as an alcoholic or heavy drinker. The correlation between violence and crime related to alcoholism was about .25. It was also associated with high A scores which are alcohol dependents scores. Longer histories of problem drinking, higher levels and severity of drinking problems and a self-definition as a heavy drinker were also positively associated with a heightened perceived role of alcohol in the crime. These relationships were not observed for drug abuse variables. High death scores and another variable indicating the number of different drug classes used in the month preceding the crime were not found to be related to the degree of violence in the crime. The correlation here was minus .12. The perceived role of drug use in the crime had a correlation of approximately .13.

Subjects with an alcohol problem are more likely to indicate that alcohol played a role in the commission of the offence. the standardized bare weights are significant at .005 levels to minus .46. This relationship does not hold for those reporting high degrees of drug dependence or drug involvement, here the P values were .09. Whether subjects have a drug problem does not influence whether alcohol and drug plays a role in the crime, but it does have a slightly negative relationship with the degree of violence observed. If alcohol and drugs play a role in the crime, there is more likelihood the crime will be violent.

It is important to note that in this analysis we are accounting for only about 9% of the variance in the violence variable although this is a significant amount. Many other factors are important if we are to understand the phenomenon of violence in inmates. Thus far we have not examined the relationship between the amount of substance used on the day of the crime and the degree of violence. What this data does suggest is that with use of alcohol, crimes are more likely to be violent. Given this relationship, it seems imperative that both treatment and secondary prevention programs be provided to offenders in order to reduce the probabilities of high levels of alcohol use and thus ultimately reduce the risk of violent crime.

PART X

NUTRITION AND VIOLENCE

NUTRITION AND VIOLENCE

Douglas Quirk
Ontario Correctional Institute

There is no such thing as violent behavior. Violent behavior comes from the use of the term violence to another. Behavior is potentially dangerous to another person and may do violence to another person. The notion of violent behavior complies with the notion that somehow the person has qualities which are going to create a violence in another person. The term violence is basically an irrelevant one when trying to deal with people as behaving organisms.

Much more appropriate to that is dangerousness, a term I would prefer to deal with rather than violence. I noted that the term violence as it refers to behavior is relatively meaningless. Essentially, the term violence refers to the opinion of a judge, a third party, an observer looking at a piece of behavior. The behavior act is essentially the same whether it be target practice or shooting another person.

The difference lies in the judged consequences of the behavior, but the dangerous action, in order to be implied as having a violent intent, must imply something about the motivation of the individual. For example, ramming another person with your car and ramming a person as a result of a flat tire are basically the same actions. Shooting another person, discharging a firearm accidentally, tripping and knocking another person down, striking another in rage or striking an unseen person when waving your arms around in a wild gesticulation are all the same kinds of actions qualitatively. One has the implication of intent or motivation, and the other has the implication of accident. A violent action is therefore both a judgment by another and a state of intention.

Another element involved in violence or dangerousness is whether this intention or motivation to be dangerous is overt or covert, voluntarily intentional or involuntarily intentional.

I would now like to make a distinction between physics and psychology. Behavior, the subject matter of psychology which may be involved in danger or risk-taking action, is to be distinguished in some way from the physical substance which is spatially distributed. Chemicals, nutrition, nutrients, the anatomical state of the body and the physiological state of the body as a structure are all spatially distributed.

Behavior is distributed in time as a force field is distributed in time. That means, if you look for a piece of behavior at the wrong time, you will not find it. If you look for it at the right time, anybody can come along and examine it. It is extremely unlikely that one is going to find a one-to-one correlation between some of the behavioral levels of analysis and a spatially distributed entity like a nutrient.

One way there may be an association is that the behavior of the organism depends upon the weight of the body as a physically distributed entity, how it works, how it functions.

Increased dangerousness can occur under certain physical conditions of action. Dangerousness will increase with the velocity or speed of an action. The faster you are going,the more risk there is of harm happening. This is true with a car. A thing which has velocity in it is more likely to have a high speed and is likely to be more dangerous than that which has a slow speed. With a slow speed there is more time for control or regulation of the action.

Velocity, the first variable of a physical action I want to address, has no relevance whatsoever to nutritional control either in terms of instigating it through malnutrition or controlling it with good nutrition.

The second physical property of an action that may increase its dangerousness is its kinetic energy, the amount of force or weight involved in an action. If a person who is doing something is stronger and heavier than the thing against which it is done, there is a greater risk of dangerousness.

Kinetic energy of the body, the amount of weight and force and effort that the body can evoke or use in action, does have some relevance to nutrition. Essentially, the greater the person's involvement with the fast food culture, the greater the risk of high kinetic energy output. This is a fairly obvious statement, but it is important to note. Risk of dangerous behavior increases.

Offenders, particularly dangerous offenders, are likely to come from a lower socio-economic level of society where the fast food culture is a part of life. Anybody working in the correctional system can evidence this very easily by merely watching the lines for food in the cafeteria. If you watch an offender fill his mug with coffee, half the mug is full of sugar. The next quarter is milk, and he colors it a little with coffee. That is a standard approach for these chaps. They take piles of white bread and leave the brown bread untouched.

They are heavily into the joy of fast food living, and we can see this while they are incarcerated. If you follow them around a bit on the street, as occasionally I have done, you will also find that they do the same sort of thing on the street.

The fast food culture, in addition to being earmarked by a heavy reliance on alcohol and coffee, is characterized by the five elements of the white plague. The white plague elements are white sugar, white flour, white salt, white milk and white people. In order to prevent dangerous behavior, it would be helpful for all people at all times to cease further involvement with all five elements of the white plague.

The third aspect of an action which makes it dangerous is the firmness of the object used in the action. A bullet, a knife, a fist or a baseball bat are firm and impenetrable, and obviously this bears heavily on how severe and dangerous the consequences are. There is no relevance whatsoever of nutrients to the object used in a dangerous action.

There are four dimensions to an action which make it risky or dangerous and give it potential energy. Potential energy may become excessive resulting in dangerous actions if the individual is too highly aroused for the level of able control. If the individual is artificially activated beyond effective control levels by exogenous substances like drugs and alcohol, potential energy may be increased.

Normal drives at normal levels are supposed to be adaptive. Simple reactive fear is the motive which signals appropriate escape from real dangers such as getting out of the way of a car bearing down at high speed. Anger is a feeling derived from the experience of frustration, from anxiety about the energy output which may result in normal and adaptive assertiveness or from an increase in constructive energy to be used in useful work.

Normal depression or mourning is a reconstructive process to permit the person to heal a personal wound before once again entering into other human relationships. Fear can be maladaptive if it is excessive or if it relates to an unreal or non-existing danger. Anger can be maladaptive if it is unregulated energy output and does not take into account the qualities of the object or person against which it is directed.

Artificial activation or allergens do not sound to many people to be a nutritionally relevant thing, but a great number of allergens are found in food substances. Allergens are in substances and are transmitted through food, air, water or skin contact to parts of the body. This results in an inflammatory response of the tissue.

Several means exist for allergens to affect changes resulting in an increased risk of dangerous behavior. At one level of direct functioning, an allergen may create discomfort in the body such as irritation from eczema or psoriasis. This increased state of discomfort may enhance the overall drive level and increase irritability in otherwise only mildly trying situations.

Food allergens, a common substance of such reactivity and preliminary observations, may well occur with a higher frequency in correctional populations than with the population at large. We have not checked that out much in Ontario, but there is some evidence from the States that this is true.

At another level of indirect functioning, an allergen such as a grain in an alcoholic beverage may be transmitted to nervous tissue and may create allergic inflammation especially in the limbic lobes. It may result in emission of blind drive behavior, such as rage or terror, or in an excessive sex drive. Susceptibility to blind rages probably represents one of the main causes of dangerous violent behaviors. It may be seen in a person's reaction to a particular kind of alcohol.

It would be wise for people, especially for those who have a history of dangerous behaviors, to be able to identify the allergic substances and to treat them as toxins to be avoided at all cost. The most common instance of this is with the person who responds with violence only with a particular kind of alcohol, usually rye or beer. If the person is responding to alcohol with rages, our data so far shows that 95% of the time the person responds to one kind of alcohol or to an alcohol with a particular grain in it.

Toxins are substances which destroy tissue or interfere directly with organ function. Examples are Dioxin, PCP and LCD and a host of psychotropic medications.

Stress activated by toxins operates in the body to increase drive states and irritability in a manner which is essentially equivalent to a reaction to sugar. Such toxins should simply be avoided if possible as its effects on behavior can range from simple distress through irritable and aggressive behavior to psychosis.

Pain operates in the same way sugar or toxins do in activating the stress reaction of the body and increasing drive level and thus irritability and potential dangerousness. Some pain results from the nutritionally relevant factors. Among these are gastric disorders ranging from gastric acidity from the body's efforts to digest meat or competing foods such as a mixture of vegetables and fruits through a spastic colon which may arise from hypoglycemia created by an excessive use of simple carbohydrates especially sugar all the way to gastric distress arising from the attempt of the body to digest lactic acid in milk.

Milk has only quite recently become a part of the adult diet, and this growth has corresponded with the development of antibiotics. Antibiotics used in large amounts are likely to destroy the healthy flora of the intestinal tract. If these intestinal flora are destroyed in large amounts, the ingestion of milk results in various forms of gastric distress, from loose bowels to severe stomach cramps and even to severe flu-like symptoms.

A thoughtful combination of foods thus ingested and possibly an avoidance of milk may well be the best ways to deal with these sources of distress and the possible increases in irritability and aggressiveness.

Direct arousal is a second kind of effect on potential energy. There are some disinhibiting agents which are perfectly obvious. Among the recognized disinhibiting agents is alcohol which is probably the best known although cocaine and LSD and some of the street drugs have a similar effect. Alcohol is a nutritional substance along with foods. One of the prime effects of alcohol is that it effectively disfortificates the individual and thus blocks the action of normal controls supporting socialized behavior.

These normal controls are of two sorts. One kind of cortical control involves cortical coordination of behavior that permits the individual to adjust his motor actions such as those involved in steering a car or controlling its speed. This coordinating function is impaired by ingesting dishibiting agents. An increased blood level of the agent increases error actions. This may achieve the position of dangerous acts if the person is, for example, driving a car.

The other kind of control is socialized control which is probably derived from shame or guilt or desire to be seen as a good or nice person. This modulates the overt expression of anger and other disruptive feelings. People who are inclined to inhibit angry feelings or to control them too well tend also to build up resentment, bitterness and internal rage often coupled with distress.

Once such a person encounters this reduced control function, the stored rage or resentment is apt to bubble over into aggressive behavior which can often become dangerous. With people who tend to store up anger, it would be wise to avoid the use of disinhibiting agents. This sort of procedure usually follows assertiveness training.

The second direct arousal phenomenon is nutritional insufficiencies. This is perhaps the most nutritionally relevant set of things I want to talk about. They are the substances which the body needs for effective functioning, and insufficiency may result in excessive distress or pain and may require corrective use of tranquilizers or analgesic agents. The person may be become addicted and have other problems from that source.

Some nutritional substances are needed to foster effective bodily functioning, and these do not tend to be habit forming. The B vitamins tend to modulate some brain functions and may modify stress reactions in the body, and stress is one of the major causes of a general state of arousal. The person then may mislabel the arousal as though it were anger resulting in angry behavior. B12 tends to increase cognitive and perceptual clarity. According to some reports, niacin may increase bodily energy and thus reduce depression.

Zinc is probably a natural tranquilizer and may be relatively insufficient in normal American food supplies. Calcium deficiency has been implicated in a number of conditions where stress reactions are excessive and may even be a factor in relative mental retardation. Iodine is needed for effective thyroid functioning, and thyroid malfunctioning results in emotional distress and irritability very often. Sugar insufficiency in a person who either uses a lot of sugar or maintains a high level of stress results in an increased irritability associated with hypoglycemia. It also reduces the control function from associated depression and fatigue.

Of all of the substances affecting the body, vitamin C is probably the most basic need. Ascorbic acid seems to modulate the stress response and is involved in a host of bodily transformations necessary to health.

The fifth quality of a person's activity which may increase dangerousness is the behavior control he exerts. I have talked about velocity, kinetic energy, penetrating qualities and potential energy, and now I am talking about control functions that the person may exert in maintaining effectiveness, in avoiding or getting involved in dangerous behavior.

Control or regulation of behavior is necessary to impede instant response or general irritability or to instigate undersocialized action some of which may be dangerous.

As a group, offenders, especially those emitting dangerous behavior, tend to be overly emotional people who feel things like fear, anger and depression apparently more acutely than most other people. They have a hard time controlling or regulating these feelings or delaying their actions associated with these feelings.

Insufficiencies of control or regulation obviously are likely to interact strongly with increased velocity, kinetic, potential energy or feelings. Insufficiencies of control may occur from brain damage, an acute psychotic illness, through mental retardation, increased stimulus or stress hunger.

My third nutritional note has two or three subsections to it. The presence of a number of nutritionally relevant substances in the body is apt to interfere with effective control in a number of different ways. It thus enhances the risk of dangerousness.

First of all, there is control suppression. There are several substances which interfere with effective neuro-functioning and thus control behavior. Psychedelic drugs such as LSD are obvious examples of this.

One substance deserves special note because it now occurs in drinking water now that domestic plumbing has largely been converted from lead to copper. Copper tends to pool in the fatty tissues of the body, one area of which is the limbic lobes of the brain which needs to be functioning intact for effective neuro-functioning.

One study has shown that cellating copper out of the body increases the performer's efficiency and significantly reduces later delinquent behavior in delinquent subjects. We have not been able to replicate that lately.

It would appear that copper, if present in large amounts in the body, interferes with effective control of behavior. This substance is likely to be ingested from domestic water supplies and probably in excessive doses by offenders who are involved in the fast food culture since most fast foods tend to increase thirst. This substance can apparently be cellated out of the body now by use of heroic doses of an essentially safe substance, vitamin C.

Secondly, the disinhibiting effect of some substances such as alcohol has already been noted. It has already been stated that its effects also include the impairment of effective control which may increase dangerousness. Alcohol ingestion, like street drug use, tends to be associated with a cult or culture in the sense that people frequently go where others who are also drinking are, to bars.

The disinhibiting effect of alcohol occurring in a number of people in contact with one another enhances the probability of mutually stimulated reactions which escalate disinhibition and uncontrolled reactions. A social cult involved in the use of some substances may foster additional breakdown control and thus increase probability of dangerous actions.

I do not know to what extent this affects the penitentiary population. In a correctional population as a whole, the source of disinhibition is not only found in the use of alcohol, but also it is found in the disinhibiting effect of being out drinking in a bar with others.

The last category of nutritionally relevant things that I want to talk about is impulse activation. Some substances increase impulses beyond the point of control. The first group of these produces excessive arousal.

Some substances increase arousal beyond the person's capability of control. Some of these have been mentioned under potential energy already, but the fast foods deserve another comment. In some people usually having a history of hyperactivity, fast food elements, especially sugar as well as some food allergens, seem to have a stimulating effect or one of drowsiness.

The person's control functions are thus impaired by the drowsiness, but the drowsiness may feel uncomfortable to some of these people using the excess energy provided by the elevated blood sugar levels or by the stress aroused concurrently by the allergen. They tend to fight off the drowsiness with an increased activity level. Some people are often prescribed ritalin for this or find means to self-medicate themselves using street drugs in the speed family. They allow themselves a better level of control over the intensified energy level.

The second impulse activation issue is eroticism. Marijuana tends mainly to increase general eroticism which is generally considered to be pleasant. But it may also impair control functions slightly in a mildly drowsy way. Marijuana may create an intensive probability of dangerous acting out and thus probably should be avoided.

Several of the toxins and a number of the allergic substances occurring in food stuffs may facilitate an epileptic response which may result in dangerous behavior.

Essentially, nutrition does not cause criminality nor violence. Violence is probably not an attribute of behavior as such but rather a judgment by another concerning the outcome of behavior. However, if one addresses the risk-taking or dangerousness as a potential in the person's behavior, a number of statements probably can be made showing a relationship between what I have called nutritionally relevant factors and dangerous behavior.

Although many of my observations may not qualify as specifically related to the person's nutritional state, some of the observations are quite specifically related to nutrition.

Finally, on a positive side, some nutrients appear to serve helpful functions in correcting, in part, some of the disruptive effects of some of the substances mentioned above. Vitamin C, calcium and zinc may prove helpful especially if coupled with avoidance of all fast foods.

NUTRITION AND VIOLENCE

Bruce Ferguson
Carleton University

I have been interested in kids with a variety of problems including their relationship with nutrition and food. Claims have been made by people like pediatrician Dr. Ben Finegold who equate bad behavior with an adverse response to additives. Dr. Finegold arrived at that conclusion by looking at case studies of kids who came to his office, and he said, "If you put them on diets free of these substances, their behavior improved." This got into the press.

People took that seriously although the research approach came entirely under fire. The hypothesis was that large numbers of kids were affected by substances. There have been careful studies which show that kids are not affected by these substances.

Next came the white plague, white sugar. There is nothing wrong with sugar. It is a carbohydrate, a source of energy. Again we have the same kind of hypothesis called sometimes the "Hallowe'en effect" because after Hallowe'en, the kids are always terrible in school. It is just because they are eating all their candy and not their normal food. Therefore they have trouble.

Sugar substitutes are now good. You cannot tell the difference in taste. The truth is that behavior does not change. Sugar is not responsible for all those nasty little devils up there. There are now a dozen such studies and the results are all the same.

There is some beginning research that shows nutrition can affect behavior. There were some studies done in the American military via a researcher then out of Harvard, Bonnie Spring, who showed that if you ingest meals at lunchtime or breakfast high in carbohydrates or proteins, if you shift the balance, you get the differential affects. The differential affects depend somewhat on your sex and on your age. By and large, if you have a high carbohydrate lunch, your sustained attention will not be as good. Your mood will drop. You get drowsy.

Tryptophan is a pre-curser on the neuro-transmitter called serotonin. We do not make tryptophan, we are totally dependent on taking it in from our diet. The more tryptophan that gets across the blood/brain barrier, the more serotonin we make. If there is less tryptophan, then there is less serotonin. Serotonin is involved in the sleep-wake cycle.

When we eat a lot of carbohydrates, there is a perfectly sensible explanation of why we get sleepy because it affects how much tryptophan gets into our brains. It is no accident that your grandmother said, "Have warm milk and a banana before you go to bed." Sources of tryptophan makes more serotonin, and you actually do get sleepier.

What you eat can affect your behavior. There are some very subtle effects. Out of all the sugar studies with children, the most consistent finding is decreased activity after ingesting sugar. It is exactly the opposite of the gorilla hypothesis, but it is exactly compatible with what we know about the biochemistry of the brain and how what we eat affects that biochemistry. It is 100% compatible. But it is not at all compatible with the Hallowe'en hypothesis.

Why would we bother to do this research? If a mother restricts her kid's diet to make him less hyperactive, then that diet can become an incredible problem for her and the 11-year-old child who would like to attend birthday parties and eat ice cream and hotdogs and cake with the rest of the kids.

It also may keep her from seeking other forms of treatment necessary in helping her kid pay attention in school, to get through school. We know that if we can keep those kids in school, that is a key thing. It reduces both their risk of future psychopathology and problems with the law. That is one of our main goals.

Sugar is not a toxin. It is a carbohydrate. There is nothing wrong with white sugar. It is just another form of carbohydrate. Your guts and your brains don't recognize the difference between honey and sugar.

So there are a lot of misconceptions that get banged about and get passed along. And you can go talk to nutritionists. You can talk to a PhD. and nutrition biochemists, and they will tell you about sugar. They will tell you about mono and dye, and it does not really mean anything.

PART XI

HOMICIDE

HOMICIDE

Elliot Leyton
Memorial University, St. John's

Murder is the ultimate theft because the perpetrator cannot return what he has stolen. Murder is also the ultimate obscenity. The act dehumanizes the victim, the victim's family, society and the killer. I regard the homicide rate as the most reliable single index showing how civilized a nation really is. I judge a nation by the number of citizens having a chance to live life with a measure of peace and dignity.

Canada is the only nation in all the Americas that has a low European homicide rate. Our homicide rate is one-quarter of the American's and one-tenth of the Latin American's. Compared to the rest of the world, there is little chance that our children will be assaulted or murdered. Yet most Canadians do not think of homicide and violence in this way at all. The majority of Canadians feel we are in the midst of an explosion of violence.

How can there be such a disparity between perception and reality? Part of the explanation for this lies in the peculiar cultural fact that Canadians often see the world through American eyes. In our absorption of American films, books, television and magazines, we inevitably take on certain foreign perceptions, mythologies and emotional responses. This distortion is by no means confined to those lacking access to the truth.

In the early 1980s several official government reports showed an increase in crime in Newfoundland by 40%. After careful scrutiny, we discovered that there was no crime wave at all. The 40% increase in violent crime that had been reported between 1974 and 1983 was primarily an increase in reported assaults. The homicide rate had not changed at all. That increase in assaults was not a real increase at all. It was a change in record keeping.

The media is the prime source of information and cultural transmission. What I expected during my investigation was that yellow journalism would be manipulating the public's fear of violence to sell more newspapers. That was not the case at all. I found in the 1970s dozens of special interest groups, vested interest groups, political and pressure groups all realizing that the most important card they could possibly play was the violence card. By linking their special needs to the explosion of violence, they could advance their own case. The newspapers merely soberly and dutifully reported them. The sensationalizing did not come from the newspapers.

By the late 1970s and early 1980s the crime wave had become the symbol of everything that was wrong with our society. It had become the ideal argument for in-house political documents and external political documents. Violence became the ammunition for the justification of any political position. It was the necessary factor that legitimized the expansionist aims of any pressure group or profession.

The Director of Statistics Canada at that time announced a 40% increase in the crime rate. He said he could not explain it, but it must be a population in turmoil. The Newfoundland Department of Rural Northern Development, led by a group of private sociology consultants, announced the crime wave was even higher than that. The Minister of Social Services argued for an increase in his budget by saying there had been an explosion of crime. The Alcohol and Drug Dependency Commission pointed to the explosion of the crime wave and related it specifically to alcohol. They used that to ask for a 600% increase in their budget. The Atlantic Institute of Criminology argued for more funding because of the crime wave. Labor and church groups politically committed against unemployment argued that we were going to get terrible violence if we did not raise the employment rate. Many judges in open court used the crime wave whenever they wanted to justify an excessive sentence. The Association of Chiefs of Police pointed to the crime wave to justify capital punishment. The vice-president of the Status of Women and the president of the Co-Citizen's Coalition Against Pornography used it to justify their anti-porn campaign. The Newfoundland Teacher's Association wished to expand their staff because of the violent crime wave. Children's Hospital needed expansion funds to justify the hiring of staff to provide for this sudden wave of sexual assaults.

As each group made its announcement, it provided another group with further ammunition for its demands and justification. Each special interest reinforced the other. Group A would point to Group B's announcement that alcoholism was destroying the fabric of the nation and was precipitating drunken assaults. If they got a 600% increase in their budget, which I certainly agree with, we should have a 12,000% increase in our budget! Most of all, each one of these announcements confirmed the public's belief that we should be fearful.

So far as I was able to determine, there were only two institutions in Canadian society that did not announce a crime wave. One was the Royal Mint and the other was the John Howard Society. They at no point took advantage of an obvious opportunity to play politics. That was remarkable.

The Alcohol and Drug Dependency Commission announced a study reporting that the total economic costs to the province because of alcohol and drug dependency was $56 million annually. The Minister of Social Services who had financed the report said that this report was critically important. Alcohol abuse has far more consequences on the family and the social fabric of this province, he said. He said, the effects of alcohol and drug abuse are major contributors to the abuse of children, the abuse of women and "no doubt the abuse of men." He said the document will give him added support when he goes to his cabinet colleagues for money for the commission. The chairperson of the ADDC asked for an increase of 600% in their budget.

In conclusion, while there are many tragic problems regarding crime and punishment in Canada, by world standards there is no crime wave in Canada. The homicide rate has remained relatively stable for years. There is a fear of crime that is simply not justified by the actual risk. What we have done is irresponsibly manipulated the public fear. This irresponsible manipulation has been by individuals in groups which are normally responsible. We have all played a role in the premature release of statistics, in overstating arguments to draw attention to a problem, in the critical acceptance of each other's charges, in not thinking through the consequences of our actions and getting so excited and reporting what has always existed as new and accelerating phenomena.

HOMICIDE

Singe De Silva
Centre for Justice Statistics

There are all kinds of variations within the area of homicide. There are variations in month, day, season, province and region. For example, the Atlantic region had the lowest homicide rate in 1984, closely followed by Ontario. Both had a rate lower than the national rate. Northern homicide rates were four to five times the national level with a rather small number in the Yukon and Northwest Territories.

It is general knowledge that the United States has a very high murder rate compared to Canada. At the same time we cannot boast about our low rates because there are countries that have a much lower rate than ours. Let us accept the notion that homicide is a form of conflict resolution. One could then compare the other violent forms of conflict resolution with the numbers and the rate of homicide. In resolving conflicts, some people kill others, other people, themselves. Others engage in physical fights, and the police count many of these fights as a source. Perhaps one could compare the homicide rate with the assault rate. For example, in 1984 there were about 600 assaults per 100,000 population reported by the police. This only represents a fraction of assaults taking place in society. We can compare this with a 2.65% homicide rate which shows that homicide is rare.

One can say looking at the historical homicide rate that it has risen considerably over the last 50 years. Right now we are stable although this is not a very good sign. With respect to homicide, the three types that generate most fear in the community are the homicide committed by strangers, the homicide committed in public places and the homicide committed during the commission of other crimes such as robbery and sexual assault.

The victim/suspect relationship regarding homicides that took place in 1984 shows that the extended family represented 38.2% of the homicides. Fifty per cent of the homicides were committed by friends; 11.6%, by strangers. Has the situation changed over time? Between 1974 and 1984, the stranger component was 14.2%. If anything, the stranger homicide in Canada has decreased very slightly.

With respect to homicide locations in 1984, 46% occurred in the victim's home, and 17.5% occurred in public places. Between 1974 and 1984, the percentage of homicides occurring in a public place was on the average 20.3%.

While many fear walking alone in a park, perhaps it is safer to go there than to stay at home. If we isolate the homicides taking place in the victim's own home, the numbers drop to 8.4%. In the victim's own home, 58.4% of the homicides are committed by family members.

Ironically enough, in 1984 80% of the homicides in public places took place by persons known to the victim and 20.9% by strangers. There has hardly been any change in this proportion over the past 11 years.

PART XII

SUICIDE

SUICIDE

David Phillips
University of California

My paper deals with the effect of mass media violence on self-directed aggression in the form of suicide. I will also discuss the effects of mass media violence on other directed aggression in the form of homicide.

Just after heavily publicized suicide stories, there is an abrupt increase in daily and monthly suicide rates. The more publicity given the story, the greater the increase in suicide. The increase in suicides occur primarily in the geographic area where the publicity occurs. One of the explanations for this finding is the possibility that the coroner is subsequently motivated to record deaths more often as suicides.

Many people feel that some suicides are disguised as automobile accidents. For example, in automobile accidents which follow a suicide, the driver is unusually similar to the person described in the suicide story. The passengers in those car crashes are not. In single-car crashes which occur just before a suicide story, the same holds true. While a suicide might trigger other overt suicides, there are also some covert suicides which are apparently disguised as single-car crashes.

When someone kills himself, there seems to be an increase in single car driver deaths. After a murder/suicide in which somebody kills other people as well as himself, there is typically an increase in multi-car passenger deaths which suggests that murder/suicide stories trigger one kind of car crash, and pure suicide stories trigger another.

Mass media violence triggers people into hurting themselves. In the laboratory people have been seen to behave more aggressively after seeing a violent movie. This is particularly true with males rather than females.

In the laboratory people have found that the kind of violent story most likely to trigger aggressive behavior has the following characteristics. The perpetrator is not criticized, but he is presented as being rewarded. His behavior is justified rather than criticized. Furthermore, the perpetrator is presented as intending to injure his victim. One type of story that meets these criteria is the heavyweight championship prize fight. The perpetrators are heavily rewarded, and millions of dollars are given to them for doing something which they would otherwise be arrested for. They are not typically criticized. Their behavior is justified.

After careful investigation, I found that daily homicides increase significantly after heavyweight prize fights. They increase more after the more heavily publicized prize fights. In the laboratory it also turns out that you are likely to behave aggressively after seeing a prize fight film if the victim available to you is similar to the victim on the screen.

Subsequent to this study on heavyweights, I investigated non-heavyweight prize fights which occur on the average every nine days. What I found is a significant increase in homicides in the United States just after these fights.

Fights involving two ethnic groups have a markedly larger increase in subsequent homicides. When the winning fighter is American, homicides rise markedly. When the winner is foreign, there is no visible increase in homicides.

In the laboratory, the only way to trigger people into violence by violent movies is to provide them with helpless victims. In the real world that would most likely be a child under five years of age. What seems to happen is that after fights, the murders of young children rise proportionately.

What kind of story do we have in which violence is heavily punished rather than heavily rewarded? One kind of story we have is one in which a person is given a death sentence for murder or when a person is given a life sentence for murder or an execution. We know that homicides go up after violence is rewarded. What happens if violence is punished? In a study of England from 1858 to 1921, I found that weekly homicides decreased by about 35-40% in the two weeks following publicized executions. I also found the more publicity given to the story, the greater the drop. Similar statistics were found in a study of the United States from 1973 to 1979.

SUICIDE

Dick Ramsay
University of Calgary

Suicide is still considered by many of us an act of violence. It is self-murder even though it no longer is a crime in our criminal code. Others who are more inclined to relate suicide to the concept of merely killing or at least to the notion of the right to take one's life see it as a compassionate and justifiable response to the terminally ill and to oppressive social situations. Others have interpreted suicide as a very complex coping behavior designed to accomplish or preserve some part of the individual's integrity and at the same time to possibly harm or destroy something in others.

There are therefore some interpretations which say that suicide is an act of violence against someone else and not necessarily against the self. The term suicide has been widely used to describe a wide array of suicidal behaviors, all the way from the superficial gesture of self inflicted harm to the self destructive behavior that results in death.

For the purposes of my presentation, I will deal with the concept of suicidal behaviors and refer to it as a continuum of behaviors that constitute deliberate self-harm resulting in death, the intention to die and the lethal behavior or means used.

The other way of demarcating suicidal behavior is to look at deliberate self-harm where there was a high intention to die, but for some reason there was a life outcome. Some may refer to this as accidental life. That would be called attempted suicide, and there are other deliberate self-harm behaviors where the intention to die is low or quite ambivalent, and life is the outcome. This is now often being referred to as para- suicide.

Finally, there are those undetermined death situations where death is the outcome from a deliberate self-harm behavior. It is very difficult to determine whether the intention to die was there. You can set this up on a matrix system in order to see four ways of classifying deliberate self-harm behavior. This behavior occasionally results in death.

Most societies recognize suicide as homicide, and constructive social policies to prevent this from happening have been very slow in developing. It is probably not unlike changes in the law which usually take up to 100 years. Very few societies have taken the responsibility to change the negative attitudes of its members or to develop large-scale action strategies aimed at preventing or reducing the incidence of suicidal behaviors.

Despite this lack of formal policy, suicidal behavior is clearly recognized as a subgroup of two major preventable public health disorders, poisoning and injuries. If this be true, then the elimination or at least the substantial reduction of these behaviors should be amenable to organizing prevention strategies.

A report on the social policy and program responsibilities has shown that the public and voluntary sectors in Alberta have tried to develop innovative strategies to reduce the incidence of suicidal behavior. From the statistical information available, it is easy to see why Alberta might be one of the provinces concerned about suicidal behaviors. We have consistently had suicide rates well above the national average, somewhere in the order of 18 per 100,000 compared to the national rate of 12-14. Add this to the fact that the Canadian rate has been consistently higher than the American rate. There is reason to believe that self-directed behavior is a self- directed violence and is a problem of some concern for us. We seem to be directed more inwardly than our neighbors.

Our rate in Alberta has been increasing steadily although not quite like the Quebec rate. Over a 20-year period, we have doubled our rate from approximately 9 per 100,000 to 17 or 18.

Relating that figure to attempted suicide and para-suicide behavior, you find that although there are no accurate figures for the ratio, two Canadian studies have come up with estimates from the general population surveys that the rate is at least 100 to 1 of a combined para-suicidal behavior and attempted suicidal behavior.

If you take those behaviors and relate them to the people who are affected by suicide, families, friends, co-workers, and use a figure, a minimum of five people in any suicidal behavior that are affected, you can mathematically determine the magnitude of suicidal behavior in a given population. For us in Alberta, that approximates one in seven individuals who are annually affected by a suicidal behavior. So it is widely prevalent in our society.

What has been done in Alberta dates back to 1973 when the government commissioned a task force on highway accidents and suicide. The Boldt Report made recommendations that we should approach the problem at three levels, prevention, intervention and post-intervention. It recommended that we tackle the problem from four areas, clinical outreach, education, program information and research.

In 1981, the Minister of Social Services and Community Health in our province, increased its social policy commitment to the prevention of suicide. The minister committed an additional half million dollars a year and set up a suicide prevention provincial advisory committee. They were given the responsibility of coming up with programs that would address this general mandate.

In doing that, we set up in Alberta an advisory committee with a budget and authorization to proceed on its own to meet the guidelines set out by the government. It is one example of what I would call participatory democracy where an initiation is made at the political level and is transferred to the community action base for implementation.

In the first year of this program, the committee was asked to develop an information dissemination system for all Albertans, to develop a provincewide education and training program, to facilitate the development of a coordinated inter agency outreach program and to improve the knowledge base of suicide through establishment of a research centre within a university setting. Within a couple of years, all of these activities had developed quite dramatically.

What has happened now is that we have developed an information clearing house resource centre that is to house all of the literature written on suicide in the English language since 1955. We now have something in the order of 8,000 documents on file and available to people in Alberta and across the country. We also set up a standardized suicide prevention training program across the province. Over a period of between two and three years, we piloted a co-curriculum training program for over 400 people.

We then developed a system where we can train trainers who could act as local resource people in their own communities and run the training programs within their home areas. That involved another 27 presentations to over 1,200 people. We now have a system of about 50 or 60 trainers who can run a two-day co- curriculum workshop within the province of Alberta. They have presented the program to over 4000 people, and currently we are presenting roughly one program or one workshop a week.

The program that I have referred to in Alberta is now being implemented within the federal corrections system.

PART XIII

TERRORISM AND HOSTAGE TAKING

TERRORISM AND HOSTAGE TAKING

Ronald Crelinsten
University of Ottawa

My four basic axioms deal with violence by people in power and by people without power. Terrorism is a weapon of the weak, and people who cannot hope to gain their political aims by force resort to random targeting of what we call innocents. The State also does this as well. This is a sign of weakness in terms of legitimacy where the State must use torture and death squads and does not have a certain form of legitimacy which is embodied in criminal law. The State will inevitably deform its own institutions.

Terrorism is a tactic of communication which combines the use of violence with the threat of violence. Both are important because unless you can prove that you can use it, your threats are not credible. While the threat and actual violence are generally directed towards one group, the demands for compliance are usually directed at different targets. Once the threat and violence go towards victims or hostages, specific demands go to governments, and implicit demands go to followers of the people you want to attack. You try to change allegiances. It is all communication, which is basically my first axiom.

My second axiom deals with the meaning attached to this communication strategy which I just defined as terrorism. The meaning attached to this communication tactic can vary according to the legitimacy of the actor and his order in the social structure. The word terrorism tends to serve as a pejorative label which deprives the actor and his actions of any legitimacy. If we call someone a terrorist, he is not political, just horrible. Therefore, we tend to find that the word terrorist has become equivalent to what I call the insurgent terrorist, the terrorist who is trying to overthrow a government or change government policy. I will use another term which is becoming more frequent, the state terrorist. The meaning attached to the communication strategy I define as terrorism varies according to who is using it. That brings in the notion of illegitimacy.

My third axiom extends this a little bit. State actors who use terrorism as I define it are better able to resist the terrorism label. Non-state actors who use terrorism are more likely to be labelled in ways that counter their claims to legitimacy. One label is terrorist. If you use it only for illegitimate actors, it will work. The other one is criminals. We tend to call insurgent terrorists criminals. We do not agree that they can use violence for political ends. Therefore, they are not accepted and are criminals.

My fourth axiom from a theoretical perspective leads me to say that if all the first three are true, then a complete study of political terrorism must analyze its use by both the controller and the controlled in domestic situations. The controller includes the actor and all the agents and bureaucrats who work for the State. To isolate the terrorism used by one actor from the reactions of its audiences and targets is to ignore the communicative nature of the phenomenon.

My whole approach to prevention and control of terrorism in a domestic context is going to be working from these four axioms. Even the phrase "the prevention and control of terrorism" must now be translated into "the prevention and control of insurgent terrorism." At what point do our attempts to control insurgent terrorism lead us into state terrorism? Can a state use terrorism forever? Can we argue that state terror will ultimately lead to insurgent terrorism?

There are three images of terrorism. We can use terrorism to maintain a status quo. I would say that most state actors do this. We can use terrorism to change the status quo. This is the controlled. The relationship between these two groups of actors is equal to a relationship between social control and social process. For instance, terrorism can be a tactic of social control, a means to control populations. It can also be a form of social protest or social change. It is the controlled, the insurgent terrorist, who uses terrorism.

Government, criminal justice and internal war are the three controller versions. We have government. It rules people. Then we have the criminal justice system with all its divisions. We have our police, and we also have legislation. We create our laws. We enforce our laws. We jump over to the extreme right, and we have internal war.

Our three bureaucracies can be the apparatus of government which is traditionally viewed as non-violent. We have our apparatus of criminal justice. This is traditionally viewed as repression. We do not use the word violence generally, but we can see the deterrent model of punishment as a form of terrorism. The use of violence is threatened against certain people to keep the rest of the people within the law.

In internal war there is our military which is a totally different institution. Soldiers with their hierarchy of training are responsible for dealing with very serious internal violence.

We can agitate for change through what we call the electoral process. I would also include interest groups that try to affect political decisions. I would try to make it as broad as possible. I would include labor unions. I would include all public pressure groups. The dimension of politics becomes exceedingly complex. I do not include only traditional political parties. We can write letters to the editor. We can make political films. There are many ways we can join politics outside the corridors of power in order to influence people.

We could then decide to use violence, crime or violent protest. Crime connotes a means declared illegal in a society.

That leads us to the third image with which I use the word revolution. This is where you use military models, uniforms, weapons, and you try to overthrow the government through extreme violence. The word generally used is force. The three images most often used in discussing terrorism are politics, crime and war. Each of those images are reflected by the controller as government and as the military. The definition of terrorism is so difficult because we always wonder whether terrorism is crime.

In between this image of crime and war falls what we traditionally call insurgent terrorism. This is the classic image we all have of the person blowing up something to gain attention for his cause. He does not have power. It falls right in a grey zone. It is politically motivated. It aims to change without the sufficient force to do so.

In political crime literature there are general distinctions between political crime and common crime. If you do something for personal gain, it is common. If you do it for political reasons, it is political. And we know that now the Irish Republican Army (IRA) is getting into the drug trade because it is fun to make money. The Tamil separatists in Sri Lanka are involved in the drug trade. In Colombia, the state terrorists are involved in narco-terrorism. The recent attack on the Supreme Court in Colombia was surely related to the fact that the government really wanted to crack down on their drug runners. We find that these grey zones do appear. That is why we have definition problems.

The state actor who responds to violence uses the police as his first defence. Why do the police respond? Blowing up a bomb is declared illegal in the criminal code. We do not care about the political motivation. We use the criminal justice system.

The reason the deterrent model of punishment is not viewed as terrorism in general is because we have something called the rule of law. Deterrence in the true sense of the word is when you threaten people with violence if they do not comply.

With the utilitarian approach to punishment, the only people the State is allowed to punish are the ones proven guilty according to the due process of the law. You must lay charges. You must inform them of their rights. You must have a right to a fair trial. You must have a right to a defence lawyer. You must have a public trial by your peers. You must be found guilty with proof. There must be a retributive limit to the utilitarian purpose of punishment. The rule of law limits the target of violence by the State. That is why we do not call it terrorism.

What we find in fighting insurgent violence is that these rules tend to become relaxed. You tend to get special legislation and broad police powers. You can dispense with arrest and search warrants. You do not have to go to a judge. You can keep them up to 60 days instead of 24 hours. France is debating holding people for four days instead of 24 hours in their new anti-terrorism legislation. Ireland has the same thing. As you relax your laws and your due process, you open up the possibilities of abuse.

This is the challenge for the State. Can we deal with this problem without becoming terrorists ourselves? According to Nietzsche, "He who fights with monsters must take care that he not become a monster himself." This is the challenge a democratic state faces. Our police are under pressure. Our prison officials are under pressure.

The Canadian Government in 1970 tried to avoid this trap. They started illegally arresting people. They brought in their emergency powers. They redefined the insurgent actor as a revolutionary threat and changed the image of terrorism from crime to war. They avoided the grey zone completely and switched over to another. This is another thing we have to be aware of. Perrin Beatty's decision to create a special emergency response team for the control of hostage situations and terrorist events triggered outrage in terrorist circles. Why? He used the Royal Canadian Mounted Police (RCMP). That is the crime model. A decision was made to put it under the jurisdiction of the Solicitor General who was responsible for the crime model. Many people criticized him. They wanted the military to step in. In the criminal justice model you have that course of redress. The idea is that you can sue and have accountability. The two models are very different. Government decisions include these problems.

Another issue involves controlling clandestine activity. A 1978 bombing in Germany is one example of this. The prison bombing was carried out by the German government. Force was used to combat force. Those opposed claimed that no state should commit violence to fight violence. They thought it a moral issue and wanted to sue the government. In other cases with secret clandestine activity, we find that our criminal justice system allows people to get away with murder hoping they will help them catch the leaders.

The problem we have here is that the state allows violence and terrorism in certain cases in an effort to catch the worst people. This creates a huge moral dilemma.

TERRORISM AND HOSTAGE TAKING

Michael Wallack
Memorial University

My topic deals with political terrorism as an instrument of foreign policy. While the use of terrorism by Third World countries is growing we have not yet successfully developed a way of thinking about it. I will point out some of the problems with the current responses.

Our usual first response to terrorism is dictated by our moral views. We must naturally regard it as morally abhorrent behavior. Paradoxically, this kind of response, not only on the part of citizens but on the part of governments, may make matters worse. It may prompt a line of policy that encourages terrorism.

Terrorism is a form of political violence. It is violence or the threat of violence where the aim is to influence political decisions by inducing fear. The political strata of society which will be the target of political violence is going to differ depending on the kind of society investigated.

There are some characteristics of political terrorism that distinguish it from other forms of political violence. The political terrorists are unable to achieve their policy objectives by the direct use of force. They simply do not have the capability to change the leaders' minds by direct force. Therefore, the terrorist violence will be directed at random targets rather than at targets of influence. This characteristic together with the ferocity of the attacks certainly tend to amplify the power that the terrorists have. Certainly, the psychological effect on the public will amplify the effect of violence.

The process that terrorists hope to induce is a kind of identification between the leader and the victim. Leaders will come to say, "That could have been us." Political authorities will then feel compelled to intervene in terrorist violence because of the general psychological effects.

The result tends to be a circle of fear surrounding the terrorist act. This increases the power of the terrorists to command the attention of, and response from, authorities. The terrorists hope they are sufficiently ruthless and persistent so their target government will bargain with them rather than use repressive violence themselves. Terrorists hope to show that the authorities cannot protect their citizens but can only avenge the terrorist act. If they can show that authorities cannot defend their citizens, the authorities may come to believe that they will have to bargain with the terrorists.

The costs imposed by terrorism are not simply those direct costs carried by the victims. There is the additional cost of the changes that are necessary in the mechanisms of social control. There are additional expenditures on security forces. People's routines change. Then there are the costs of the fear and stress. There is also the cost of time and energy in responding. The government, while focusing on the issue of terrorism, will put in the background other important issues.

I want to move to another perspective on the role of violence in politics. We are in a fortunate situation. Unless we are reminded of terrorist acts or other incidents, we tend to forget that violent acts are a real danger.

By experience, they have learned violence does not pay. They agreed to control violence and to live by laws. Each individual would give up the use of violence, and the authority to use violence would rest solely in the hands of the public authority acknowledged by all.

On this account, society is based on fear and harm. More than that, that society is held together by fear. People agree to live in society and to abide by laws only because they fear the consequences of reprisals. The indirect argument included the notion that those who do not agree to lay down the violence remain legitimate targets for violence. This would include citizens of other countries. This would also include slaves within the society who are lawfully, and rightfully treated as enemies. It is right, according to some theorists, to use people who are outside of this political bargain for whatever purposes necessary. If the advantage of the State would lie in this direction, it would be perfectly fine according to these same theorists to kill someone else or to use his labor.

One view about violence is that it is at the centre because it has come down to us through our political tradition and is a part of our background. At the beginning of the modern age of political thinking, political theorist Thomas Hobbes systematized in his Leviathan this notion that society is based upon fear. Hobbes argued that societies should be arranged in such a way that governments could threaten with death people who disobey the law. This fear of violent death is the strongest force that could keep people social.

Hobbes said, "Covenants without the sword are mere words and have no strength to secure men." So promises, Hobbes thought, including the promises that are inherent in living in a civil society, only work because of the fear of punishment. There is another side to Hobbes that is usually ignored because Hobbes was a theorist of the absolute state. We in a liberal democracy do not like to think of absolutism as being a good form of government. Hobbes was also quite a reformer. He argued that punishment should not be used in order to avenge a crime. Punishment is to be exacted in order to restore, for example, the moral values of a society or to provide an outlet for the desire of revenge "in order that the will of men may thereby be better disposed towards obedience." The purpose of punishment is obedience and not revenge. He continues, "The aim of punishment is not revenge, but terror." This quote directly acknowledges that fear is a legitimate means for political life when used for social purposes. This is part of our political tradition.

If we move a little bit further into the political tradition, we recognize that violence is not simply acknowledged as legitimate for the State for social control. It is also understood to be inevitable during certain periods in political life, particularly during periods of political change. Among classical theorists, Aristotle was one who stressed that political change or revolution would frequently involve the use of violence by all sides. A revolution would usually take place whenever opponents of a regime recognized that the regime was potentially threatened. Coming a little closer to the centre of our tradition, Locke believed that political violence could be justified when regimes themselves acted outside of their legitimate roles. Locke primarily talked about the legitimate use of violence against tyranny.

The reason I raise these issues is to show that throughout the political tradition, violence has really been at the centre of thinking in our political life. We tend to forget the underlying importance of violence as a subject matter for politics throughout history. We tend to do this because we have forgotten the past. It is true because our political circumstances are unusual in the world. Most in the world is not free from fear and violence.

Relatively speaking, in terms of a scale running from communication and persuasion at one end to violence on the other, our society is very close to the top end of those societies in the world which are relatively free of political violence. This may lead us to reactions to political violence that are very unrepresentative. They lead us to misunderstand the character of international political life. Force is acknowledged by our policymakers as a last resort. We know our governments use force sometimes in international life. They must justify it with reasons of national interest. We expect the rulers of other states who regularly use force themselves to view force in international relations as a means of last resort. It is more or less commonplace in their lives. We have to understand that our projected hopes about the international character of international relations are only hopes. They are probably resting on suppositions about politics. They are largely going to be contradicted by political lives in many places.

We can equate this to an orchestra. On one end we can put traditional instruments of diplomacy which are communications and bargaining. These are instruments that have relatively low costs. States can use diplomacy without it costing them too much. It is also low in violence. At the other end of the continuum are instruments of foreign policy, we have the use of threats and force ranging on up to war. That line which separates communication from the threats and use of force is most important.

What we have to recognize, however, is that the choice of foreign policy instruments is very strongly determined by the character of the country. In other words, when two similar societies bargain about their future course with each other, it can be rich in its potential. They have many avenues of access that can be used in bargaining. Diplomacy and bargaining can predominate. When two countries do not have much in common and quarrel, each country's influence is going to be quite low after the original presentation of communications and diplomacy. If a disagreement is reached, there will not be much else to do. Violence may be the alternative. The more powerful the country is, the more relations it has in the world. The United States and the Soviet Union are powerful because they have many relationships which can be used in the course of diplomacy. Smaller countries have fewer. The advanced industrial countries have a fairly wide range of choices. There are many countries in this world which do not have many instruments to use beyond diplomacy unless they are willing to turn to force.

This is where the issue of terrorism as an instrument of foreign policy surfaces. As I stressed earlier, terrorists are people without a great deal of power. They have a means or a technique that they can use to amplify their power. They have the psychological effect that they can produce in the target population. Terrorism is a low-cost instrument of foreign policy. It is likely to be attractive for that reason to countries that do not have very many resources in the world.

Terrorism should not be thought of in terms of individual acts or organizations of terror. We have to recognize that modern war has a distinguishing characteristic. The target of war is not simply the military regime or the establishment but the whole society. Modern war is a war of one society against the other. It is not simply a war of specialists.

This characteristic of modern war came into prominence after World War I when air power made it possible for strategists to believe they could defeat the opponent by inducing fear, by bombing them, by destroying their productive capacity and by undermining the enemy leaders. Many strategists have talked about air power which would revolutionize warfare. You would not have to defeat the enemy army. You could leap over them. In World War II, mass bombardments of populations became the practice for both sides. It was justified by the war aims of the Allied powers. It was accepted that the psychological consequences of mass bombardments would be justified. Innocent civilians were to be spared. Only armies could be attacked. These moral constraints were given up in World War II because of the nature of the conflict and because of the ability of modern warfare to induce fear in the population.

During the postwar years there was a tendency to drift from this doctrine. This was inevitable with the invention of atomic weapons. Atomic weapons made it difficult to distinguish between the innocent who must be protected and those implicated in a war of aggression. Therefore, the doctrine of deterrents came to the fore. Deterrents simply carry the threat of force while atomic weapons bring along the notion of balance of terror. We accept the balance of terror as a doctrine.

A new doctrine was elaborated when the availability and use of atomic weapons became more flexible. This is the doctrine known as compellence where force is used as persuasion rather than as destruction. The problem here is that if the atomic powers cannot use their force because of deterrence, then how can they influence the world. Threats could be used instead. Risks could be imposed. These risks would influence the adversaries. Essentially this doctrine of compellence has been the driving doctrine of American foreign policy in the postwar years since the 1960s. The tendency has been to use compellence when all else fails. It does not involve use of force to directly achieve the objective. Compellence essentially attempts to use fear or violence as a psychological tool.

Certainly the use of violence against innocent people should be condemned. The term terrorism is only used in certain instances. Compellence is used when these activities are carried out by those who make the decisions. The problem is that terrorism as a political term can lead to a great deal of confusion. Another phrase that is used sometimes to avoid the word terrorism is coercive diplomacy. In this case society allows leaders to use force for psychological purposes in foreign policy. In other words, total war and coercive diplomacy are bound to include terrorism.

I will now discuss use of compellence against terrorism. The American action involving Libya is an example of coercive diplomacy. There are many states in the Middle East, for example, that may be captured under the American definition of terrorism. It is highly unlikely that if the United States were to use force against such a state in response to its terrorism, that state would be a future partner in negotiations with the United States in resolving the disputes of the Middle East. When you cross the borderline and punish a country by using violence in international affairs, it is very difficult to come back in the other direction. That is a cost of this doctrine of compellence.

Another problem is that compellence imposes greater risks on others. The problems with this, as applied to international terrorism, is that it is not likely to be true in liberal democracies. That is simply a fact about the character of liberal democratic societies. In liberal democratic societies we prefer governments which allow us some degree of personal freedom to travel and communicate. Effectively responding to terrorists would impose on us great costs in terms of personal liberties. Furthermore, we are an industrial society. There are many targets terrorists can find which are very difficult to defend. Our societies are not designed for internal warfare. It would be very difficult to protect more than a few people or places. Responses which stress protection against violence have to be regarded as basically symbolic.

Most people in our society will not be protected. When we authorize, or when our government endorses, a violent response in international affairs, we should realize that we are not completely protected. It is true not only because of the character of our society but also because of the character of the terrorist societies. They are likely to be authoritarian societies accustomed to violence. The leaders have already been able to insulate themselves from the people. They can resist whatever harms we choose to impose on the larger society.

The only way we can effectively respond to terrorism by proxy would be to overthrow that regime. History teaches us that this is very difficult to do. It is very costly. It is probably more costly than bearing the terrorist attacks. Therefore, I would suggest that this doctrine of using force in response to international terrorism is likely to be counter-productive. It is likely to induce terrorism. It is likely to cause greater risks than we can bear. I suggest we should not support it ourselves. We should be careful about the ideology that tends to convince us to support it.

Where does that leave us? Unfortunately it leaves us in a more complicated world than we would like to live in. It leaves us in a world where even the superpowers cannot protect themselves without undermining their own values. Cooperation among countries can perhaps reduce terrorism. We have to turn to the causes that stimulate nations in the first place. This is a long process. It is a political process as it requires bargaining. It is not a pleasant circumstance. We have to tolerate violence to a greater degree than we would like to. I am afraid this is the real world.

TERRORISM AND HOSTAGE-TAKING

Tom Mitchell
Independent Researcher of Political Science

This paper deals with the role of the media in the terrorist strategy and the ways in which the terrorist attempts to use the communications media to his advantage. The second part will deal with more practical problems and specific types of incidents.

I cannot imagine a subject more controversial than terrorism. Probably no aspect of terrorist analysis is more controversial than that of the terrorists and the media. It is important to be as objective as possible in assessing this phenomenon. Approaching it as a social scientist, I am neither condoning nor condemning it. I am trying to understand how terrorism works and the role the media plays. I am not a journalist, a law enforcer nor a terrorist. Therefore, I can be as objective as possible. There is no question the media role is very controversial, and there are many perspectives on how the media plays into this. Some very controversial statements have been made by politicians and scholars.

While it is very difficult to know the root cause of terrorism, I can suggest how the terrorist strategy operates. The central appeal for those who wish to challenge the political order is its economy. A terrorist campaign requires only a handful of activists and a modicum of resources. A few dramatically and carefully planned acts of violence can give the group an aura of power and strength.

It would probably take a comparable non-terrorist group years of tireless agitation to achieve the same amount of attention that one terrorist act can. For nearly 50 years the Armenian community passed out leaflets describing the genocide of 1915. People were not interested. One single act of terrorism in 1973 in California galvanized attention.

The impact of terrorism is based upon its dramatic character and its ability to generate fear and insecurity. Bombings, taking hostages and assassinations are spectacular events. Any group which carries out such acts is almost guaranteed receiving extensive publicity and attention. At the same time of course, such events tend to spread a sense of insecurity and vulnerability among the populace.

If the incident is skilfully executed, the psychological impact can be enormous. Fear can have a corrosive effect on society. In 1985, according to the most complete survey that is available on transnational terrorism conducted by the United States Department, there were approximately 900 deaths from transnational terrorism in the world.

Yet there will be 22,000 homicides during the same period in the United States. These are other routine crimes such as family disputes. Over 50,000 Americans are killed on highways. The amount of injury and destruction by terrorists is quite insignificant. What makes it have such an impact is that it is carefully planned and aimed at specific symbolic targets, and the media has a role in exaggerating the impact. The likelihood of being struck by lightning is greater than witnessing a terrorist incident.

We cannot really put terrorism into any perspective in terms of the history of mankind. The first major terrorist organization was the Jewish zealots of the first century A.D. There have been incidents ever since. It is difficult to put it into perspective as to whether we have more terrorism now or less. What appears to have given terrorism a greater impact is our modern technological society.

At least four elements of modern society have given terrorism its impact. It has been made more economical, more effective and more efficacious in terms of pursuing a political cause. Our modern society provides easy targets. There are oil refineries, nuclear reactors and communication links of all types. Targets of this variety are particularly appealing to a terrorist because there is virtually no risk. They are basically not defended. They have great symbolic as well as practical value in a terrorist campaign. Terrorism has thus become a very attractive strategy because it is more economical in modern society than it ever was before.

The second feature is a vastly improved transportation system. Advances in transportation have literally shrunk the world. It has become possible for a terrorist group to get to its target. Once the incident occurs, the terrorists can readily escape from that target. This has made it much more difficult for law enforcement personnel to keep track of terrorists.

The third feature is the existence of a vast array of weaponry now at the disposal of terrorist organizations.

The fourth feature overshadows the other three. The most important feature of modern society which has given terrorism its impact is the existence of a mass communications network. In the 19th century if a bomb went off in a crowded place, only those in the immediate vicinity would know about it. Today, because of satellite communication, it is possible for an incident to occur in one part of the world and be immediately broadcast around the world. This has given the terrorist groups enormous impact.

No single factor is more important than the terrorists' ability to manipulate the media. The publicity which even a few minor incidents of terrorism can generate is the reason for the economy of terrorism as a political strategy. Terrorists tend to strike at symbolic targets in order to attract popular support and create a climate of fear and intimidation. They strike at symbols. The media serves as the vital link in the impact of terrorism publicizing the attack on the symbolic victim.

Government and law enforcement authorities complain bitterly that extensive media coverage leads to contagion. While the media has not created terrorism, it has significantly affected the impact of terrorism and has enhanced it as a political strategy. The question is how can publicity for these kinds of events be carried out.

The psychological impact of terrorism is often, as I have mentioned, far greater than the actual injury. What is required for terrorism to have an impact is a series of events over a period of time. To protect themselves people will create barriers both in a literal and figurative sense. Over time the social stress which terrorism causes can lead to polarization of society, an undermining of social trust and a curtailment of civil liberties.

Democracy could easily be overwhelmed either by the acts of the terrorists themselves or by the Draconian measures that are adopted to defeat the terrorists.

The likelihood of publicity is a crucial factor guiding the terrorist in the selection of tactics and targets. To facilitate media coverage, terrorism tends to occur in or near urban locations that have major communications facilities. To obtain and hold media attention, terrorists must either use increasingly sophisticated tactics or must inflict mass casualties. The repeated use of the same tactic on the same targets will discourage coverage. The terrorists have therefore learned they must constantly improvise. The terrorist event must be characterized by drama, danger and unpredictability, or the media will quickly lose interest in it. They are constantly figuring out what twist will grant them attention because they realize that the media is very fickle.

Publicity itself is often a key demand in a bargaining situation. Frequently the terrorist insists on the broadcast or the publication of a manifesto before substantive negotiations can begin for the release of hostages or victims. Most of these manifestos tend to be very long documents and poorly written. The media tries to determine whether to publicize this manifesto. Consultations usually occur with the law enforcement authorities. Within the last five years the media has tended to ignore the entire manifesto but has chosen to quote specific passages.

Much of the coverage accorded to terrorism seems to be fragmentary and superficial. The media generally focuses on the violence itself. Rarely is an effort made by journalists to place the incident into context. This is very frustrating for the terrorist organization. Terrorists know that publicity is indispensable to their strategy. They also know that the type of coverage will probably not assist them with their long-term goals.

The whole nature of the relationship between the terrorist and the media is a very controversial one. It could be called a symbiotic relationship. I would suggest that the terrorist is probably the exploited one.

I will now deal with more practical matters such as highjackings, hostage barricades and kidnappings which take place over a period of hours, days and weeks and in which a bargaining situation is created. There is a confrontation between the terrorist and the law enforcement authorities. The journalist is in the middle. There is no bargaining situation in an assassination or an attack. There is one where a hostage has been taken and negotiations ensue.

Particularly controversial is police media relations during these incidents. In these kinds of incidents precise location of the terrorist is known. In a kidnapping it may not be known. You know that someone is held. A bargaining situation is created and is given. Such situations involve hungry reporters and photographers. The media defends the reporting in terms of the public's right to know. At the same time, the law enforcement authorities insist that the safety of hostages must be the paramount concern. In my view, both of these goals are essential. Unfortunately, there is a potential for conflict. The two goals will collide, but it is important that the media is not looked upon as an enemy. The media can be most influential in setting the tone for a proper response by civil authorities to acts of terrorism and political violence. The media can provide an outlet for legitimate public concern on important issues. It can also bring pressure to change official policies. The media's presence may make it unnecessary for a group to engage in terrorism. If they can get their message across by having a vehicle like the media to express it, this may prevent terrorism from even occurring. In any case, a free and responsible news media is an important device in a democracy. In these situations it is important to have minimum intrusion of the media and non-inflammatory coverage. This principle was derived from the President's commission on disorders and terrorism in the late 1970s in the United States. A large report was produced assessing hostage incidents in the United States and suggesting that the public interest was best served by complete, low key reporting. To achieve this, the President's commission in 1977 made some suggestions.

One of the suggestions was to use pool reporters to cover activities at the scene which would reduce the number of people at the scene and eliminate the possibility of a circus atmosphere. Another suggestion made was to limit interviews with terrorists holding hostages. Another suggestion was to focus on an official spokesman. Rely on a police spokesman to be the source of information.

Basically, journalists in Canada handle these types of situations responsibly. Only a few incidents have been tense. At the same time, law enforcement authorities have responsibilities as well by providing the media with information while maintaining public order and safety. They should respect the confidentiality of media sources.

PART XIV

DRUNK DRIVING

DRUNK DRIVING

Alan Donelson
Injury Research Foundation of Canada

The subject of drinking and driving can be made so complicated and so broad that you cannot really digest it. The reports produced within the last year number in the thousands. There are literally dozens of conferences devoted full-time to drinking and driving, but it is the task of a researcher to boil it down into a few words if the public is going to understand where we are.

The magnitude of this particular problem is now in question. At the same time, the problem is complex, and the solutions are many. The first law against drunk drivers was passed around 1872, and we have gone through cycles of tougher laws and stiffer penalties ever since in the Western world.

The solutions may be many, but the problem has been so complex and so simplistically presented to people that we have failed to make the kind of progress that we are now making. Progress has been made, but further progress is going to depend on three elements.

To date we have relied primarily on punishment to get our point across to people so they will behave themselves. I think the time has ended where we can just rely solely on that. There is also going to be a pressing need to coordinate the many active agencies and many active groups that now exist. The resources are limited, and we have to somehow pool them and coordinate our activity. Public participation is going to be essential. The system is not self-aware. However, there are fragments of information that occasionally become available to indicate that some things have made a difference. For example, in Ontario the Attorney General's office has been very interested in knowing whether or not the province-wide effort has paid off.

Between 1973 and 1982, the two major groups of driver fatalities were those where the drivers had been drinking and where they had been drinking a lot. In 1983, there was an abrupt departure from the statistics of the past 10 December periods. For 10 Decembers, 1973 through 1982, in Ontario about 20 drivers had illegal Blood Alcohol Concentrations. This is about 42% annually. It remained fairly constant with drivers who were impaired and who had died on the highways.

In 1983, the 42% dropped to 18%. Only six of the 33 drivers killed in Ontario during that month had illegal Blood Alcohol Concentrations. The following December 1984, only eight of 32, or 25%, had illegal Blood Alcohol Concentrations. In the most recent December, an even more remarkable statistic emerged from Ontario. Only two out of 27 drivers, 7%, had illegal Blood Alcohol Concentrations. This is a remarkable result. The result for December 1985 was the lowest number and the lowest percentage of impaired drivers ever to die in Ontario during December.

What happened in Ontario is a real question. In November 1983, the office of the Attorney General took a leadership role and held a conference focusing on the community response to impaired driving. There was a province wide call to action to deal with this problem. New legislation was being put forward and was simply less intensified.

Interestingly enough, with the exception of January 1984, during the 11 months intervening between December and December, everything went pretty much back to normal. The combined effects perhaps of the new legislation and tougher penalties introduced federally and provincially in Ontario may have contributed to an even greater decline in December 1985.

There are many tactics and interventions that can be used other than through the criminal justice system. Public participation is coincident with the realization that until people get involved at the community level, the police are going to have a very tough time with it.

When having social problems, we must turn to the criminal justice system for solutions. Whether it be child abuse, vandalism, marijuana or sexual assault, this is the only tool we have. This is a realization that has come about in the area of drinking and impaired driving.

We know the law alone is not going to reduce the problem as a whole. Neither education nor treatment and rehabilitation in and of themselves will work. Nevertheless, there is a certain lesson that the public education materials have not stressed. When you have a hammer, everything looks like a nail. Our hammer is the criminal justice system.

If we want a society predicated on the notion that we need a police state to get our social act together, or if we want to have the ultimate in deterrents, it is just a short step from where we are now with life imprisonment, other lengthy terms and with executions to reduce the burden on society. This is not the scenario I would like to pursue. The question, is what are the alternatives?

Our emphasis has always been on doing something to or for people. Passing and enforcing laws is doing something to and for people. It is not encouraging people to become self- sufficient and self regulating. The distinction then is action by the community to the extent that there is community awareness. There can be community action. If there is one lesson that has been brought home by a number of ministers, it is that in the absence of concerted social action and broadbased community support, we can expect little or no progress in the area of impaired driving. We can look forward to change because change happens. We cannot necessarily look forward to differences because differences are made; they do not just occur by accident.

The response is that we should have more public participation. Government has never been known for its effectiveness in dealing with pressing and persistent social problems. We must look at the number, the type, the level of organization where participation can occur. Public participation means participation by individuals in terms of a simple decision not to drive after drinking too much. Community groups can at least provide alternative transportation to their summer picnics where alcoholic beverages may be consumed. Nongovernmental organizations, government agencies and industry can as well. There is so much to be done in this area that participation is not limited by opportunity.

There is no one group in Canada that can carry this ball by itself forever and get the job done. There has to be co- operation, co-ordination, pooling of resources and sharing in order for the effort as a whole to be more than the sum of its parts.

The issue really boils down to responsibility. Responsibility is simply the ability to respond to this problem. We become part of the solution as individuals whether we be researchers, government employees, professionals, industry representatives or private citizens. The principle that has to be accepted is that each individual does make a difference. If you do not believe that individuals make the difference, then you will completely rely on government for solutions. That is exactly the opposite of what we are talking about. For individuals who make the difference for themselves, for their families, friends, neighbors and community, the difference will be shown in the provincial and federal statistic levels. The cost seems to be almost impossible although sociologists will have very ornate models which describe how social change occurs.

How do we translate the kind of unprecedented awareness that we have now into public action? We can only appreciate it from our own individual and personal perspectives, and I would say that it becomes this simple. Know the problem, and know what you are up against. If you decide to be concerned about impaired driving, then do something about the problem. Understand the problem to the best of your ability. There is a tremendous amount of material concerning this problem. To own the problem simply means to make a personal and individual commitment to do something, whether it is simply not driving after drinking too much or making sure your friends do not drive drunk.

There is always a place for participation. Take personal action, whether it be through your community groups or through your organization.

Finally, support others. You can make donations to non-profit registered charities concerning this problem, or you can encourage others to also take action within the community. The point is that we can treat this problem because it has been done at least for a month in a couple of provinces every other year.

DRUNK DRIVING

Brian Jonah
Department of Transport

I have laid out a framework for the prevention of impaired driving. The framework is consistently two dimensional. In one dimension, the point of intervention, you try to deal with it in primary and secondary degrees.

Primary means that you try to terminate the problem of getting too drunk before the accident. Secondary intervention deals with removing the impaired driver from the road. The technological advantages under primary intervention are in bars. The patients can go to a breathalizer, blow in and find out whether or not they are over the legal limit. This popular study was started in Vancouver in the 1970s. Unfortunately the feedback did not have any impact on the decision to drive. They still drove impaired.

Secondary interventions are things like alcohol airlocks, devices put on vehicles so that if the person were impaired, the vehicle would not start. This is either based on breath tests or based on the performance tests done on the vehicle.

The first approach taken to deal with impaired drivers is the legal approach. That includes legislation dealing with issues such as the minimum drinking age and a rise in the license age. There have been three amendments to the criminal code since 1969. The first one was breathalizer legislation requiring drivers suspected of being impaired to provide a breath sample, In 1976, the criminal code was amended to allow for roadside screening of drivers who were suspected to drinking. The most recent amendment was passed last December and is embodied in Bill C-19 which deals with new offenders for impaired drivers who cause death or injury. The fine for a first offence increased from $50 to $300 with a mandatory blood test.

The second approach is the educational approach where you can have a mass media campaign oriented towards all drivers. You can also have a campaign geared more specifically towards high- risk groups such as young drivers. With the public education approach, in the primary kind of intervention, there are programs like the 1971 Edmonton study which was basically a mass media campaign. They found that not only could that program increase awareness of impaired driving, but also it could reduce it.

The third approach is the health approach which deals with the treatment of impaired drivers who have an alcohol dependency program. The technological approach refers to the technological hardware to predict impaired driving. With this third level, there is a warning system which is given to convicted impaired drivers. After conviction, they are allowed to have their licenses back as long as they have this device on their vehicle. If they try to drive the vehicle while impaired, this particular device will detect it, the headlights will flash, the horn will honk and it would be clear to everybody including the police that the person was impaired.

The final approach is a systems approach which is a combination of two or more of these approaches. The most common systems approach is a combination of enforcement activity and public education.

Another step that can be taken is that of general deterrence, trying to deter people who are impaired before they actually drive. Canada does not have that step, but in Australia they have had it in for several years. The way it works is that they set up roadblocks and request drivers to supply a breath sample. Since this particular program, there have been reductions in alcohol-related accidents. It seems to be fairly successful.

In Canada, people with short-term license suspensions can have their licenses suspended immediately for 12 hours if the police claim the driver at the roadside has had alcohol, 50 ml in 80.

Intervention programs are being currently conducted as part of driver education, and the idea behind it is that students participate in a nine-hour program which consists mainly of role playing in various extreme situations. They learn how to dissuade their friends from drinking too much. Evaluation has indicated that it is successful by increasing knowledge, changing attitudes. There is also some indication that students who are brought to this peer program are more likely to intervene and stop their friends from driving while impaired.

The impaired drivers program evaluation shows that the program increases knowledge and awareness of impaired driving, but it really does not have any impact on recidivism, whether or not people are convicted again of impaired driving.

Finally, the long-term approach to impaired driving is education in schools. It is similar to peer intervention but perhaps of a different quality.

PART XV

CHILD SEXUAL ABUSE

CHILD SEXUAL ABUSE

Chris Bagley
University of Calgary

It has been nearly two years since the Badgley report came out. It was an evidence-based report which made 52 recommendations, none of which were accepted. Badgley had made major proposals for the office of commissioner to coordinate research, demonstration projects and standardized protocol for the investigation and treatment of child abuse across the country.

One of the things the press picked up on was his National Incidence Survey. He had asked people across the country about their sexual experiences during childhood and adulthood. He discovered that 50% of adult females had experienced some unwanted sexual act including exposures and actions after childhood. I think there was a certain degree of skepticism about these figures. Unwanted touching, manual interference or further types of sexual assault against a person 16 years old or younger yielded a figure of about 15% for females and about half that for males.

I am able to support Badgley's findings with some of my own research done in the context of a community mental health study in Calgary. The study was originally conceived to investigate child sexual abuse. My colleague, Dick Ramsey, and I randomly sampled 780 adults from the population using the Calgary telephone book. We gathered comprehensive community mental health information about current mental health according to standardized measures, suicidal ideas, psychiatric admissions and suicidal actions in the past. The Badgley Report subsequently came out, and I decided to again interview the women in the sample to ask them about their experiences of sexual abuse in childhood. Our results were similar.

Of the 379 women interviewed, 82 reported serious sexual abuse prior to their 16th year. Serious sexual abuse was defined as at least manual interference with a child's unclothed genital area through to the more serious sexual abuse cases that involved intercourse. Approximately 22% of women and 10% of men in our survey experienced serious sexual assault. We found that the perpetrators in at least 80% of the cases were known to the child, often related to the child and in the child's household. Contrary to some clinical impressions, the classical type of incest was relatively rare. The most frequent type was either someone distantly related to the child or a stepfather or live- in boyfriend. This suggests that having an unrelated male in the household puts the child at a very high risk for sexual abuse.

What is new in our work is that we were able to fit our study into the context of a community mental health study which used systematized measures for looking at mental health outcomes in adulthood. We were able to examine the mental health of the abused females in comparison to those who were not abused. In every single case, the sex of the perpetrator was male regardless of the sex of the victim. I have yet to come across a single female perpetrator.

The highest scores on this mental health scale were disproportionately occurring in the group of abused women. Abused women were twice as likely to have serious mental health problems. There is a 10% incidence in the population for this. The measure we used was the Middlesex questionnaire which is standardized in England and is considered valid and reliable in a variety of cultures. Abused women also have a higher incidence of suicide attempts and are more likely to have poor self-esteem.

Other childhood factors included emotional and physical abuse. The women who reported child sexual abuse were also more likely to report various punitive behavior on the part of the parents. They were more likely to come from broken homes.

Many different types of research have concluded that sexually abused children are not a random sample of the population. They are a risk group. At risk is the child of an authoritarian, punitive type of upbringing where he is not given options and does not feel confident in going to adults. With the situation in which the home is broken, the normal father and mother situation does not exist, and you have new people having access to the child.

So far our findings from this study have supported Badgley's as far as incidence is concerned and as far as casting child sexual abuse as a very serious problem causing long-term mental health problems for at least a quarter of the victims is concerned. These are profound problems that, if not treated, will stay with a victim throughout.

Badgley also included in his report a survey of juvenile prostitutes. He studied some 250 juvenile prostitutes across the country and found that although the homes from which they came were often disrupted by marital quarrels, problems of alcoholism, physical abuse, child sexual abuse, there was no greater an incidence than that encountered in the general population. This was in contradiction to an American study where sexual exploitation definitely affected the decision to become a prostitute.

Badgley concludes, "Young prostitutes were at no more risk when they were growing up than other Canadian children and youths having been victims of sexual offenses. It cannot be concluded on the basis of the information available that having been sexually abused as a child was by itself a significant factor that accounted for the subsequent entry into juvenile prostitution."

Clearly, we have to inquire why the findings are different. If we look at the methodology of Badgley's work and that of the Fraser Committee, we find a fairly typical pattern. The research is commissioned by national enquiry, and the results are required very quickly. Nobody is terribly concerned with methodology.

In the case of the Badgley survey of prostitutes, students were recruited over the summer period. They located the prostitutes on the streets and interviewed them under conditions of unknown standardization. Included in the interviews were students from a criminology course which included experienced RCMP officers. These are not the kinds of conditions or people who are likely to engender relaxation, confidence, and openness of these subjects. The work done for the Fraser Committee included surveys conducted across the country in different regions. In the Prairies, they found prostitutes by means of newspaper advertisements. Again, this is a method of unknown reliability.

It is clear that research with prostitutes is difficult and hazardous. A random sample is really impossible, and the dangers of working on the street are obvious.

The Silva questionnaire which deals with people leaving prostitution takes about three hours to complete and can only be completed by someone who knows the person well. There were internal reliability checks in that measure. It is quite likely the results will be different.

I published a critique in the Canadian Journal of Public Health on the Badgley findings on juvenile prostitution in terms of child sexual abuse. The methods of research are not specified, and the questionnaire is not available. The average age of his prostitutes was 17 years; of his adult population group, 30 years. While he asks each group to recall prior events of child sexual abuse, different ages perceive sexual abuse in different terms. Sixty-three per cent of female prostitutes were sexually experienced by age 13 compared with 2% of the national sample. They became sexually active and left home much earlier. Their exposure to sexually abusive family situations was much shorter. The various pieces of evidence in the Badgley Report make it look as if two-thirds of the children who became prostitutes were hardly present in homes after the age of 12.

My colleagues and I have been using, in the past two years, Silva's questionnaire in working with ex-prostitutes, women who have left the street and are now going mostly through vocational training programs. They were interviewed by women whom they knew well and who were involved in their counselling and support. I was able to pull out two sets of controls for these prostitutes from our community mental health sample. One was a group of age-match controls without reference to any abusive experience. The other control group was to compare the prostitutes who had been sexually abused with women in the community sample who had been sexually abused. All the ex-prostitutes had worked on the street at some stage. Some had also worked in bars and massage parlors. None that we knew of had worked in escort agencies or highclass callgirl groups. We have no research data on that kind of prostitute.

Within the group, 36 of the 45 were white. Three were black, and the rest were Indian or Metis. These women tend to have different lifestyles and patterns when they leave prostitution. They do not stay in the city but move back to rural areas and reserves. They are difficult to locate.

My sample of prostitutes, more often than our controls, grew up in inner city areas. Forty-two per cent of the prostitutes grew up in normal family situations where mother and father were present most of the child's life, three-quarters of the controls. Seventy per cent of the prostitutes reported a drinking problem with at least one family member during their developing years, 10% of the controls. Sixty-two per cent reported serious sexual abuse compared with 8% of the controls, and 40% of the prostitutes reported physical neglect compared with 2% of the controls. Two-thirds of the prostitutes witnessed fights between their parents and other family members, 5% of the controls, and reported some sort of emotional abuse or neglect compared with 7% of the controls. By age 16, 80% of the prostitutes had left home permanently.

With child sexual abuse, 73% of the prostitutes reported serious sexual abuse up to their 16th year compared with 29% of the controls. The 29% incident rate with our control subjects is higher than the overall population rate of 22%. This reflects the fact that the younger respondents in the general community are reporting more sexual abuse than the older respondents. I interpret this as indicating that there is an increased incidence of child sexual abuse. This child sexual abuse reflects family disruption. Many more younger families are disrupted by divorce or separation than families of older people.

Thirty-three out of 45 of our prostitutes were sexually abused. The prostitutes experienced more serious profiles of sexual abuse than the controls. They were assaulted by more than one person and over longer periods of time than the controls and in more serious ways. The child abuse sometimes involved being photographed for pornographic purposes, or for sadistic activities. This also did not occur in the controls. Consequently, the community controls experience sexual abuse at a less serious and degrading level.

The reactions and recollections of the prostitutes include feelings of shock, disgust and self-blame at the child sexual abuse. These children became promiscuous within their peer culture. Approximately 25% of them, by the time they were 14, had had more than 20 sexual partners none of whom involved stable attachments. They rapidly moved out of the home onto the streets and drifted into prostitution. Everybody hated being a prostitute and left it as soon as they could. Clearly, prostitution is a constrained and helpless role.

The average age of entry into prostitution is 15 years. By the time they reach 18, most of them are leaving the game. Virtually all prostitution is juvenile prostitution. We did mental health profiles of prostitute groups and found that they had very poor mental health. The mental health did not improve after leaving prostitution.

I agree paradoxically with the strong conclusions of the Badgley Report except in suggesting that juvenile prostitution should not be criminalized. These kids have been victims enough, and I do not see anything under any new law that will prevent this. We allow child sexual abuse through prostitution, through the present laws which allow voluntary contract between a 14-year- old child and an adult man for sexual purposes. We construe that as not being an illegal act of child sexual abuse.

CHILD SEXUAL ABUSE

Hillary McCormick
Crown Prosecutor, Ottawa

In the Criminal Code there are a number of different sexual offenses which can be laid involving children, and there are different offenses depending on the relationship to each child. Yet many of the offenses currently in the Criminal Code have been held to be unconstitutional with the new Charter of Rights. There are also just straight sexual offenses which can be laid with respect to offenders whose victims are both adults and children. Although some offenses are specifically set out in the Code with the idea of protecting children, the new sexual assault sections are applicable to situations where children have been sexually assaulted. In fact, this has been the preference of the Crown Attorney's office since January 1983. We use these new sections because they are far less complex than some of the old sections. If the offence took place before 1983, we cannot lay charges under the new sections.

I am an assistant Crown Attorney, and our office deals with many situations involving historical sexual abuse. Quite often these offenses date back 10 years which is one of our biggest problems. With historical offenses, it is very difficult to prosecute when there is a difference of a number of years, where the person who is 17 is relating offenses which he experienced when he was 7.

One of the greatest legal hurdles is that the documents require we set out the charge in what is called an information. We are required to set out with some specificity when the offence took place. An information alleges that on a particular date in the City of Ottawa, in the Province of Ontario that A did sexually assault B contrary to the Criminal Code. With these historical abuse complaints, we are setting out information with a time gap of sometimes three or four years because the person cannot tell you what year he/she was actually assaulted. He/she can tell you with great specificity how it occurred and how often, but he/she cannot remember if it happened when he/she was five or six. A number of these informations that are alleged over such a long period of time have been thrown out by the courts. They say this is not fair to the accused. You have to give him/her some idea of when he/she is alleged to have committed the offence. That argument depends on how long the period of time is, and it is within the discretion of the judge whether to quash the information. Some judges will agree to a two-year period. Others have held that even a six-month period of time from even January to June 30, 1979, is not good enough. There is a wide spectrum among judges.

This is one of the greatest technical problems we are faced with. It seems very unfair because these children have no real sense of chronology. In my view, when it happened is not as important as the fact that it did happen. If they are able to tell exactly what happened, it should not have any bearing on whether they can remember the exact date. Part of our job in prosecuting is to try and help them pinpoint the date. We have some techniques. I often ask children, "Do you remember where you were living at the time?" "Do you remember what school you went to at the time?" "Do you remember the grade?" Sometimes you can help them work back and close down this six-year gap to maybe a two-year gap. It is a problem because it is a technical defence and is not addressed by the Badgley Report or by the newly proposed amendments recently released.

On a more practical nature, the other problems we face with children who are testifying is their legal competence to testify in the first place. It can be distinguished by whether they are going to be able to give sworn evidence and by whether they are going to be able to give evidence at all.

With sworn evidence, it is presumed in Canadian criminal law that persons 14 years or older can give sworn evidence, and they are presumed to be competent. The corollary is that if you are under 14 years, you are not presumed to be competent. The court must then enter into an investigation as to whether or not you can be sworn. This is determined by asking the child questions to see whether or not the child understands the nature of an oath and appreciates the moral obligation. Involved are the moral consequences of taking an oath. With the old law people would go around asking what kind of religious training the child had because if the child went to school and had religious training, he would know the religious consequence of taking an oath. It became apparent that a child may have no religious training and may still understand the consequences of taking an oath. Going into the child's religious training may still help to determine whether or not the child understands the nature of an oath, but it is not necessary. You cannot have a situation where children of atheistic parents are automatically excluded.

The child can also be instructed on the nature of an oath prior to giving testimony. We often explain to them exactly what an oath is. There is an obligation to do this. There is a big consequence as to whether the child is sworn or not. If the child is sworn, a conviction can be registered on that child's evidence alone. If the child is not sworn, it requires corroboration. It is important to get the child sworn because it has very serious legal repercussions to the prosecutor. If the child is not sworn and is of sufficient intelligence to justify receiving its evidence and understands the duty to speak the truth, then the child can give evidence. This is the two- tier test. First of all, the child must be of sufficient intelligence to justify receiving evidence. Secondly, the child must understand the duty to speak the truth.

This is also determined by an inquiry entered by the court. The judge will ask the child questions to see how much understanding the child has. The end result is that if the judge is not satisfied that the child is of sufficient intelligence or understands the duty to speak the truth, then the child will not be heard. Charges involving children who are sexually abused are done in private. There is generally no other evidence. In any event, without the child testifying you are not likely to get any further. This particular problem does not arise often.

The age that children are being sworn in at is getting lower. In some of the old cases, you would see children of 12 and 13 not being allowed to give sworn evidence. In my experience, it is not unusual to have children of 8 giving sworn evidence. I doubt our office has ever prosecuted a charge involving a child under five. Five is the youngest that I have ever dealt with. It is unfair to subject younger children to testifying. There have been a number of decisions in Ottawa in the last couple of years where the judges have held that children four and five years old were not of sufficient intelligence to justify receiving their evidence.

Obviously there are consequences. Nothing can be done in terms of a criminal prosecution for a child of that age who is sexually abused. The most recent case is one that I dealt with involving a five-year-old girl sexually assaulted by her natural father. I was confident because it was one of those rare occasions where I felt there was corroboration. The corroboration was that he had also sexually assaulted his own stepson but not his natural son. There is a provision where you can use other sexual activity to corroborate sexual assault on one child.

This particular incident came to light when the child was observed performing fellatio on a baby. She had been observed doing this by the babysitter who asked, "Where did you learn to do that?" She said, "My dad does this to me all the time." This was a very cogent way of corroborating a sexual assault. It had never been tried before, and I was interested in seeing if it would be allowed as corroboration. The judge dismissed it. He said the child was not of sufficient intelligence because she was five and did not seem to understand some of the questions being put to her. It was felt she was relating an event that had happened when she was as young as two and had been continuing up until she was four. He felt this was not reliable. He ruled that she could not give any evidence, and that was it. There was nothing else we could do. It is a real difficulty if you do not get the child in to give evidence at all. If the child is permitted to give evidence, but is not sworn, then corroboration is required. I will deal with this in three headings.

What amounts to corroboration will probably cause everyone a great deal of difficulty. One example of what can amount to corroboration is that if the child is unsworn, by law there has to be corroboration. Both the Criminal Code provides for it as well as the Canada Evidence Act which is a statutory act governing some of the rules of evidence. Even if the child is sworn, the judge can, and some would say must, give a warning. He can give a warning with respect to the frailties of a child's evidence. This relates to children who are either eight or who are presumed to have competency. If the child is sworn, the judge can still say to the jury that when weighing the evidence they must bear in mind a number of things simply because children are involved.

The four things that are specified are the child's capacity to observe, the capacity to remember, the capacity to understand and frame intelligent answers and the moral responsibility of the witness. They may not have the same ability to express themselves or the same capacity to observe things.

What constitutes corroboration presents many difficulties to the courts. Often they go to the Court of Appeal because the accused's lawyer thinks the judge got it wrong the first time. The test for corroboration has also changed through the years. Before, there had to be independent evidence that implicated the accused and also showed a crime had been committed. Not only had there been a sexual assault, but also it was the accused who committed the sexual assault. This became a very difficult test. The case law has been ameliorated somewhat by some recent cases that have indicated that at least one material truth of the story can implicate the accused.

It is sufficient if one part of the child's story is true. If that part of the story is true, then all the child's evidence which implicates the accused is reliable. This has changed the text for corroboration for prosecution. With corroboration, medical evidence is probably the best and most often available.

One particular case not involving children was a case of sexual assault. There was bruising around the vagina. All the doctor could say was that it was consistent with "very passionate intercourse." Of course, the defence was consent. The court said this is not corroboration because it was as consistent with passionate consent as non-consent. They decided that was equivocal. If there are marks on a child, most of the cases indicate, that will be corroboration. Similarly, you can have little bits of medical evidence that perhaps individually constitute corroboration such as if the hymen is perforated. It is corroboration if there are bruises on other parts of the child's body, and she is saying, "Look, he did this and at the same time he hit me across the face." Similarly, seminal fluid on the child and on the accused's clothing at the same time can constitute corroboration as well as can the distressed condition of the child. If you have a child crying and accusing a neighbor of doing something, the fact that the child is distressed can be considered corroboration. That is the law in Ontario. It differs in other provinces in Canada.

The next big area is what is referred to as similar fact evidence. If you can lead evidence that the accused performed a very similar sexual act with another child, you can call that child to relate what the sexual act was and use that to corroborate the child that you are actually prosecuting. There are some limitations on that. They have to be very similar in nature. They have to show a course of conduct that identifies the accused rather than identifying the way the sexual intercourse took place. Also, there is circumstantial evidence concerning the opportunity of the accused to have access to the child. Witnessing the accused coming out of the bedroom doing up his shirt and his pants, with the child left in the bedroom in the bed is held to be sufficient.

There is a new line of cases arising out of Manitoba where they have been calling psychiatric expert evidence with respect to child abuse. Some children tend to show a certain kind of pattern after they have been sexually abused. They very often become promiscuous. They have other difficulties. They lie. They steal. In three cases in Manitoba, the Crown called an expert in sexual abuse and related that this kind of promiscuity really was an indication or a manifestation of the kind of abuse. That was held to be corroboration. Similarly, it was also used to explain some of the difficulties children have in testifying. A child only learns at a certain age that A comes before B, and that is why they cannot tell you when they were sexually assaulted or what year they were sexually assaulted. The expert can explain the levels of development of the child and can explain discrepancies in his or her evidence. One thing that is very obvious in a child's evidence is that he or she will change the story on cross-examination. You may ask how many times something occurred, and the answer might be 10. When asked again, the answer may be five. Experts in child abuse will explain why children do not have this ability to tell you exactly how many times something occurred. It does not mean that the children are lying. It is because of their developmental milestones that they have not reached. What it means is that it happened. They cannot really tell you how many times it happened because they really do not know. This, of course, is quite helpful because normally if you have someone who does not know how often it happened, you begin to wonder if it really did happen.

PART XVI

TREATING THE VIOLENT JUVENILE OFFENDER

TREATING THE VIOLENT JUVENILE OFFENDER

Al Leschied
London Family Court Clinic

Twelve years ago the view of treatment of juvenile justice would have been a motherhood statement. Rehabilitation was pretty well synonymous with corrections. Certainly it was not juvenile justice. John Conrad, a veteran criminologist at the time, recently stated that he knew what correctional treatment was. He said it consisted of a dollop of counselling here, a dab of group therapy there and a diagnostic interview with a psychiatrist for those for whom dollops and dabs did not suffice to avert really serious trouble. Presto, there was correctional treatment. The statisticians caught up with us, and there were those lurking in the bushes waiting to prove that dollops and dabs and psychiatric interviews were not working. They proved it. They found that the mere programs, given the title treatment, did not favor the youth as they were supposed to.

There was further dissatisfaction with rehabilitation. Not only was it declared ineffective, but also the mere application was seen to contravene individual civil rights and liberties. In 1949, Justice Hugo Black of the Supreme Court of the United States stated in reference to rehabilitation that "this prevalent modern philosophy of penology, in 1949, emphasizes that punishment or treatment should fit the offender and not merely the crime. Reformation and rehabilitation should be the important goals of criminal jurisprudence." John Howard, exhorting the rehabilitative ideal, is still the benchmark of the 18th Century, but John Howard and Hugo Black are out of style.

The place of rehabilitation has also been taken not only by the skeptics and the cynics who bought the "nothing works" doctrine but also by those that felt that if you cannot do anything good, at least do no harm. At least make a system of justice fair and equitable. Let the punishment fit the crime; time is spent more wisely examining deeds and not needs. Imagine what they would be saying today if they could hear that. We should be mindful of the words of Francis Allen who said in the Decline of the Rehabilitative Ideal, "If a theory of rights prevents the achievement of social purpose, then there is something amiss either in the theory of rights or in our conception of social purpose." So what do we have with its pervasive hopelessness and the ability to bring about change in our young offenders and with our present preoccupation with individual civil rights?

Many of us may have believed that the sun has set on the rehabilitative ideal. When you reread the catch phrases, there is a certain seduction in the nifty phrases like nothing works, do no harm, least intrusive intervention, justice is fairness and proclamations that exhort us to recognize that young persons have civil rights too. Let us look beyond the catchy phrases. As an example, I give a few perspectives on the Young Offenders Act (YOA) in Canada. The YOA was proclaimed almost two years ago, and it embodies many of the provisions of the justice system, that is fairness or "just desserts" school of criminology. It too is liberally sprinkled with emphasis on due process, rights to counsel, rights to appeal. What are the results?

Although two years is a short time in the life of any legislation, there are three trends emerging that are quite significant. The first one is that rates of incarceration and lengths of stay have increased considerably. Rates of custodial dispositions have increased from 100% - 150% in five provinces reporting statistics. Our own research at the Family Court Clinic in London, examining dispositions in a nine-county area of southern Ontario, an area which includes 40% of the adolescent offender population, indicates that committals to training school under the Juvenile Delinquents Act accounted for five per cent of dispositions. Committals to custody under the YOA now account for 11%. Second, the treatment disposition under Section 22 of the YOA has rarely been applied. Since April 1, 1984, only six treatment orders were made in the entire province. Under the JDA in 1982, there were 300 young persons given dispositions by the court to receive treatment in a children's mental health centre. The most obvious explanation for this dramatic decrease lies in the necessity for the court to receive the consent of the young person before a treatment order can be made. Kids do not consent to their own treatment needs. They do not seem to have that necessary critical insight. When we examine what treatment has in terms of our present context of the YOA, we must remember civil rights and social purpose and how those two seem to work at odds.

The third trend deals with Section 16 of the YOA which allows for the court to consider an application to transfer a youth to either adult or ordinary court. In two years of the YOA, such applications have increased in Ontario, four times over a similar period under the JDA. Approximately 89% of those applications were approved for advancement. The primary test for transfer as identified by His Honor Judge Henry Vogalsang in London who made the precedent-setting decision, stated that the primary purpose around a Section 16 hearing is for the protection of society and not the consideration of the needs of the young person. With the JDA transfer applications, it was just the reverse.

There are three questions we have to answer related to treatment with the young offender particularly with reference to treatment with the violent young offender.

Are the goals of rehabilitation mutually exclusive from the protection of society? Juvenile justice in Canada and the JDA suffer from the criticism that it was soft on young criminals. It seemed never to rise above that criticism, and treatment was equated with a general slap on the wrist. Perhapsit was because the expectations of the rehabilitative ideal could never be met. Cullen and Gilbert, in 1982, reported that justice is fairness, the equitable justice business or the deterrents model has not evidenced any discernible change in crime rates when compared to periods when rehabilitation was the preferred mode of intervention. In some states south of the border it has failed even worse. Of course saying that one model is not any better or worse than another does not give great confidence in the former approach. What it does implore us to do is to go back and re-evaluate previous approaches to examine what did work and what was effective.

When treatment is provided, does it always result in someone's rights being transgressed? In a recent article entitled Children's Rights For or Against Treatment by McConville and Bala, they point out that it often seems that lawyers are arguing the patient's right to avoid treatment while mental health professionals argue in favor of a patient's right to receive treatment. It is a strange marriage of authors as Dr. McConville is one of the former chief psychiatrists at the Kingston General Hospital, and Nicholas Bala is a law professor at Queen's University.

We are in an age when civil rights is paramount. Experience tells us that universal application of civil rights may hold more ethereal wisdom than knowledge. Witness, for example, Canada's adult criminal system which, as a result of liberalized mental health justice legislation, has saved offenders from becoming the victims of the mental health system only to have them victimized further by the correctional system. Even noted Canadian lawyer Barry Swadron, architect of much of Canada's mental health legislation during the 1970s, recently stated in the Globe and Mail, "The influence of civil libertarians has been a little too successful." Barry says that the presence of mentally disturbed people in prisons across the country is one warning signal that the laws have become so liberal that some people are not getting the treatment they need.

TREATING THE VIOLENT JUVENILE OFFENDER

Vicki Agee
Paint Creek Youth Centre, Ohio

After 19 years of treating the most violent juvenile offenders, I found that the only way to even consider changing their behavior is to forget everything you have ever learned about helping ordinary, disturbed kids get rid of their problems. You have to overcome certain "thinking errors" if you are going to treat properly.

The first thinking error is the victims stance. Yochelson and Samenov use the term to refer to the tendency that criminals have to claim they themselves are the victims of whatever crimes they committed. Anybody who works with delinquents knows that is the case. They will blame their behaviors on everybody and everything, their parents, their friends, their neighborhood, the weather, their teacher, the judge. Usually they reserve the greatest part of the blame for themselves.

For example, one youth that we just took into the program had twice burglarized the same elderly lady in the house. His reason was because the first time the woman had decided out of the kindness of her heart to drop charges against him, and he decided that meant she deserved to be robbed again. A problem with the victims stance is that we "treaters" often either agree with their excuses, or we give them new ones.

Parents are favorite targets for blame. Any youth who has been in counselling for longer than half an hour knows that he can get his counsellor's attention if he recites tales of how terribly he has been misunderstood at home compelling him to commit crimes. My contention is that often we are not hearing the true story. When there really is an abusive situation, there is no excuse for the youth to abuse other people. If you dwell on this in treatment, he will feel he is justified in continuing to do what he has been doing.

When we were treating the most violent sex offenders in Colorado, many of whom had indeed been sexually abused themselves, we spent the majority of the treatment time working with what they had done to harm others. We painfully found that if we first addressed how they themselves had been victimized, they remained stuck there feeling sorry for themselves and not for the people they victimized.

The next thinking error is minimization. This term is used to describe the tendency to make light of serious situations. This is another common tactic delinquents use. They make their actions sound minor and not very harmful to the victim. They minimize the crime.

I used to believe the kids, as did many others within this system, and that was another critical mistake we made. We minimized the crime right along with them. I believe we did it because we never saw the victim. We never even read a victim impact report. I gathered my information from a kid who was telling me he had not done too much. I wanted to believe him.

There is a strong tendency among sex offender therapists to normalize what they hear from their patients. The information is so bad that they try to pretend that they do not hear right, or the person did not really mean what he said. That goes on all the time with those of us who try to work with delinquents. We try to get some distance emotionally from the victim because if we do not, the job of changing the kid would seem so much harder. We would have real trouble dealing with the youth's anger. I have learned a great deal about crime victims over the years. I have been one myself, and I believe there is no such thing as a minor offence. All crimes hurt, affect others and disrupt their lives. I am sure that anyone who has been robbed, who has had his house broken into, who has received obscene phone calls or even who has been cheated and lied to would think that the world would be a better place if the perpetrator would change his behavior.

Unfortunately, with our limited resources we often do very little to deal with people who commit minor crimes. We have to put our resources on those who commit major crimes. But the one thing we can do to change our behavior is not to agree with them when they believe that what they did was only a small thing. If we do that, once again the youth feels he does not have any reason to change.

Psychiatrist William Gaylin writes about the dilemma that we in this field are in. He feels strongly that the balance between victim and criminal has not been achieved, and society's sympathy has been strongly with the criminal for many years. There is an old joke about two criminologists walking down the street who find this terribly beaten man lying on the sidewalk and immediately exclaim, "Oh my God! The man who did this needs our help." Most of us know this has been the sentiment for many years. Only in the past few years has there been much attention paid to crime victims. Dr. Gaylin summed it up by saying that society has been guilty. We minimize the crime. We glorify the criminal, and we forget the victim.

Another thinking error is ventilation or the hydraulic model of people. Most people do not deal with anger in very brilliant ways. Most people still think our feelings build up inside of us like a steam engine, and if we do not find a way to express it, we will blow up. Obviously, current research and approaches seriously question that assumption. There is quite a bit of evidence to suggest that ventilation or practicing anger might even rehearse, solidify or intensify the anger, and this is certainly the case with the violent offenders we work with. Rather than expressing anger by merely letting off steam, it becomes like a war dance with them. It escalates the anger. I strongly recommend an approach where they do not encourage aggressive kids to express their anger.

Samenov, for example, says that effective change agents should not be apologetic moralists, and I agree. If your values are consistent with the core culture, you should feel strongly about teaching your values to delinquent youth. In order to teach values, you must hold similarly high ones for yourself. One of the finest practitioners in the country, David Barenson at Maine Youth Centre, talks about how he personally changed since he started working with delinquents. He mentions how you have to take a look at your thinking errors and behavior errors if you are going to be a role model for these kids. He stresses that we must practice what we preach. We too have to control our anger.

Another thinking error is the mistaken assumption that treatment and discipline are two different things. I have never been able to figure out why mental health professionals act as if learning to be a responsible human being can take place without setting limits. They must feel that these youths, most of whom have been so out of control that they or their parents have sought mental health assistance many times, can change with the proper person talking with them. Teaching self-discipline is a critical part of the change process.

The last thinking error is the assumption that mentally disturbed youth need treatment but delinquent children do not. There are several grave errors in this reasoning. One error is that the diagnosis is not accurate, reliable, valid or connected to reality. We have seen that no two diagnosticians agree on anything. One of the last kids in my old program before I went to Ohio had five different diagnoses in five months, and they changed miraculously with the different medications given. The other error is faulty assumption that there is nothing emotionally wrong with youths who engage in delinquent activity; they are just bad. Bad kids, presumably, just need limits to be good. It is not that easy.

Schizophrenia, for example, is a disease of young adults. Sometimes the onset is in late adolescence, but it is most common in the early 20s. There are very few young schizophrenics. We had only three in our program in the past 13 years. They are usually not dangerous. It is only cost effective for society to concentrate money on those who are most likely to make the quality of life worse for the largest group of people. That is juvenile delinquency.

My new program is Paint Creek Youth Centre in Ohio. It is one of three cooperative efforts of the Department of Justice. We were given a grant to test out the theory of community rehabilitation. In juvenile corrections they want to see if a community program can provide youth correctional treatment as effectively and efficiently as the state system.

The three programs receiving money are the RCA Corporation in Acarper City, New Jersey, the Associated Marine Institute in Florida and the New Life Youth Services of Cincinnati where I work.

New Life Youth Services initially was started by a group of black church women 16 years ago who wanted to do something for kids. They started the very first group home in Ohio called the March Group Home. New Life is now one of the largest private community-based youth services organizations in the country. There are 10 programs such as the Shot Group Home and the first runaway shelter in Ohio, the Lighthouse Runaway Shelter.

Their program which has gotten the most national attention is the Freedom Factory which is essentially a wood products industry. They take kids coming out of the division's youth services and teach them the wood products trade. They learn good skills and get paid at a good rate.

They have one factory called the Therapeutic Aids Factory. They go into the homes of handicapped people and make wheelchair ramps and other therapeutic aids such as breathing boards for babies at no cost. They have another factory making pallets from which they make quite a bit of money. It helps pay for the therapeutic products division.

In addition to the Paint Creek Youth Centre, we also have a Freedom Factory in Bainbridge. We have the treatment program plus a strong vocational component to our program.

The Youth Centre was an old abandoned sports camp located in the foothills of the Appalachian Mountains at Bainbridge. Paint Creek runs through it and has tennis courts, swimming pools, baseball fields, football fields and other recreational facilities. It is a program for serious offenders who have committed felonies.

The research is run by the Rand Corporation in San Francisco. Youth Services calls and tells them if the youth is control or experimental. The experimental ones come to our program. The controls go to one of two large institutions in Ohio, Teco or Riverview.

Serious offenders have a mandatory one year stay. They may possibly stay longer, but it is very unusual for them to get out in a shorter period of time. The Divisional Youth Services reimburses us for each youth referred to us.

Our treatment approach has four major components. The first is the intensive program based on a positive peer culture, the only way to work with adolescents. The second component is a victim awareness approach.

The third major component of the program is a very strong educational program. In addition, we have a very strong recreational therapy program, and finally we have the work program. After they have been in the unit for about eight months and have worked their way through the program, they can go half days to the Freedom Factory where they get paid and actually learn the wood products industry. They earn this by first working on the grounds and doing community service work.

A portion of the money earned at the Freedom Factory, goes towards the restitution that the court has ordered to their victims as well as towards support of offspring. After the program, they move into the community and are given a job at one of the Freedom Factories in either Cincinnati or Bainbridge.

In the area of victim awareness we have to be careful we do not make value judgments before a youth walks through the door. We realized we had to learn more about the victimization process because if we did not, we could not share it with our kids. The way that we chose to do that was to meet the victims. After, we went into the victim organizations which gave us a better understanding of the victim. After learning that, we changed our program so that it now has much more of an emphasis on victimization. I hope we have achieved a balance of sympathy.

The first thing we do in treatment is to build up their anxiety for the first 2 1/2 days. They can use it as a cue to stop their behavior. We keep the isolated from the peer group. They have several scheduled raps during that time with positive kids, higher team kids and also with staff. They talk about what they did to get there with emphasis on what they have done to hurt other people. At the end of 2 1/2 days they come out to the community group and talk about all the things they did since they started getting into trouble.

Usually what they get out is about one sentence, and the kids interrupt them. They are kept in line by the other kids. It is informative rather than hostile, but it does blow them away because all the previous little rationalizations they had been using to deny responsibility for what they had done does not work anymore. They realize very quickly that they are going to have to take a whole new approach to working with their problems.

As soon as they hit group therapy, they again detail their crime history. The kid relates the crime, covering the details. The other kids continually penetrate the denial. They constantly bring up the area of empathy for the victims, and if a kid has a hard time, they use role play.

After they develop some remorse, some self-disgust, desire to change their behavior, they learn their violence cycle. They learn what it is that incites them to go out and hurt people.

After learning the violence, they learn alternative behaviors. We use conflict negotiation, assertiveness training somewhat and Yochelson and Samenov's thinking errors.

Our kids are scored twice daily in the thinking errors. When they bring up a problem in group, they have to identify what the thinking errors are. Obviously they are much quicker to learn other people's thinking errors than they are their own. It is amazing how quickly they are able to point them out with the rest of the group members and how difficult it is to point them out in themselves.

Outside of the group, we also have a continuing emphasis on victim awareness through television, the papers and anything else dealing with victim impact. We use any input possible.

They have to write papers. It sounds like what we do is hang their victims around their necks like an albatross, and in many respects we do that. With the violent offenders, we learned a long time ago that one of the serious problems was giving up too soon in doing that. We had to keep doing this throughout treatment for them to continuously be aware of their impulses to hurt people.

After they get much higher up in the program, at the CATC, they usually return to the scene of the crime. What we do is have them go through the whole situation again. That brings back all kinds of similar stimuli, and it is amazing how new details come back to mind. They go through a very similar thing which the victim goes through. Because the first stage of victimization has a blunting effect, taking him back to the scene of the crime does make it very clear that it did happen. Another thing we do is show them pictures of the murdered victims which brings back many similar stimuli and really shocks them into reality.

Continually throughout the program, we have a restitution model. We tell them they owe their peers. They have to help other people. We have them do things for the community.

TREATING THE VIOLENT JUVENILE OFFENDER

Joe Borgo
Shawbridge Treatment Centre, Montreal

What we have learned over the past 12 years since we first began dealing with the very violent offender in need of secure treatment at Shawbridge Youth Centres has been largely experiential. We have learned a great deal about ourselves and about the needs of the children.

Shawbridge is a treatment centre for emotionally disturbed and delinquent children. It was founded in 1907 and has been in existence for the last 78-79 years. It was founded originally by a group of men including two physicians from the Children's Hospital in Montreal.

One of the experiences that led to the founding of our agency was the testing for tuberculosis among the general population. One of the physicians had had the opportunity to test two young schoolboys. From the time they took the tests to the time the culture grew and showed that the kids did indeed have tuberculosis, the two boys were in prison for having stolen apples off a push-vendor's cart. One of them was six years old and the other was 12. They were both prisoners in Joliette with leg irons and manacles. When they went to take them out of the prison to bring them into the hospital, they were so appalled by the conditions and by the numerous young children living in those conditions that they came back and convinced their friends on the Board of the Children's Hospital and the boards of other social agencies in Montreal to set up a program for protestant young offenders in Montreal.

As was the fashion at that time, they bought 250 acres in the country, 45 miles north of Montreal and hired someone who had been the first superintendent at the Verjean School in Verjean, Vermont, one of the first juvenile delinquent programs in the United States, and began the treatment program.

The reason I go into that is because until the 1950s Shawbridge was in a rural setting. We actually exploited a farm, and the old name of the agency used to be The Boys Farm and Training School. Our cattle won prizes all over Canada, and we furnished breeder stock to Western farmers.

The entire program was based from the very beginning on a family model of treatment rather than building a large institutional structure. The Board of Directors built small, family-like units that would house a family of about 10-12 kids which was common in the early part of the century in rural Quebec. The homes the children lived in resembled other children's homes. It was organized around a common green and was essentially a very small community.

We were asked in 1974 by the Ministry of Social Affairs to assume responsibility for children in need of secure treatment because of a temporary crisis in detention facilities. The Ministry said "All we want you to do is to do it for six months." Twelve years later we no longer have a detention unit. We have three treatment units as well as a detention unit for girls.

Our early experience was atrocious. We did not have any facilities physically equipped for dealing with the youngsters. We had staff turnover ratios that were over 450% per annum in our closed units. We were burning out people almost as fast as we could hire them. We had quiet room incidences, at least six or seven a day, and it was a general mess. We responded to that by petitioning the Ministry to at least provide us with adequate facilities.

At one point, the girls unit was housed in an abandoned motel in St. Marguerite du Lac Masson, a former 1920s brothel. It was made entirely out of varnished logs and was of a similar style to that of Chateau Montebello. You can imagine the problems we had with fire prevention and security in that facility. The Ministry finally financed the remodelling of some of our buildings, but as is always the case when you attempt to run a secure unit in a facility not specifically designed for that purpose, the expensive remodelling was not very effective. Those are still the same units that we have today. It is possible to run extremely good security programs in settings that are not all that secure and in settings that are not designed to be secure.

The facility is important, but you can run good programs despite it. The purpose of a security program and the first step in beginning to treat the violent, young offender is to create a milieu for that person with security for both the staff and the client. The static aspects of the security which include the locked doors, the fences and the rest are only one element and the least important element in terms of being able to create an effective treatment program. You have to have them when they are necessary, but the better you are at carrying out your treatment program, the less you have to rely on them.

In 1974, for instance, the secure units had the least use of the quiet room and ran on an average of about four episodes a year. This is with the most violent and most disturbed kids in our care. It is therefore possible to do it, and it is possible to do it because of the dynamic factors of security. That has to do with staff and with the program.

Staff selection is one of the most important aspects of running an adequate security treatment program. It is very important to be able to select staff who have a good sense of self, who are not threatened by anger, who are not threatened by violence, who can cope well with violence and who do not respond aggressively and violently towards the juveniles who are expressing that behavior. All of the staff working in our security units are now the most experienced. The average length of stay in our security units is 12 years. It has become a badge of honor to be chosen to work in a secure unit because it is like a testimonial to your competence and to your ability to do your job well.

The other important element is adequate programming which structures a child's day. The important thing is that we have tried and have allowed time for some learning curves. It took us from late 1974 through 1977 before we had an adequate treatment program going. We went through a large number of staff. That takes a great deal of confidence on the part of the administration, the Board of Directors, the Ministry and the public which is paying the bills. You must convince them that eventually you are going to put together a combination that works, enabling you to run an adequate program. You need at least two years to develop the kind of culture in a unit that will enable it to be self-sustaining and where the staff set the tone for what is permissible.

Our programs also have very rocky beginnings. There lies the difficulty when you are trying to justify a program to funding authorities and to other people within your own system. It takes faith on the part of the people in charge, and it takes dedication on the part of the people who are involved to make sure that the program happens.

We started out in our security units with 12 kids and 15 staff. We are now down to 11. At the beginning we relied on the extra security and the extra personnel to be able to deal with the problems.

Striking the proper balance is somewhat a matter of trial and error, but I think it is important to realize that you do not need a huge staff or large ratios in order to make these programs function effectively.

What kind of kids are we talking about? We will deal with three case histories of kids who are currently in our closed units and have been there for a long period of time. The first case concerns a young woman who is now 18 years old. She came to us at the age of 17 after having murdered her sister and after having assaulted her father when he discovered the body lying on the bed. She murdered her sister because they got into a fight over a pair of her new jeans. She comes from a very successful upper-middle class family and is with us under a Young Offenders Act Order (YOA) with a three-year limitation on treatment.

The second case involves a young person who was written up in the Montreal Gazette and the Globe and Mail and who is with us again under a YOA Order for one year. He is almost 18. He comes from a family where he was abused and raped by his father at the age of five. He had been continuously molested by his father until he came to us at the age of 16. His father married a woman with two children from a previous marriage, and he was forced by both his father and his stepmother into sexual molestation of the younger children. There is a great deal of anger and resentment in this young man, and he will be leaving us when his sentence expires within a month.

The third is a recent case. He came to us from the emergency room of the Children's Hospital where he was admitted for antrum metria. He had punctured his colon with a broom handle while inserting it into his anus during masturbation. He too had been raped. He was raped by his grandfather from the age of five. His grandfather had sexually molested his mother, all of the children in his mother's family and all of his male and female siblings. The family has been known to social service agencies in Montreal for the last 30 years, and almost every child from both generations has been involved in treatment. This young man who is 13 years old has also been involved in the sexual molestation of younger children in the neighborhood.

These are the kinds of cases that we are talking about. I am not talking about kids who are put into secure units because they run away from other kinds of facilities, and nobody can hold them. I am not talking about kids who are in secure units because they gave staff a hard time. We are talking about kids with a very serious level of personal disturbance, very disturbed family histories and a history of violence both against themselves and others.

How effective are we in dealing with them? I do not know. We are good at controlling their behavior while they are with us. I know that in a large number of cases, we are even successful in terms of changing attitudes and in provoking some new perspectives about life, about the meaning of their own lives and the way in which they interact with other people. How effective we are in dealing with the root causes of the violence of which they have been both the victims and the perpetrators, I cannot say. Paradoxically enough, one of the reasons for that is that we do not get enough of the kids. They do not come in batches of 12 or 15. One of the dilemmas is how to vary the program within the facility to be able to address the needs of those most in need while not infringing on the civil rights of the other kids.

One of the other dilemmas is staff. For years our staff would deal with these kids without ever dealing with the reasons that brought them to treatment. Nobody ever talked to a kid about his offence pattern. Nobody ever talked to him about what he did, why he did it and what the meaning of that behavior was for him. They talked about his behavior in the unit. They talked about conforming to the rules of the program. They talked about all kinds of other things, but they did not deal with the fundamental issue of why he was there. We still do not do it consistently.

Very often my staff are still wrong because they do not deal with the issues that have brought the kids into treatment. They are less afraid to deal with the offence behavior than they are with some of the behaviors where the kids have been the victims of violence.

Of the girls that we see at Shawbridge upon admission, 15 per cent have a reported family history of incest. In the course of treatment it comes out that 85 per cent of the girls that we see have a history of incest. Thirty-three per cent of the boys have a history of homosexual incest. Staff, and particularly male staff, have a very hard time dealing with that. They do like to explore those issues although they are not comfortable issues to explore. Until you explore them and then help the kid to explore them, it is difficult to know what kind of treatment to use.

There is some behavior learning, cognitive learning and some changing of social attitudes that go on, but we still do not do enough of that consistently. It takes almost four years to be able to adequately deal with the kinds of issues that these kids are faced with. Yet we are dealing with legislation that says to a child, "Yes, you acted all wrong. Yes, you acted against your own best interests and the interests of society therefore we are going to take your liberty away from you. In taking your liberty away from you, we are also going to give you the right to refuse treatment. You do not have to be treated. We will just lock you up, and you can do your time." There are many self-righteous defence lawyers and social workers giving just that message to kids which I think is the wrong message. It is a distorted message and a misconception about what we are all about. It is a misconception about what the needs of those children are all about. It is really adults who refuse to accept the fact that they are adults and who refuse to accept the fact that they have a responsibility towards children. Under the guise of children's rights, they want to walk away from the responsibility of caring for someone. It takes a great deal of commitment and emotional energy.

Burn-out is a very real factor in these kinds of programs, and there has to be emotional support so staff can be able to carry out their responsibilities. The fundamental issue is not children's rights but adult cowardice. The first and fundamental right of every child is to be loved and to have someone care. That is what secure treatment and particularly the treatment of our kinds of kids is about. It is about caring, accompanying a child, being there with him. This is a very important part of adequately running this type of program. It is also difficult to sustain it. It takes people with experience, dedication and commitment to carry it out continually. In order to be effective, you have to have strong and supportive staff relationships. It is easy to tip the balance in favor of responding to staff concerns rather than client concerns because we are concerned about team morale. The only way to maintain that balance is by putting the emphasis on the child's needs and effective treatment.

I have four different treatment philosophies, but one of my drawbacks as an administrator is not being able to establish a consistent philosophy of treatment. This is consistency in terms of delivery and fundamental philosophy.

The other area where we need work is in terms of preparing the kids for when they leave us and enter the work force.

We have invested time and resources in dealing with the emotional and educational problems of kids. The average age of boys entering Shawbridge is 15 years five months, and their average grade level is six years four months. The average length of stay in a security unit is nine and one-half months. Within that time, on the average that is two and one-half academic years. Individualized instruction, education and cognitive learning skills are important parts of our treatment program.

While we deal with some of the attitude problems and help them acquire self-control in terms of the violence, I am not quite sure we have helped the most disturbed ones deal with the underlying causes of violence.

Consistently enough, we do not prepare them well for an entry into the job market. We have some programs that attempt to deal with that, but because of the very nature of the issues that have brought them to us, we have taken a choice to focus on those emotional and psychological issues more so than training issues. In a way we are letting the kids down because while we may have helped them cope more adequately on an emotional level, we are also putting them out into a job situation where their skills place them in an immediate disadvantage. Therefore, if there were component parts to our program that I would like to strengthen, that is one of them.

PART XVII

VICTIMS OF VIOLENCE

VICTIMS OF VIOLENCE

Ezzat Fattah
Simon Fraser University

Although I have not been a victim of a violent crime, I have been victimized over the years with all sorts of property offenses. Also as a child I was assaulted and beaten by friends, enemies, siblings, cousins, neighbors and school friends. I published my first paper on victims in 1966.

Those who are unable or unwilling to see beyond their ideological position often accuse criminologists and victimologists of caring too much about the offender and not enough about the victim. This is simply untrue. Criminologists and victimologists care as much about the victim as the offender. They are seen as human beings who need our love and sympathy, our support and compassion.

I know of no criminologist or victimologist who is insensitive to the pain and suffering that many victims and their families go through. They are sensitive to the fear and anxiety that is generated by crime in the minds of the general public and in the minds of certain groups, especially the elderly and women.

I think humanitarianism is indivisible, and we cannot be humane to one party and not to the other. If we are genuinely concerned about victims and about the society in which we live, then we have to promote love not hate, forgiveness not vindictiveness, reconciliation not retaliation.

Unfortunately, many of the victims groups seem to be more interested in attacking the offender than in defending and protecting the interests of the victim. They are more interested in harsher punishments and the reinstating of the death penalty. They seem more interested in the abolition of parole and mandatory supervision than they are in preventing victimization or insuring compensation.

Under the guise of serving victims' interests, all kinds of regressive measures are being advocated. One of the major recommendations of President Reagan's Task Force on Victims of Crime was to abolish the exclusionary rule. Ninety-five per cent of the cases in which the exclusionary rule is invoked by the defence council are drug cases, prostitution cases and gambling cases. These are cases in which there is no victim, I therefore do not see how the interests of victims can be served by the abolition of this rule. This is not to minimize the plight of victims. Although there are many brutal rapes, vicious killings and unprovoked assaults on defenseless, helpless people, the incidence is neither typical nor average.

Typical mundane cases do not make headlines and are judged by the media as not newsworthy. The media likes to sensationalize and focuses on the bizarre, the unusual and the extraordinary.

I seriously doubt whether victim advocates who are generally self-appointed speak on behalf of victims of crime. At best, they represent a very tiny minority of all victims. At worst, they represent only themselves.

I also question the present attitude of portraying victims of crime as a herd of weak, helpless, defenseless and unsuspecting lambs who fall prey to a bunch of hungry savage wolves. I question the present tendency to look upon victims as a group that is in need of guardians. I question our current inclination to intervene and to intervene intensively with victims of crime.

I do not understand why we force victims to reluctantly report their victimization to the police. Why do we have to urge them to mobilize the criminal justice system? Since when is the criminal justice system the appropriate agency or the appropriate vehicle for conflict resolutions? We are willing to open a whole new field for state and for professional intervention without studying or even reflecting upon the dangers or the side effects of such intervention. Do we know what impact this is going to have on the family, on society, on human relations, on human interactions, on future generations?

We seem always to forget that the human side has enormous healing capacity. While in some cases our intervention might do some good, in most cases it is likely to interrupt, delay or block the normal healing process.

We cannot talk about victims in abstract terms. We cannot look at violent crime situations in isolation. We have to compare them with situations in other countries and compare the risk of criminal victimization with other risks.

In Canada, property crimes have increased substantially, but crimes of violence have remained relatively stable. Homicide is decreasing. In 1984 there were 667 homicides compared to 701 in 1975. The suicide rate is about five times the criminal homicide rate, and, according to Statistics Canada, traffic accidents are about six times the criminal homicide rate. When compared with other forms of violence, un-natural causes of death such as traffic deaths and suicides, homicide in Canada is relatively rare.

In 1982, compared with those who died from homicide, approximately six times as many people in Canada were killed in traffic accidents, and just over five times as many people died as a result of suicide. If we are genuinely concerned about victims and the loss of lives, we should pay equal or more attention to those who die as a result of suicide, traffic accidents and drunk driving.

A large percentage of homicide cases take place within the immediate family. More than 40% of all homicides in Canada are domestic, and if one combines domestic homicides with homicides that are committed by acquaintances or relatives, they constitute about 90% of criminal homicides.

This situation is not unique to Canada. The study of criminal homicide in Denmark showed that the rate of homicide within the immediate family is 60%. The chances that the victim will be an acquaintance are 30%; the victim a stranger, 10%.

Although the immediate family is the smallest circle, the chances are overwhelming that the victim will be from this small circle. Acquaintances are in an intermediary circle, and the chances are intermediate that the victim will be chosen from the circle. The circle of strangers is by far the largest. Only 10% of the time will the victim come from this huge circle.

Generally, fear of crime is essentially fear of strangers and fear of violence. This is the way it is portrayed in the media.

Our crimes of violence in Canada account for only 9% of criminal code offenses. When we compare our violent crime situation with the violent crime situation south of the border, we realize how much better off we are than the United States.

What we have learned now from the victimization surveys that have been carried out in Canada and in many other countries in recent years are the characteristics of victims and the earlier stereotypes of black and white. The earlier stereotypes characterized the victim population and the offender as distinct and different.

Victimization surveys have greatly enhanced our knowledge of the victim population and have confirmed what many victimologists have known for a long time through mere intuition. They showed, among other things, that the risks of becoming a victim of crime are not evenly spread, and victims of violence do not constitute an unbiased cross-section of the general population.

This reality is constantly ignored in current debates on victims which continue to stress and thus help perpetuate the bad lot level. These debates divert attention from the fact that individuals are at risk because of certain personal factors such as lifestyle.

Singer points out the idea that victims and offenders are part of the same homogeneous population which runs contrary to the public's popular impression that criminals are distinct from their innocent victims. In the current retrospect of victim movements, victims and offenders are portrayed as totally different and totally distinct populations.

Such portrayal is difficult to reconcile. The knowledge we have gained from victimization research reveals a striking similarity between the two groups. If we examine the two groups, the offender populations and the victim population, along a series of variables such as age, sex, marital status, employment status and race, ethnic origin, we find that similarities are almost perfect.

If we look at age, for example, and exclude very young children, we find that the young age group is overrepresented both in the criminal and delinquent population and in the victim population. The elderly as a group have the lowest rates of crime and delinquency and the lowest rates of victimization whereas intermediary age groups have intermediary crime and delinquency rates and intermediary victimization rates. Males commit more crimes and are criminally victimized more frequently than females are.

This is also a constant pattern revealed by both official crime statistics and victimization surveys. Sexual offenses are the only exceptions since they are predominantly committed against women. Married people commit fewer crimes and are less victimized than single, divorced individuals. This difference is reflected in age and in lifestyle associated with the marital status. Because crimes of violence are to a large extent inter- racial races and ethnic groups with high crime and delinquency rates such as the Blacks and Hispanics in the United States have also high victimization rates. The white population, on the other hand, registers lower rates on both counts.

Committing the crime increases the chances of further involvement in delinquency. If someone commits an armed robbery, a burglary or an act of shoplifting, the chances that the same person will commit a second offence are much higher than for the rest of the population. The same is true regarding the risks of victimization.

Criminals are more frequently victimized than non-criminals. In the follow-up survey to delinquency, Singer examines the extent to which victims are also guilty of serious assaults, and he reports that sample members who were shot or stabbed were not often non-white, high school drop-outs, unemployed and single when surveyed.

This coincides very well with the findings of the Canadian Victimization Survey. Using the victimization data, we can draw a profile of the victim of crime against crimes of violence. The victim is young, unmarried, male, living alone, probably looking for work and with an active life outside the home. This is not very different from the profile we might draw of the offender.

In Finland, Aroma reported that victims had much in common with the offenders. They were often, especially when the gravest crimes of violence are concerned, closely related to each other. He also found that even in less serious crimes of violence, perpetrators and victims very often were not complete strangers, and he noted that it is often a matter of pure chance in these encounters which party ends up as the victim and which one turns out to be the offender.

It is understandable that the frequency with which some individuals become involved in violent situations will affect both their chances of using violence and of being recipients of violence. Who will end up being the victim and who will qualify as the offender depends quite often on chance rather than on deliberate actions, planning or intent. Thus, victim offender roles are not necessarily antagonistic or incompatible but are frequently complementary and interchangeable.

This is particularly true of brawls, quarrels, disputes and altercations, and these are the typical contests in which crimes of violence take place. The affinity between the victim population and the criminal population should not come as a surprise because crimes of violence do not occur in a vacuum, and motives for these violent crimes occur when people interact with one another. That is why we find that there is both social proximity and geographical proximity that brings these people together in situations where the motives of violence and actual use of violence ultimately end up in situations where people are injured or are killed.

Looking at crime in a different way from other social risks is hurting rather than benefiting victims of crime. We should look upon and treat criminal victimization as one of the many risks of life in modern society, risks to which we are daily exposed. The fact is, that modern life is a hazardous life, but while other risks are more or less adequately covered in the welfare state by some public or private insurance, the risks of becoming a victim of crime is not.

I have a hard time understanding that if someone is killed as a result of a traffic accident, then the family gets adequate compensation because of the insurance. If someone is hurt or suffers injury or loss of life as a result of medical malpractice, then they get more than adequate insurance.

Other risks such as unemployment are covered by insurance. Old age is covered by insurance. Labor accidents are covered by insurance. When it comes to criminal victimization, we have only symbolic compensation for victims of violence. And we have imperical evidence showing that fewer than 1% of all victims receive compensation. When compensation finally comes, it is too little and too late.

In many provinces, the ceiling on such compensation is $20,000. If the accident were unintentional as a result of a motor vehicle, than it can extend into millions and millions of dollars.

In England, rape payment is set at $1,650. The government's Criminal Injuries Compensation Board said a woman could expect to receive $1,650 if the attack left her with no significant physical injuries and an average psychological reaction. That is the price that is put on rape whereas for other injuries the compensation can be more or less adequate.

If we are genuinely concerned about the plight of victims, we are genuinely concerned about alleviating the pain and suffering and the agony that victims or victim's families go through, then we have to go ahead and not make an excuse for the costs of the system because these costs have not prevented us in other areas of social risks of setting up adequate compensation schemes. We must try to have this universal system which ensures that there is some financial compensation.

VICTIMS OF VIOLENCE

Gary Rosenfeldt
Edmonton

Since the creation of victims organizations a number of years ago, people have come to believe that we are opposed to other agencies which provide services and help for those who commit crimes. This is not true, and I plan to discuss this myth as well as others.

The victims organizations in Canada began at about the same time as many American organizations. These organizations such as Victims of Violence in Edmonton, Alberta were developed in response to the need for better or improved services for victims of crimes in Canada. We started mainly as support groups.

In my own particular case, my 16-year-old son was one of 11 children murdered by Clifford Olson in Vancouver, and at the time that my child was abducted and murdered, I found very little community support. We, the parents of the abducted children, were given very few services or really anything by the criminal justice system. When our son was discovered missing, we went to the Coquitlam RCMP and told them we had a missing child. We were told he was only one of many, many missing children in Canada. He was considered a runaway, and they would not even enter his name in the computer for 48 hours.

On May 11, 1981, we received a telephone call from the Coquitlam RCMP. My wife answered the telephone, and they told her that our 16-year-old son had been found murdered. The RCMP arrived a few hours later. They talked to us, told us very little about what had happened to our child and went through the normal procedure of investigating us. That was the last we heard of the RCMP or anyone within the criminal justice system.

Everything we learned from that point on was from the news media. This included the fact, for instance, that our child had been sexually assaulted. I can remember talking to Inspector Larry Proque of the RCMP one day after they had released information on some of the other children who had been sexually assaulted, and I told him that I would appreciate it if they would tell me this sort of information. I had two other children, nine and eleven. I wanted to have the opportunity of being able to discuss sexual assault and murder with them prior to them hearing about it on the press. Larry assured me that they would contact me, and they did not. The next day we read in the newspaper that our son had been sexually assaulted prior to being murdered.

Victims of crime, especially secondary victims of crime, have been totally neglected or forgotten by the criminal justice system for many years. The development of agencies such as Victims of Violence was a natural result of this neglect.

Things have changed considerably all across Canada as a result of lobbying. We cannot bring about change unless we start to look at some of the mistakes that have been made in the past. This is the reason for the development of victims groups across Canada. These victims groups developed basically as support groups for each other.

In the Vancouver situation, at the time when a number of children were being abducted and murdered around the lower mainland of British Columbia, we got other parents together. We formed a little group out there and are still together. In fact, we are presenting our case to the Supreme Court of Canada to try to have the money taken away from Clifford Olson. I think that we have been effective in supporting each other overcome the traumatic effects of violent crime.

There are myths I would like to clear up regarding victims groups. For one thing, when we first set up an office in the provincial courthouse in Edmonton, Alberta, there was a great outcry that was heard across the country from the Criminal Trial Lawyers Association. They stated that we were comparable to the Klu Klux Klan and were vigilantes. They claimed we were going to be using the courthouse to intimidate victims and witnesses prior to giving testimony in the courtrooms.

At that time, a few years ago, there was still an awful lot of fear as to what we were really after within the criminal justice system. We did talk at specific times about capital punishment which frightened a great number of people within the criminal justice system. We were not vigilantes wanting to set up systems of hanging people as they left the courtroom.

I have spoken many times in favor of capital punishment. The interesting thing about the capital punishment issue is that we have done a census of all the people within our organization, and we know of only one case out of thousands where a person has actually changed his attitude on capital punishment after experiencing the victimization or murder of his child. It is not common for people to suddenly stand up in favor of capital punishment after having a child murdered.

Another myth that developed immediately upon the forming of our organization was that we were out to build more prisons, and we were looking for longer, stiffer sentences for all criminals. This is not true. One of our objectives as a victims group is to reduce the number of prisoners within our systems today. We feel that our prison system is a training ground for young people to become violent criminals, and we would like to see more restitution programs out in the community.

By incarcerating young people convicted of vandalism and theft, we are simply developing the violence that seems to be becoming more common today. Especially for young offenders, we would like to see more drug and alcohol treatment programs.

The truth of the matter is that violent crime is increasing in Canada. One does not have to be a statistician to figure out that, for instance, Statistics Canada figures over the last number of years show quite an increase in the murders. We have had in the last number of years serial killings that just did not exist a number of years ago.

Child abduction has become very common today. We deal with that all the time, and it is a relatively new phenomenon. With violent crime such as terrorism, one would have to be naive to suggest that it is not on the increase in Canada.

How do we reduce violent crime in Canada? I believe we have many agencies in Canada, but we are expending too much wasted energy on treatment and rehabilitation of violent criminals within our system. There are some people for which there is absolutely no possibility of rehabilitation.

We have only a few violent criminals in the country, and a great many of these criminals are released back onto the streets in too short a period of time. We would be better off locking these people up. I would rather see the money used to deal with the young people living on our streets. In Montreal, for instance, there are 5,000-6,000 homeless children living on the streets.

Most of these kids become involved in prostitution and drugs when they reach the streets. There are pimps waiting for them. We have a 16 year old girl working in our Edmonton office who was on the streets at 11 years old. This is not unusual. She was a victim of violence and sexual abuse within the home, and our systems out there are not adequate in dealing with these kids. If you stop and look at where our violent criminals come from, the majority of them have been on those streets and have learned to become violent.

Another problem is drunk driving. A number of victims of drunk driving have spoken up since the creation of a group called MADD down in California. What we have done over time is really phenomenal, and I think it is something worth looking at. We have, in the last number of years, changed public attitude totally around.

Society's attitude towards impaired driving has changed. I honestly believe that we can do the same thing with violent crime. It will take a concerted effort on the part of many community groups to make violent crime as repugnant as drunk driving has become in the last number of years. Criminal code amendments themselves will not be sufficient. Attitude change is necessary, and we can change attitudes towards violence in our society if we work together.

We also have to do something about the problem of runaway youth in this country. The Canadian Council on Children and Youth is one area where people are involved, and they would welcome any assistance. I suggest that agencies such as the John Howard Society and Elizabeth Fry begin to talk about the victimization of children and the numbers of children that live on our streets. It would assist in doing away with the problem of violent crimes.

PART XVIII

APPROACHES TO PREVENTION AND TREATMENT

AN OVERVIEW

APPROACHES TO PREVENTION AND TREATMENT: AN OVERVIEW

Rick Mosley
Department of Justice

The subject of violent crime is one which I find very difficult to deal with. While there is no lack of consensus that violent crime is the object of the law, it is not always clear what the form of the legislative response should be.

There is a widespread belief that the law is not doing enough to protect. Opinion surveys consistently report to us there is an overwhelming feeling among Canadians that the law and courts are not harsh enough on criminals. I expect that that sentiment is directed primarily against violent offenders. I know that it is, and I suspect that it is more directed to the application of the law by the courts rather than to the law itself.

We find frequently that when we take the opportunity to explain to someone the range of penalties, they are taken somewhat by surprise. They expect the ranges provided by the law to be much lower when they discover that you can get life imprisonment for something like armed robbery.

Nevertheless, from the representations we receive at the Department of Justice, there appears to be a continuing degree of public faith in the law to reduce the level of violence within our society. This objective could be achieved if those within the system had the will to do something about it. For those of us within the criminal law policy development business, the results of those public perceptions, whether well-founded or not, are that we are expected to come up with solutions to problems for which there may be no clear answer or at least none consistent with the operation of the civilized society.

There is a continuing effort to improve the law's response to violence. It would be extravagant to predict any extraordinary successes from those efforts. They are directed primarily at rationalizing the current law, achieving clarity in the statement of the law and improving and updating the procedures to meet modern conditions. Those efforts range from the proposals in working papers 33 and 38 on assault and homicide prepared by the Law Reform Commission to initiatives directed against single problem issues within the system. Those initiatives are normally developed outside the field of institutionalized law reform. They are developed within the Department of Justice. As examples, I would point to the criminal law amendment act of 1985 and two specific provisions that were brought into effect. One was the new offence of hostage taking. The other was a revision to the crime of threatening to include threats made directly between the parties.

The hostage taking amendment was adopted to comply with the terms of the United Nations Convention which Canada adhered to in 1980. To further carry out our obligations under that convention, the 1985 legislation extended the jurisdiction of our courts to try persons found in our territory who have allegedly committed these offenses abroad. The principle objective of those amendments was to deal with the problem of international terrorism as expressed through aircraft hijacking. The efforts of the United Nations are continuing in that direction, and I expect there will be another convention in the near future which may call for further amendments to our criminal code in the area of jurisdiction and in the creation of new crimes.

The amendment, with respect to the offence of threatening, is perhaps a very minor change in the criminal law, but it may play a significant role in providing the police with an instrument to defuse potentially violent situations in which there has been a threat of death or of bodily injury. In those circumstances, a criminal charge would be available and would permit an arrest and removal of the person who has threatened. It may have an effect on reducing or permitting a timely intervention to avoid the problem that might otherwise occur.

This type of single issue legislative policy development is a necessary part of our criminal justice system despite its piecemeal and somewhat ad hoc nature. In recent years we have responded to demands for changes to the criminal law by the appointment of special committees or by the referral of the subject matter to the Law Reform Commission. Special committees include the Committee on Sexual Offenses Against Children and Youths, the Badgley Committee, and the special committee on pornography and prostitution under the chairmanship of Mr. Paul Fraser.

When such committees are in operation or when the Law Reform Commission has taken the subject under consideration, we wait until their work has been completed before we take a further view on behalf of the government.

That approach reflects our basic faith in the results that may be achieved from research, from consultation and from careful deliberation. The Law Reform Commission currently has under consideration work on the law of assaults and homicide. That work will be included in the draft criminal code that is to be expected in the Fall. The working papers have proposed a restructuring of the law on assault and homicide.

In respect to assault, the Commission would change the emphasis of the law to focus on the type of assault which has been inflicted. The scheme of assault offenses would be changed from the current tiered approach which increases the penalty to reflect the degree of harm or other aggravating circumstances. They would create new offenses of assault such as touching an unwilling victim, assault by hurting an unwilling victim or assault by causing harm or injury. All of these could be aggravated by the manner in which the assault occurred or by the relationship between the accused and the victim.

The law of homicide, the Law Reform Commission has proposed, should be defined in terms of the state of mind of the offender and his purpose. Unintentional killings should never be treated the same as intentional homicide. They would abolish the concept of constructive murder currently found in our code. This is based on the reckless causation of death in the pursuit of an unlawful object or in the commission of an offence.

The commissions, in their earlier work on sexual offenses, were influential in developing the assault provisions currently in the law. That legislation which was introduced in January 1981 was carried through Parliament in the Summer and Fall of 1982 as Bill C-127. It created parallel, three-tiered structures of assault and sexual assault.

In respect to sexual assault, the intent of the legislation was to place the emphasis on the violent nature of the offence rather than upon its sexual aspect. Limits were placed on the evidence that could be introduced and on the defence available to an accused. Those limits such as the limit on cross- examination of a complainant, the Shield Law, had been the object of successful Charter based challenges in recent months. Those are now under appeal. The Attorney General of Canada has intervened in support of his provincial counterparts to defend the legislation.

It remains to be seen what the outcome of those proceedings will be, but they highlight a new reality in criminal law policy development. In addition to the other factors which may influence a policy decision, each proposal must now be assessed in terms of its charter viability. Does it conform to the letter or to the spirit of the Charter guarantee? If it appears to be in contravention, does it constitute a reasonable limit within the meaning of Section 1 of the Charter? That would, no doubt, be a familiar concept to Americans but,it is something that in Canada is a departure from the previous principle of Parliamentary supremacy. Parliament could do what it chose in enacting the law. At present, we are constrained by the terms of the Charter, the court interpretations of the Charter and by our assessments of the direction that those interpretations will take in the future.

That is not to say that the government is shirking from proceeding with legislative initiatives which will likely be challenged under the Charter. It is expected that most of the proposals that come forward in the foreseeable future will indeed be challenged as the limits of the Charter are explored, as each opportunity is taken by defence counsel to find a basis under the Charter for a defence for his client.

The Minister of Justice introduced two new pieces of proposed legislation which will give rise to very significant Charter issues. The principle one deals with the limits of the guarantee of free expression in the Charter and what the effect is of Section 1 on that protection. That question will be the focus of much debate in the coming months, and no doubt it will be the subject of consideration by the courts if the legislation is adopted by Parliament.

For one who works within the system, there are other practical considerations. For example, with respect to the recent child abuse legislation, it had been the recommendation of the Badgley and Fraser Commissions that we restrict the defence of mistaken age when an individual is charged with a sexual act in relation to a minor. In view of a recent decision by the Supreme Court of Canada, we felt that we could not do that, that the Charter demanded that the defence of mistaken age be limited only insofar as the mistake was shown to be reasonable.

That is the form of the proposed legislation contained in the Bill. There are many of these small or minor points, but they influence each stage of the policy development process as we attempt to explain what options are available and what the considerations are which will bear on whether those options can be adopted.

There is belief that the proposals with respect to pornography will go some way in reducing the level of sexually violent materials circulating within our society. They go much further, but a significant aspect of that package of amendments is the treatment of physical harm and sexual violence.

Several initiatives sponsored by the Solicitor General have a direct relationship to the subject of violence and violent offenders. One is Bill C-67 which proposes a legislative version of the gating practice to allow correctional authorities to detain inmates who pose a high risk of recidivism beyond their remission release date. The Bill also proposes one shot mandatory supervision for an accused released on mandatory supervision who is revoked for cause. He will not get a second chance for release on mandatory.

Bill C-106, on the amendments to the Young Offenders Act, contains proposals for amendments which would allow a court ordered exemption from the Act's restriction of publication where there is reason to believe the young person is dangerous to others. Publication of a report is necessary to assist the police in apprehending the young person. The Act would also be amended to permit imposition of a consecutive disposition for an offence committed after the commencement of a previous disposition. That may result in a combined duration of disposition in excess of the three-year custodial limit otherwise applicable to young offenders.

Any comprehensive legislative attempt to respond more effectively to violence in Canadian society would have to consider sentencing practices, sentence administration and proposals developed by the sentencing project of the criminal law review introduced in Bill C-19 in 1984.

Those proposals included codification of sentencing principles, rationalization of existing sanctions, creation of new sanctions and procedures and revised provisions for dangerous offenders. They were met by a lack of consensus within the criminal justice community. Only some proposals were favored by certain sectors of that community. Changes proposed in Bill C-19 respecting dangerous offenders were intended to affect a fundamental realignment in the orientation of the current provisions and move away from the predication of future dangerousness.

There may be some question as to whether or not that is a harmful or improper practice regarding the violent and brutal nature of the offenses or the pattern of offenses that have been committed. A finding today that an offender is dangerous may result in an indeterminate term of imprisonment.

PART XIX

LIMITS TO TREATMENT

ETHICAL AND CHARTER CONSIDERATIONS

LIMITS TO TREATMENT: ETHICAL AND CHARTER CONSIDERATIONS

Ted Keyserlingk
Law Reform Commission

I will try very briefly to lay out what I think are some of the basic legal and ethical issues involved in the subject of treatment, particularly the limits of treatment. From the legal and largely from the ethical point of view, what particularly limits medical treatment whether it is physical or psychological in intent is the principle of autonomy of the individual person. This principle is now very much underlined in section 15 of the Charter of Rights and Freedoms. This is a principle which courts have always been eager to underline and protect.

From this comes the subsidiary principle of self-determination because individuals are held to be autonomous. It is therefore concluded that they have a right to determine their own fate up to a point. In law there is a difference in terms of forms of laws as to how that right is dealt with. That raises some interesting points that I would like to touch on briefly.

In common law, the law that applies in the provinces other than Quebec, the right tends to be much more absolute than it does in civil law. In common law, in terms of how courts have dealt with this right of autonomy, it tends to be fairly absolute in that the right to contradict the wishes of a person, patient or inmate is really not possible whenever that person is considered competent, understands what is involved, is not legally incompetent, is of age, and so forth. That person is able to say no to treatment even if that treatment will save his life. This has been raised in a number of cases where a person has a right to say no to treatment as long as he understands what is involved, and he is informed of the consequences of refusal. If he still maintains his stand, then he has that right which is a fairly well established right at this point.

Obviously, it is more complicated than that because it is incumbent upon the treaters to explain very carefully what is involved with saying no if it might lead to death and or to other non-beneficial results. It is basically an expression of that same principle of autonomy and self-determination in which the individual who is competent and who understands what is going on is assumed to know what is best for him or her.

Others who feel that is ridiculous are not held to be in the same position to be able to judge. A patient will often refuse what a professional feels is the very best form of treatment offered. The professional may have every reason to refute the patient's decision. Nevertheless, in law, that is a person's right.

In civil law, it is different in that you can interfere more readily with the person's decision on the grounds that the decision seems to be against that person's own autonomy and individualization. On the same grounds of protecting the person's autonomy, you can sometimes impose treatment.

In common law, we have qualifications for the right of self- determination. These are qualifications of the principle of autonomy where you can sometimes impose treatment.

In theory at least, there is a difference in that in civil law it is held very often that a patient who refuses treatment actually is putting himself or herself in great jeopardy, and that refusal is going to lead to problems in limiting the person's autonomy. It may be a form of treatment which is directed to helping the person become more autonomous, more able to cope, more able to understand, more able to make decisions about himself or herself.

It is very hard to come to that conclusion without being very cautious because one is tempted. It is tempting to override the refusal, even applying a kind of civil law rule. It is tempting to override the refusal and apply that kind of rule on the grounds that this is going to interfere with that person's capabilities, freedoms, ability to be autonomous and so forth. In fact, what we may be doing is simply imposing treatment in a form of paternalism.

What we deal with in a common law context is exceptions to the general rule that a person is always autonomous, always able to refuse. The exceptions are very limited and again are carefully applied. One of them is that the person is not competent, and that is a decision which in most cases is taken by the professionals treating that person. It has to be on good grounds because it is tempting once again to declare somebody incompetent simply because they are refusing to do what we, the professionals, think they ought to do. Nevertheless, it is possible. It can be declared in some cases by a court.

It is not as if one therefore just imposes treatment, but one goes through a fairly careful series of questions about who then can decide. This depends entirely on the context. Generally speaking, the family remains involved. It is certainly true for juvenile offenders now, and it is true in most cases that the family of anyone who is mentally incompetent makes the decisions for that person. If the family is not available or refuses on grounds that are judged to be frivolous or would put that person in jeopardy, then courts can become involved.

Just because a person is incompetent does not mean treatment decisions are foisted on him without a fair amount of care. There is a limitation on the ability to refuse treatment, a limitation on the limitation of treatment itself or on the provision of treatment.

Secondly, there are the situations where people left untreated will be dangerous to themselves or others. That is a favorite in any institutionalized context. We have to be aware that from the legal point of view, it is not something that is condoned without a fair amount of care.

Third, there are good grounds for thinking that the treatment, if applied and even if refused, is the only way to prove the condition of the person.

It is a tricky principle because sometimes we can easily extrude our own professional blinkers. Because that is the kind of treatment we provide and deal with under experts, obviously it is the one that is going to produce the best results. But nevertheless, as a principle, it is perfectly legitimate that in some cases we may conclude on the basis of careful consultation that the person, patient or inmate cannot be helped by any other form of treatment. There are usually fairly careful protections around this. It is not something that can happen just because I as a psychiatrist or psychologist decide that this is best. Consultation is involved. Sometimes we have to get permission from review boards. It depends entirely on the context and the particular statute which rules the context we are in.

The principle quality is the right to refuse treatment for the autonomy of persons. The person may be incapable of coping and needs treatment, and for this particular activity, a third party is entitled to provide the consent.

An important point to make about that is that it is now increasingly understood in law that the incompetence of a patient, the inability of a patient or an inmate to decide what is best for him, is not something that one can decide forever. The incompetence is something that must be verified on an ongoing basis, and it may apply to only one particular activity, a particular treatment. It may not apply to a lot of other things that that person was involved with. A lot of people are incompetent about some kinds of activities but not about all.

In the past, people were assumed to be incompetent about everything because they were determined to be that way for one kind of activity. Now we realize it just is not the case. It is much more complicated than that.

Incompetence is, in some cases, on and off. People are erratic. Hopefully the treatments that are offered or imposed by third parties are still decisions taken on behalf of that person. It is not an imposition, but it can be if it is improperly done. If it is properly done for the benefit of that person, then it is not an imposition even if a third party decides. We know now that one can be competent today, a little bit less so tomorrow, and obviously these are always going to be subjective judgments. The point is there has to be some sort of ongoing verification which is very important in terms of case decisions and so forth.

We can see how, if we look from the very basic general principles to, for instance, the provincial mental health acts which to some degree apply even in young offenders, one sees the variety of positions they take. Two provinces in the country actually have an explicit statement to the effect that the patient who falls within the terms of this act has a right to refuse, and those two provinces are Quebec and Nova Scotia. All other provinces either are more or less silent on it or imply in fact that there is no such right.

What will probably happen in the future because of the Charter of Rights and Freedoms with its strong statement in Section 15 about non-discrimination on the grounds of sex, age and mental ability to support is that all these statutes will have to be brought into line with an explicit statement that one has a right, if competent, to refuse treatment. One also has a right to accept it on the grounds that it discriminates against mental patients, inmates and others to put them in a totally different category.

On the other hand, the Young Offenders Act is quite explicit about the fact that the persons who fall within its jurisdiction fall within the protections and rights of the Charter of Rights. That is very clear in the preamble, to that particular Act, and it has been stated that they require further protections because of their particular needs and requirements as young people.

The Charter is moving towards revising all the various statutes which apply in terms of medical treatment. Referrals and the right to refuse will become much more explicit.

They all allow for the qualification that if the non-provision of treatment results in danger to a person, that becomes a justification. In each case, there are particular provisions established to verify that it is not a case of just a particular individual professional deciding. It is always a case of confirming this with others as well as perhaps going before a board. This would depend entirely on what the probation order or other conditions are that are leading to this kind of treatment. This is not to say that because these are the principles, we know exactly what we are going to do in every situation.

It is important as a first step to affirm that whatever the difficulties, the patient or inmate we are involved with gets the best treatment and is given due process, principles of autonomy, right to refuse and so forth. In many cases, that may be true. It may be more serious if we simply ignore these principles because we have to acknowledge one big factor here. We start with affirmation of principle, and then we attempt not to throw it all out and qualify it so that it does not apply anymore.

How can we now apply this principle if autonomy is the most important thing. Surely it is also important to treat in some cases for the benefit of that person, precisely to help that person's autonomy. Some of these provisions are precisely an affirmation of autonomy with the dangerous part of being that we can try and do that. We can do that with a kind of paternalism which is really not so much letting the autonomy rule but our professional instinctive desire to treat which may or may not always be totally justified.

LIMITS TO TREATMENT: ETHICAL AND CHARTER CONSIDERATIONS

Paul Gendreau
Ministry of Correctional Services, Ontario

Times have changed. There are new laws on the books and new ways of doing things and looking at things. People like myself who have a long term commitment to either being on the front line or being a bureaucrat service lawyer help us to recognize these sorts of new legislations.

A lot of my work has been involved lately in presenting treatment models and trying to bring along with that things that work with the population. Historically, in the United States, rights were enshrined, but also there was a belief that the State can do good. It can be said that all kinds of things do work, and we should be treating people and doing that sort of thing.

On one side of the far right you have the people who cheerfully believe in utilitarian deterrence. The use of capital punishment, incarceration and selective incapacitation is part of their platform. There are some who are a little soft on it. They are not too sure they are in favor of hanging. Many of them are economists, and they use a cost theory instead, and ask if the penalties are actually high enough. If the costs are high enough, then this rational approach to crime would mean that offenders will commit crimes at a much lesser rate because the costs of penalties will be high enough.

There are people on the left who believe in the big bang theory of revolution. They believe that things can change all of a sudden with the oppression no longer doing the oppressing or whatever.

We have these two perspectives coming from either end. They join up with the civil libertarian approach which has always been around arguing that much of the treatment is hypocrisy under a cloak of benevolence, and what we should do is again get out of the treatment business and make at least fair justice. That would be their issue. Nothing can be done except to make our justice system as fair as possible.

So what kind of policies do these three distant groups produce? They produce the kinds of policies that lead to some extent to our Young Offenders Act and most of the legislation in the United States. It leads to getting rid of the Juvenile Delinquents Act, leads to getting rid of the discretion in a lot of our lobbying, and it leads to policies such as restitution or victimization and the like.

It is important to see what is happening now, in this policy platform by people who argue the new liberal position. The new liberal policy is very similar to the utilitarian deterrence. This is a new philosophy that supplements the treatment philosophy based in part that nothing works and intervention is ineffective. This has been going on particularly in the United States for quite some time.

The Americans are the pioneers in this regard. They have abandoned the treatment model. They obviously have not gone for the Marxist revolution. In some places they are still keen on utilitarian deterrence, but they are keen on justice and fairness. And we must make sure that justice can always be equal.

In the last 10 years, despite the fact that juvenile crime has decreased and young people are fewer in number in the United States, the amount of incarceration in juvenile settings throughout the United States is increasing. It has increased in a number of areas. In detention centres, there has been a 100%- 200% increase in the amount of detentions spent by juveniles. Under the justice is fairness model, we are finding greater use of split sentence which is resembling something like the short, sharp shot, yet topical. All of a sudden this kind of policy has been much more important in the United States. Juveniles are also getting a little taste of prison presumably to make them straighten up and fly right. That is a fascinating policy because what is happening is that there seems to be some racial discrepancies in that Blacks and Hispanics seem to be getting a greater proportion of some of the split sentencing approach than Caucasians.

Another fascinating phenomenon is that under the split sentencing approach, it is quite likely that some low risk offenders are being placed in prisons housing hardened people. If they are left there long enough, one runs the risk of putting these lower risk people in jeopardy by this kind of sentencing policy. When you take low-risk people and leave them in an institution for a period of time, you have doubled to tripled the recidivism rates of low-risk people who are left in the community in a halfway house or in some other kind of vehicle.

Under the justice is fairness approach, one of the main platforms is ridding the discrepancies of inequalities from the system. Yet when you look at the state of juvenile corrections in the United States, you find still deplorable conditions across various jurisdictions. You find discrepancies and idiosyncracies across various states.

The same old inequalities from the states system where there is too much discretion still exists under the new justice is fairness approach where much is determined. There are still inequalities in how sentencing models work in rural areas. There is far less plea bargaining and larger sentences in urban areas and far more plea bargaining and fewer sentences in rural areas. Since the justice is fairness model has been put into effect, there has been an increase in incarceration. Discrepancies in the system still exist and there has been no better improvement.

There is one study since determinate sentencing has been put into effect in a couple of jurisdictions which asks offenders what they think about the certainty of knowing how they are going to be disposed of by the State. Long-term they do not care. They do not mind the system because it does not really matter if they are out after one year or 10 months.

There is a differential response from those who are incarcerated for long periods of time. The ones who are incarcerated for long periods of time do not like the idea that parole was thrown out. They do not like the opportunity to change their status. So there is that bit of evidence.

The argument proposed is that we in Canada are going to do things better. The kinds of things we are seeing in the United States will not apply in Canada. We can think of a host of things in the social service areas where we in Canada have been so far theoretically, conceptually and technologically advanced. The Americans think we have done a better job than they have when it comes to dealing with social problems.

The initial results, not surprisingly, are fairly similar to what has been occurring in the United States. The use of incarceration has increased under our Young Offenders Act (YOA). The amount of use of security detentions has doubled without the treatment dispositions in Ontario.

For a year prior to the YOA, there were several hundred treatment dispositions for getting help for young offenders. The year afterwards there were seven. Even for young offenders coming out of the court, delays in cases are up to several months. With this time lapse, a young offender could eventually forget the whole purpose of whatever he was up for. It is a very costly procedure.

If you want to take a strong decision on civil liberties and rights in due process, you can try to combine legislation and needs legislation. What usually happens is that the need aspects get left behind.

This kind of thrust towards criminal justice policy is exceptionally naive when it comes to dealing with rights. Not once in the last 10 years according to Lynn Goodstein and others in the United States, has there been a mood to reduce sentencing severity. What legislator in his right mind, given the United States crime rate these days, is going to reduce the penalty for a crime. If there is an option, penalities will likely be increased.

It is incredibly naive of the liberals who want to give up their traditional groups to get into bed with the conservatives and somehow think they can exist in a kind of play. In this kind of position, I believe there is no middle ground in this very different political and social-political balance.

Strangely enough, we have the right to give punishments, but we send them off to institutions increasing the likelihood of possible recidivism particularly with low-risk offenders. But in many ways we do not have equal access to the right to treatment. We can see the sort of twisted logic that you can get into. Somehow punishment works, and treatment does not.

We are confused. The issue is that under our new fairness protection, under due process, we have increased the use of incarceration and imprisonment throughout. It is almost as if you have a greater right to be incarcerated than to be given treatment services. I am not too sure what constructive action can be taken except to be very aware of some of these problems.

We are now finding more disturbed people in our institutions, and there are virtually no services for them. For example, if you take one of our most popular penitentiaries in Canada, one that is supposed to be treatment-oriented, it is estimated that if two psychologists were to spend every waking hour treating their clients, every client in that prison would get 2 1/2 hours of counselling per year. The interesting phenomenon is that we are, with our rights-oriented legislation to mental health, presumably putting more mentally disturbed people into our penal institutions. Some of society's cripples are not going to be getting the services in our penal institutions.

The other area to note is retardation. This is an area where rights are going to be defined much more closely under guardianship acts in the near future. All too often in criminal justice we have a lot of blinkers on. Often we steadfastly refuse to look outside and see what is happening in the other world.

But we are going through some interesting precedents. The new legislation is good. It is making treatment professionals more aware of what they should be doing and making them more careful. If they are going to be intrusive, they have to think it out much more carefully.

We have freedom of movement and freedom of association now under the Charter. The people in retardation centres are mobile. They can get around, and they can do various sorts of things and be constructive. Some retarded people, IQs 15, 20, 25, can verbalize that they do not want to stay. They are not declared incompetent. Treatment people are worried about their discretion, and if a retarded person decides he wants to leave, theoretically he can.

Where would he go? What would he do? There are other kinds of interesting phenomena in the retardation area. If a staff member assaults a retarded person, who is not declared legally incompetent, the staff member can be dealt with by the judicial process. If two retarded people attack each other and inflict injury, it does not go to the judicial process. It is handled internally. With the third scenario, if a retarded person assaults a staff member, the courts can deal with it.

There is also freedom of association in any retardation centre. There are occasional clients who are very, very dangerous, far more dangerous than anybody in many prisons. There are sexual assaults, and yet they are not declared incompetent. They have their rights to association, and theoretically you have this bizarre world where they assault each other, and you prevent them from freedom of movement in the institution. You would be depriving them of their rights. You can get into the issue of a sterilization of all sorts.

There are going to be some interesting future scenarios in another area which may be different from corrections but which will bring about problems that are similar to what we are facing. The kind of results that will occur in retardation are entirely different from the ones we had in corrections. It is an issue of balance, and I think the balance has gone too far.

On the other hand, I quite well agree that in days gone by, treatment professionals were far too cavalier in some of the things they did, and we have many examples of some real abuses. They hit the press and we are made aware of them on occasion.

PART XX

PERCEPTIONS OF VIOLENCE

PERCEPTIONS OF VIOLENCE

Vincent Sacco
Queen's University

My research has shown two trends in professional literature over the last several years. One is the growing emphasis that has been placed throughout the 1970s and 1980s by feminist scholars on the study of the victimization of women. There has also been a trend, since the mid-60s, which relates to the public fear of crime. As a result of both of these influences, it has become increasingly apparent that the threat of sexual victimization impairs the quality of women's lives. Their ability to participate in community life and to avail themselves of social and economic opportunities is severely curtailed.

Seen in that way, fear of victimization is a form of social control. This point has been discussed eloquently by a number of feminist writers.

We in Canada pride ourselves on the relatively low degree of violence in this country as compared to the United States. What is less clear is whether or not that lower rate of violence translates itself into increased feelings of security on the part of Canadian women.

While the fear of crime appears to be a problem that affects the public, the truth is that fear of crime is not uniformly borne by the general public. It is borne disproportionately by the members of only some social groups. The single factor that most clearly and consistently discriminates between those who are and those who are not concerned about their personal safety is gender.

Victimization data indicate that men have the highest rate of all forms of victimization, with the exception of sexual offenses. Sexism perhaps wrongfully suggests that women are too irrational or hysterical to be in such situations.

It has been suggested that exposure of the male genitals or flashing may promote fear of injury to a woman because of her uncertainty about what may happen next. Murder, rape, serious beating or sexual assault may be feared outcomes. Although women have fewer rapes, they encounter more often routine situations which potentially threaten their safety. This paradox is undermined by research into sexual socialization which indicates that much of the female socialization process exclusively emphasizes sexual vulnerability.

Research on sexual vulnerability suggests that this kind of anxiety is not uniformly distributed across gender groups. It varies with the number of social, demographic and residential characteristics of respondents. Concern about sexual assault has been shown to be related to being younger, a lower sense of mastery over the environment, a sense of attachment to local communities, perception of oneself as physically capable. But actual rape does not necessarily coordinate with average levels of fear in the same area.

Certain precautions are taken to provide protection from victimization. These behaviors include lifestyle precautions such as avoidance, isolation, the restriction of activity and, to a lesser degree, target-hardening techniques such as purchasing deadbolt locks.

The Vancouver urban survey was conducted from October to December 1983. It focused on street crime. The sample yielded 489 completed interviews, and 280 were female respondents. They were asked about their level of worry and to estimate the risk of that event happening to them the following year. We asked them to indicate their perception of the severity of that particular kind of victimization if it were to happen to them. All used 11-point scales. We included other offenses such as the use of a weapon to take something by force, break-and-enter while at home, being cheated out of a large amount of money and having one's unattended coat stolen.

The mean worry level for each of those offenses showed that the sample sexual assault had the highest mean level. Thirty-eight per cent of the respondents scored above the mid-point on that scale. Ten per cent of them had a score of 10, indicating that it was for them a constant and chronic concern. Sexual assault was also viewed by respondents as the most serious. The subjective risk of it happening again was somewhere in the mid- range.

The second thing we did was to take those measures of seriousness and those measures of risk and cross-tabulate them in order to see the level of worry risk. People who perceive low seriousness and low risk are worried. What that reveals is that both risk and seriousness assert an independent influence on level of worry. People who see sexual assault as being a relatively non-serious, relatively low-risk defence, have a level of worry of 1.71. Forty-six per cent of the respondents indicated that they perceived sexual assault as a relatively high-risk, relatively serious offence. That is startling in a sense that such a large percentage of respondents believe that they are likely to be victims of serious victimization.

Another thing we did in the analysis was to attempt to investigate the degree to which worry about sexual assault correlated with worry about other things. Victimizations do not subjectively represent themselves to people as separate and discreet incidents. Fears can be related. Looking at the relationship between worry about sexual assault and worry about other kinds of offenses, we found that there was a pretty high correlation between the two. Worrying about a break-in at home, for many women, carries the additional burden of worry of being sexually assaulted.

Studying distribution of sexual assault, we looked at a whole range of variables which we broke up into three major groups. We looked at social demographic variables, residential characteristics and finally social/psychological characteristics. The strongest demographic predictor was age, and it indicated that there was a greater worry among younger women. We found a weak relationship with a higher income might encourage greater worry. There was also a weak relationship with homemakers status. Worry was higher for people who did not perceive themselves as homemakers.

We looked at measures of attachment to the local neighborhood. We looked at their perceptions of increase in local crime. The only set of residential variables that persisted were the signs of instability. We asked people to indicate how much of a problem different kinds of conditions such as misbehaving juveniles, loitering, noise and decaying buildings were. All of those things proved to be moderately related.

While in Canada we pride ourselves on lower rates of violent conduct, it is apparent that these differentials are reflected in increased feelings of safety among Canadian women. This is in part because the concern about sexual assault is not in any direct way a product of the rates of legally defined crime. Indeed some American research shows that women's fears do not relate to variations in recorded levels of violent crime. The present data even indicates that perceptions of increases in local crime cease to be relevant as predictors of worry once other things are taken into account. It is also no doubt true that worry about sexual assault is deeply rooted in the dynamics of gender relations and in sexually coercive behavior.

The petty rapes to which many women are routinely subjected have uncertain outcomes and are thus worrisome. Women's encounters with loitering youth and public drunks frequently involve rituals of status degradation by which women experience their vulnerability. Chance is a powerful determinant of social outcome.

The findings of this research also seem to reveal several significant consequences that flow from worry about sexual assault to feelings of trust and to the adoption of various kinds of lifestyle precautions. Locking doors, avoiding teenagers in the streets and carrying objects for protection are among the routine strategies that many women employ in response to these anxieties.

The data also indicates that worry about sexual assault does not lead women to adopt the law and order or crime control posture. These worries find expression in personalized limitations of activity and movement. Ironically, while many respond to worry by adjusting their lifestyles accordingly, it is by no means clear that such actions make them safer. Data from the Canadian urban victimization study revealed that 41% of all sexual assaults involved known assailants. A significant number of such victimizations occurred in the home of the victim or of the friend or acquaintance.

The behavior which restricts interaction with strangers clearly imposes a cost with uncertain benefits. The preliminary nature of the investigation and the work undertaken by others suggest a need for a sustained research effort. We know too little of the social/psychological dynamics of sexual vulnerability.

The legal system has not traditionally defined threats to women's safety in the same way as women themselves. The vast literature on rape vividly illustrates this. The tendency to regard women's safety as a narrowly defined criminal justice problem deflects attention away from its broader structural and cultural dimensions. Effective steps have been taken by women's groups to provide accurate information about the risk of sexual assault and its psychological effects.

PERCEPTIONS OF VIOLENCE

Ehor Boyanowsky
Simon Fraser University

The mass media identifies events which are by their nature intense, exciting, arousing or extreme on prominent issues. These are phenomena which easily attack and hold our attention and which can be presented in a form easily interpreted by the average reader or viewer. They are out to get our attention and sell. That is the intention of headlines. Unfortunately, many of us stop at the headline of a newspaper. Originally, there were no newspapers. There were these moral and socialization lessons necessary for society. What did societies do? They had initiation rights which were, in those days, much more important than they are now because we have newspapers and lobbying, government and law reform commissions to deal with things.

There are all kinds of headlines I have collected over the years. One of my favorites is ANIMAL SET MAN ON FIRE. This is not dog bites man story. It was the story of a delinquent gang which poured lighter fluid on one of the kids they were having an altercation with and rode around him with bicycles while his clothes were burning. There was no concern about these delinquent gangs in the city until this particular headline made the streets. Similarly, the violent 30 second television clip attracts the viewers attention and holds him or her captive for the period it takes to view the clip and leaves a sharp memory of the event. Researchers of mass media claim that violence may not be so prevalent in the mass media, but such items remain indelibly embedded in our memory.

How violent are newspapers today? In 1922, Lipton reported that pre World War I papers devoted approximately 6% of column space to crime and violence. By the 1960s this increased about 25% in some of the tabloids in New York City. It was not commensurate with increases in crime rates but with newspaper competition. The competition with other newspapers sent the content of crime way up. If the competition dropped, the content went down. In a 1985 study of a Scottish newspaper, they found the violent content was up 10% which is overrepresented in terms of violence. It is not necessarily overrepresented in the kinds of news that is available. Nevertheless, the point here is that those are the kinds of things we remember. We remember them, and then we are motivated to respond to them. We feel we are vulnerable at that point to a conversion in terms of our ideas, mobilizing our efforts or focusing our efforts in one particular direction or another.

There is less violence in television reporting than in newspaper reporting. It is very graphic, and that is the difference. In fact, it has been raised that if the violence that was reported during the Vietnam War on television had also been made available to the public during World War I, the war would not have gone on for as long. We all keep with us a few graphic images. These graphic demonstrations of violence were things that motivated American people to realize that their identity and self-image were not congruent with what was going on in the Vietnam War. It started to produce some sympathy for the whole cause.

The point I am making here is that television communicates to us things that, because of their immediacy and graphic effects, disturb us and motivate us to action. If they were sterile, we may be willing to put up with these things.

In the mobilization against other ills such as crime, pornography or child abuse, there have been graphic images used not the representative images. The Fraser Commission, when they did an analysis of the degree of violence of pornographic video tapes versus the degree of violence in tapes, found that the amount of violence in sexually explicit tapes was negligible. It went anywhere from 40% to 50% of the images portrayed in ordinary fare. Yet the mobilization of efforts in this particular crusade was against sexually violent material. What we have ended up with, as I predicted, is an absolute ban because the definitions are so difficult otherwise.

If you create the fear, you mobilize the effort. This is true of murder. There is a mobilization in the cry for executions now with the rise in murders. This is a mobilization of effort for people to deal with their anxieties about certain events. The fear is that we may have a misplaced emphasis whereas the actual degree of concern or gravity of this problem is minimal compared to other problems. They are not sexy issues. It is very hard to mobilize an effort.

Hans Mohr asks audiences to describe a typical murder. He finds they describe a television murder. The single most common murder occurs among acquaintances in a kitchen or bedroom. The main problem lies not so much in the degree of reporting but in the type of coverage whether it is conservative, factual or sensational and whether there is different coverage of certain types of violent crimes which create distortion. If you just characterize the murder, event or action as being associated with certain kinds of individuals or certain kinds of content, then we will respond and try to eliminate that problem in the easiest way. We do not want complex explanations. We want simple solutions. We want things that will reduce our anxieties. For example, witness the common report that an individual was raped or murdered by an ex-mental patient or convict, suggesting that this is a very common event. An outcry goes out about mandatory supervision, about parole, etc. By contrast, when is the last time you remember reading that Ms. Jones, an ex-mental patient, was recently elected president of the Ambleside Curling Club? I know juvenile delinquents who were elected to bank directorships. They do not like to have themselves characterized this way when they achieve success.

We do not have this balancing kind of image about what happens even if it is extraordinary. No one likes to categorize himself as an ex-mental patient. As far as we are concerned, once a mental patient, always a mental patient. I think this is the problem that works its way into our perceptions of the characterizations of certain classes of individuals and their inability to play certain roles in our society. In smaller communities, you have two ways of dealing with deviants. Number one, they are characterized that way, the village idiot. Instead of sending them off to a psychiatrist, there is a natural public conversion experience. What happens is that when people have reached the level of community standards of tolerance, instead of kicking you out, they grab you. They haul you into a smokehouse. They crank up the heat in the smokehouse to about 140 degrees to 200 degrees, and they keep you in there until you break down. Some of them break down. This is when it comes to the attention of authorities. In the interim, what happens is that there is a breakdown of the individual's resistance to accepting the fact that he has a problem. Finally he admits he does. He starts experiencing hallucinations.

When you get the right image of a positive role model and role identity, then the community comes together and hauls you out of the smokehouse, cleans you up, hoses you down, washes you, feeds you, cheers you up. They then give you a new prescription for your new role and identity which is commensurate with proper living and support within the community. This has been vastly discouraged by the authorities for the last 100 years. The cure is usually worse than the disease when you get people who are out of shape, overweight, suffering from the ravages of alcohol. But the mortality of subjects notwithstanding, the success rate is very high because it does involve everyone.

The point I am making here is that where you have this kind of closed community, people have to cope with people's past ideas, and they have to change that identity. You have to work together. I suppose the John Howard Society could adopt some of these procedures. Because they are only one element in a very complex society, they are restricted in the repertoire they can use. Grave in its implications for any society is the fact that the media can serve as a tool for terrorists as well. There are positive and negative effects to this phenomenon. It is claimed that it would not have been possible without the presence of the media to raise common murders or kidnappers to an equal bargaining position with the prime minister of the country.

The media does not tend to cover peaceful demonstrations. For example, a Texas television crew revealed that it packed up its equipment and went home when a demonstration turned out not to be as violent as predicted. So we do not get the reporting of peaceful demonstrations. We get reporting of violent demonstrations. This is much more exciting. By the same token, it has been reported how the media has fueled feminist causes to make the justice system more sensitive to women's issues. When you have a minority trying to communicate, television is a good medium in the sense that if you are vocal enough or you are dramatic enough to meet the criteria, you will get coverage.

Concentrating on a small part of a city where riots or demonstrations occur can make it seem to those who are relying entirely on television for their conception of reality that such conditions are universal.

The 1980s has shown that the people who respond and who experience the most fear of crime are not necessarily those who are living in the high crime rate areas or who have been personally victimized. It is those who have had their experience of crime mediated either by television, by a personal acquaintance or by a relative who experienced the most fear. Those who have been personally victimized experience a reduction in anxiety and fear of crime when watching crime programs on television. The reason is because our actual victimization is very different from what happens on television. It does produce in these individuals a great deal of agitation, but it does not enhance fear. This phenomenon also changes the threshold of tolerance.

PUNITIVENESS, FEAR OF CRIME AND PERCEPTIONS OF VIOLENCE

T.C. Caputo & Richard A Wanner
University of Calgary

In this paper we attempt to develop a multivariate model explaining attitudes of punitiveness among a random sample of adults in Calgary. We discovered that the only factor that has a substantial effect on the degree of punitiveness expressed by our respondents is the nature of the crime, i.e. whether it is violent or not. From a policy point of view, the issue that should be raised is the distinction between violent and non- violent crime. Since violent crime represents such a small proportion of all crime, this may give us cause to re-examine our policy on sentencing those convicted of non-violent crimes. Our findings further suggest that those individuals with accurate information about the occurance of violent crime were significantly less fearful. As well, those with accurate information tend to favor less severe sentences for the convicted. Our respondents attributed a far higher level of harm to acts of violence, suggesting that their reactive attitudes of punitiveness are rooted in their perception that violent crimes are far more serious than property crimes. Consistent with this is our finding that respondents were considerably more likely to support alternative release programs for property offenders than they were for violent offenders.

The public's perception of crime and the operation of the criminal justice system have been the subject of a great deal of recent research in Canada. The results of this research are important for the potential impact which they can have on public policy and legislation in this area as well as on the behavior of ordinary citizens. Fear of crime, and in particular of violent crime, have been thought to lead to more punitive attitudes among the public. An assessment of this relationship, however, has not been entirely straightforward, as many studies in this area have uncovered a number of anomalies concerning people's perceptions of crime and related attitudes and behaviors.

To begin with, a large number of Canadians identify crime as a serious problem. A recent national victimization survey showed that 81 percent of the respondents believed that crime had increased in their cities during the two years prior to the survey. Yet the type of concern with crime expressed in these surveys and the public's perception that crime is increasing does not appear to be filtering down into people's everyday lives. Thus, while 80 percent of the respondents in the national victim survey believed that crime had increased, only 33 percent felt that it had increased in their own neighborhood. In fact, 80 percent of those who participated in this study felt that their neighborhoods had a low or average amount of crime. Similar results have been reported in a number of studies which found that perceptions of crime are affected by a variety of social, psychological and environmental factors.

A further paradox involves the apparent incongruity between fear of crime and victimization rates. In this case, women and the elderly are consistently found to have higher levels of fear while experiencing lower levels of victimization. In addition, the experience of being a victim does not appear to have an effect on fear of crime.

To some extent, these inconsistencies reflect the type of information that people have about crime and the workings of the criminal justice system. Doob and Roberts, for example, found that in Toronto the public grossly overestimated the amount of crime which involves violence. Wright argues that this lack of accurate information has an important impact both on the formulation of policy in this area and its acceptance by the public.

A similar type of contradiction exists in people's attitudes towards sentencing. A number of studies have documented public support for severe sentences and criticisms for leniency by the courts. However, Bertrand argues that while there is ample evidence that the Canadian public is desirous of more severe sentences, people are less punitive when given information about specific cases. This is consistent with Chandler's study of capital punishment as well as Boydell and Grindstaff's work on sentencing.

This raises a number of serious questions concerning the relationship between perceptions and fear of crime and public support for various policy measures. The nature and extent of punitive attitudes among the public is of prime concern in this context if these make a policy of 'getting tougher' more attractive to politicians. With these concerns in mind, this paper presents an attempt to develop a model explaining attitudes of punitiveness using data from a survey conducted in Calgary in 1985. In developing this model, we were particularly interested in how fear of crime, knowledge of the prevalence of violent crime in Canada and victimization are translated into punitiveness, defined as willingness to support a prison sentence for various categories of offenders. We were also concerned about the degree to which levels of punitiveness are related to several demographic variables, specifically age, sex, educational attainment and occupational status. In the next section we describe the data and measures of the concepts used in building the model, as well as our specific hypotheses based on the existing literature.

The research reported here is based on a telephone survey conducted in the city of Calgary during the period March 11 to March 25, 1985 in which a total of 498 interviews were completed. The sample was drawn by means of a random digit dialing procedure that permits weighing of the sample by the number of telephone numbers in each city exchange, since it is unreasonable to assume that each exchange is of equal size. This entailed drawing a simple random sample of residential numbers from the most recent Calgary directory using a table of random numbers, and recording the first four digits only. The remaining three digits were added by means of a random number generator programme on the computer. This procedure has the advantage of being not only self weighing, but it permits the inclusion of unlisted numbers by randomly generating the last three digits. While not all commercial phone numbers were excluded, by selecting only residential numbers in the initial sampling they were kept to a minimum.

For purposes of this paper, the focus of interest is on two endogenous variables, fear of crime and attitude of punitiveness. In the model to be described both are measured by means of four indicators. These indicators were identified by means of a preliminary exploratory factor analysis which screened a large number of items to determine which were most highly correlated with these dimensions. The items selected provide scales of these constructs with relatively high reliability levels.

The exogenous (causal) variables used to predict both fear of crime and punitiveness are listed. The three variables we concentrate our attention on are knowledge of violent crime, and whether or not the respondent has been a victim of crime and whether or not respondents' friends or relatives have been victims of crime. The first is response to an item which asked, "In your opinion, what percentage of crimes committed in Canada involve violence — for example, where the victim was beaten up, raped, robbed at gunpoint, and so on?" We attempted to construct a multi-item scale of "knowledge of crime," in the manner of the scales of fear and punitiveness. Unfortunately, our effort failed in this case, suggesting to us that the level of knowledge of the workings of the criminal justice system in Canada is itself shockingly low. Nevertheless, we felt that respondents with correct information on the small proportion of all crimes in Canada that involve violence would likely be less fearful of crime in general and less likely to express attitudes of punativeness toward offenders.

As for the victimization measures, we simply asked if the respondent had been a victim of any crime in the past year and if any relatives or close friends of the respondent had been victims in the same time period. We hypothesized that not only should victims and friends or relatives of victims express greater fear of crime, but they should also be more punitive toward offenders.

Several demographic variables found in other research to be related to both fear and punitiveness are included in our models predicting these variables. Sex has been repeatedly shown to have a strong influence on fear of crime, with females exhibiting higher fear levels. Age has also been shown to influence fear level, although preliminary analysis of our data indicates that this relationship is not the direct one usually assumed to be present. We found evidence that fear level is high among the youngest respondents, declines in middle age, recovering to a higher level again among the elderly. We therefore include in our model not only age in years, but also the square of age to capture this parabolic relationship. We anticipate that age will also influence punitiveness, with older respondents exhibiting more punitive attitudes.

As for the remaining variables, education is measured as years of schooling completed, and occupational status is measured by means of the Blishen-McRoberts Revised Socioeconomic Index for Occupations in Canada. As well, fear of crime is included in the model predicting punitiveness.

By far the largest effects on fear of crime are associated with age and sex. As expected, women are more likely to express fear than men. In the case of age, however, we find that, as our preliminary analysis suggested, fear first declines with age and then increases, indicated by the negative slope associated with the age variable and the positive slope associated with age squared. As we hypothesized, knowledge of the prevalence of violent crime in Canadian society is negatively related to fear. As expected, having had a friend or relative who has been a victim of crime increases fear level to a statistically significant extent, although being a victim oneself does not have a significant effect.

Our major interest in this paper, however, is in the punitiveness equation. As we indicated, only a small portion of the variance in punitiveness is explained by the model. Nevertheless, both knowledge of violent crime and having had a friend or relative who has been a victim significantly affect the level of punitiveness. No other variable in the model influences this variable. In the case of knowledge of violence, more accurate knowledge tends to reduce punitiveness; knowing a victim tends to increase punitiveness. In neither case is the effect a powerful one. Although we hypothesized that fear of crime should have a positive effect on punitiveness, the estimate indicates no such thing.

The analysis so far leaves us in a quandary; fear of crime appears to be a systematic phenomenon accounted for quite well by the variables in our model.

The main message of our findings is that Canadians are quite inflexible in their condemnation of violent acts and overwhelmingly favor prison terms for those who perpetrate them. This unwillingness does not vary to any considerable extent by age, sex, or socioeconomic status. While a knowledge of the prevalence of violent crime in the country softens this attitude somewhat, it is unlikely that a public information campaign will go a long way toward altering public attitudes toward violent offenders. That is the pessimistic message of our research. On the optimistic side, our respondents were considerably less likely to call for a prison sentence for a nonviolent offender. Indeed, they expressed very strong support for alternative release programs for such offenders. While fear of crime is strongly related to knowledge of the prevalence of violence in our data, suggesting that informing the public on this matter might well reduce the general level of fearfulness, there is no evidence that a less fearful public will be any less likely to advocate prison sentences for violent offenders.

PART XXI

EMERGING TRENDS

EMERGING TRENDS IN CORRECTIONS

Robert Levinson
American Correctional Association

There are many theories about the causes of violence. This suggests that the pursuit of valid, positive factors may be of a long duration which presents no difficultly if you are a research or academic type. Actually it may lead to a protracted career in making talks and lectures. However, instead of being employed in academia, you work in an environment into which society extrudes its violent offenders. Logic would suggest that until valid theories of causation are demonstrated, there is little that one can do to prevent or treat individuals who engage in violent behavior. Despite the rationality of such a formulation, correctional workers cannot wait for our academic friends to tell us what to do. On a daily basis, prison staffs are required to manage populations containing a large percentage of violent offenders.

Violent crime has been defined to include such things as homicide, robbery, assault, arson, residential burglary, child abuse and molestation, sexual assault, kidnapping and all felonies involving narcotic trafficking. Individuals convicted of committing these crimes are deemed to be violent offenders.

Other categories of prisoners can be added to this litany. For example, there are inmates who initiate or engage in riots, who attack or murder staff, who intimidate and/or physically or sexually assault other inmates, who attempt to commit suicide and so forth. At least part of the difficulty in coming to grips with how to best manage a population of violent inmates stems from the fact that we do not clearly identify which group we are talking about.

Will the operational definition of violence be limited to acts inflicted on others, or will it also include those directed against oneself? Will threats or only accomplished deeds be included? Some contend that even precise definitions will not help. They cite our extensive literature and conclude that dangerousness or violence cannot be predicted. However, a recent monograph by John Monaghan indicates that the literature in this area leaves much to be desired.

A wholesale dismissal of the concept of being able to predict violence may be premature. In addition to this definitional issue, a number of other elements contribute to the problem. As the American Psychiatric Association notes, dangerousness is an attribute not only of persons but of situations and of environmental factors. More correctly then, dangerousness should be regarded as an outcome of the interaction of these facts. This interactive complexity has led too many to conclude that there is a .40 sound barrier for predictive accuracy in this area.

If this is correct, it means we cannot even hope to identify the majority of violent individuals. While some cite explanatory reasons such as low base rates, many other commentators delight in pointing out that clinicians are even more likely to be wrong than right when predicting when a particular individual will be violent.

Nevertheless, there is some good news. Another line of inquiry has produced encouraging results using an actuarial approach to the development of prediction categories. It then becomes possible to assign individuals to groups which have different varying likelihoods of committing violent acts. Consider two particular categories. The first consists of individuals who are most likely to be violent while the second consists of those least likely. In the first category, approximately 80% will be violent. Approximately 90% of the second group will be non- violent.

Valid criteria can be developed which will enable a given individual to be assigned to one or the other group with a high degree of reliability. We can replace the less accurate prediction for individuals with the more accurate prediction for groups. This approach has some important implications with a management of violent inmates. The causes of institutional violence are as difficult to explain as the causes of crime.

Among contributing factors are overcrowding, inmate idleness, institution size and age, level of security of inmate population, education and training levels of staff and the extent of warden/inmate intervention. Recreation facilities, extensive opportunistic uses of administrative and punitive segregation and lack of an effective inmate grievance procedure are also included. If the causes of prison violence are difficult to explicate, so too are the remedies.

"Keep the lid on" has been the time-honored strategy or repression which usually reproduces a resumption of order and quiet at a very shallow level. It is viewed as a stop gap measure which often contributes to the vicious cycle of repression, protest against repression and increased repression.

So what can be done? One illusion was described in the March 1986 issue of Core Health, a newsletter published by the American Correctional Health Services Association. It reprinted an Associated Press news item from San Jose, California. "The hollering, handcuffed man kicked arresting officers as they led him into the pink room. They tossed him in with knowing smiles that his screams would subside. Within minutes, the prisoner turned to calm; he had been pinked."

Rather than color, I recommend classification. We can better manage our prisons and the violent individuals they contain through more effective objectives. Classification systems like system classification is something that everyone knows about, and that some even practice with idiosyncratic flare. Objective classification is not a revolutionary idea. A variety of approaches exist.

Increasing numbers of states and local departments in the United States are implementing this approach. What is failing on the correction horizon is an objective classification program which combines both unit management and internal classification. Unit management restructures the administrative organization of correction institutions by subdividing a single prison into semi-autonomous units.

Under this arrangement, the inmate population is sorted into smaller, more manageable groups. Prisoners assigned to each housing area become the caseload of a more permanently assigned staff. These line and professional personnel whose offices are located on the living unit have specified decision-making authority. As a consequence, prisoners have greater access to significant correctional staff. Better relationships develop, and control is more easily maintained. This proximity which leads to better coordinated staff efforts also reduces the possibilities for inmates to manipulate one staff against another.

A more recent refinement of unit management is the adult internal management system (AIMS). It has been developed over the past 25 years by Professor Herbert Quay of the University of Miami and is an example of an internal management classification system. It holds that all prisoners are not alike. Based on an empirical factor and an analytical approach, five dimensions have been identified along with several different name types.

Just as it makes managerial sense for correctional systems to designate incoming prisoners to maximum, medium and minimum security institutions, the same logic applies. Within a single institution, using AIMS, prisoners can be grouped into three basic categories of aggressiveness, heavies, violent prone and manipulative predators. The lights are anxious, inadequate, victim-prone individuals; the moderates, reliable, hard-working inmates.

By housing these prisoner types in separate living units, a series of benefits accrue. It becomes possible to more appropriately and differentially allocate available resources. AIMS offers specific guidelines regarding both inmate program assignments and treatment strategies AIMS also offers management recommendations regarding which matches between staff and prisoners will be most effective. As a consequence of employing this system, institutions experience a reduction in the number and seriousness of management problems.

For example, some time ago at the United States penitentiary in Louisburg, Pennsylvania, there was an inmate vs. inmate murder once a month. Implementing a modification of the AIMS approach resulted in a 13-month span without a homicide. In South Carolina's Central Prison, AIMS reduced a ratc of serious incidents by 18%. This led to its adoption on a statewide basis.

Using another approach with a similar intent, an institution for young adults in Tallahasee, Florida reported after one year a 46% decrease in assaults. After two years, the total number of incident reports had dropped 16%, and referrals to disciplinary committees decreased 22%.

These examples illustrate the fact that both inmates and staff benefit from a safer and more human climate of confinement. Such an environment results from the implementation of this suggested management strategy.

In conclusion, the problem of violence in correctional institutions can be approached on three levels, focusing on the inmates, modifying environmental conditions which foster violence and implementing more effective administrative policies and management procedures.

The major treatment goal with violent persons is to help the individual deal more effectively with anger. For example, they learn that it is okay to accept help, that feelings can be expressed verbally rather than physically, and that there are more efficient coping techniques.

Environmental modification which helps reduce violence consists of such things as placing cubicles in dormitories and making changes which reduce noise levels and/or increase privacy and safety. These tend to lessen levels of contention, and all of them help decrease the frequency of violence.

Changing the ways in which institutions are organized and managed can dramatically reduce violence by, for example, using such things as an objective external and internal classification system.

One of the main problems is with overcrowding, and I know of no method of reducing this other than raising our standards for admission. It has been noted that corrections is the only institution that cannot say no. We let everybody in.

While corrections cannot control its admissions, crowding can be better managed. For example, the system can choose which level of security will be most overcrowded. In other words, let us not overcrowd the maximum institutions. We know how to better manage violent behavior. What is required is the will to use what we know.

EMERGING TRENDS IN LAW ENFORCEMENT/POLICING

Alan Grant
Osgoode Hall

Of the many topics on law enforcement and balance that I could concentrate on, I have chosen just two. First, I plan to discuss the effects of having made the prevention and detection of violence a political priority in law enforcement. Second, I will discuss the use of modern technology to improve police investigation of violent crime and to reduce and perhaps eliminate police violence in investigating crime.

I have argued that when we talk about resource allocation and law enforcement, we often think about police chiefs and others making decisions on where to send policemen and policewomen. That is not a very accurate reflection of what happens.

Domestic violence is a justified primary topic because it is the next generation which unfortunately learns that violence is an unacceptable way of life. In this country around 1983, several provincial and federal levels started speaking out against domestic violence. To the extent they were able to do so, they directed police officers under their control to investigate these cases and lay charges on the basis of reasonable and probable grounds that an offence had been committed. On February 11, 1983, the Attorney General in Manitoba gave a direction to the police that the criteria for laying charges be reasonable and should take into consideration probable grounds of the event having occurred irrespective of the wishes of the victim or of others involved.

The Solicitor General of Ontario told police chiefs later that year that he was looking to them to lay charges in appropriate cases and to investigate all such cases. The Attorney General of Ontario, in a memorandum to his council, talked about vigorously prosecuting incidents of domestic violence.

What we had was a change of political climate where police resource allocation in domestic violence was no longer a question of the whim of the complainant. I think the police were very quick to respond to that political direction in the reallocation of their resources by laying more charges, prosecuting more cases and by the crown attorneys taking a more vigorous approach towards the prosecution of domestic violence in Canada. Certainly that seems to be justified by some research published this year. In 1986 in Manitoba, following these recommendations by the Attorney General, this new prosecution was taken. We had many more charges laid by the police.

The expected response was that the police laid more charges in cases of domestic violence. There was the negative aspect of some women in Canada going to prison for declining to give evidence against a person charged. We had the rather odd situation of the victim going to prison while the alleged assailant walked free. We can never quite determine what the outcomes of some of our great policy initiatives will be. It seems that judges are trying to send a message that you cannot stop the wheels of justice by refusing to testify.

This is not the message being received by the community. I see this politicization of the directive, the police and the crown attorneys on the use of resources as a very important trend. If the Manitoba research is right, this trend has had some positive as well as negative effects.

The Manitoba research claims the following. In a survey of the affected population, wife abuse was seen as a serious crime along with other crimes against a person. In other words, there had been an attempt at heightening the public perception of the fact that this conduct was criminal.

The Ontario minister responsible for women's issues stated in 1983, "What I want to do is raise public awareness of domestic violence as a crime." Detection and prosecution cannot, in an intelligent, rational society, be the only solution but it is one solution. Secondly, it is true that there is a reluctance to prosecute in some of these cases, and that results in a somewhat lower conviction rate in these domestic violence cases. The research tends to show that though a bit smaller, the conviction rate is not significantly lower.

Another major finding from the Manitoba initiative this year is that while legal intervention had the positive effect of having more charges laid and more convictions entered, the law was playing some maudlin educative role in specific deterrents by police arrest. There was a lack of tailored referral services. In the Manitoba studies, in 61% of the cases, the reporting police officers did not identify alcohol as a problem in the particular cases, but all of the referral services used in court were through alcohol related referrals.

There was a mismatch with the underlying problem and with some of the attempts being made to undertake remedial operations. We need researchers across Canada to find out if these findings can be replicated elsewhere. Another study in Toronto raised some of the same issues.

The Toronto study was not involved with domestic violence but rather with violence to women and children in public places. It found that in respect to violence in public places, there really were no particular situational zones such as a transit service or an underground subway station where people were at special risk in respect to public violence. We seem to be dealing with violence that occurs randomly as opposed to domestic violence occurring in the homes of the participants.

One of the areas to which the Toronto study drew attention was the need for cooperation among police, crown council, hospitals who undertake these examinations of victims particularly in sexually related matters and various victim assistance and referral services which help victims cope with victimization.

An overhaul occurred in Toronto. There is now a much more coherent approach on the part of the police, the Crown, the hospitals and referral services in trying to do more to sensitize each other to the needs of the victims and to the needs of effective law enforcement. Sometimes gathering evidence on violent offenses, particularly sexual offenses, can often oppose sympathetic concern with the victims. This was recognized in a very large study in Scotland in the last few years.

The Scottish study is not necessarily applicable to the Canadian scene, but some of their advice bears pondering. For instance, they took a look at hundreds of cases that have occurred in Glasgow and in Edinburgh. They said that the primary consideration of the police consequent to a report of sexual assault ought to be the well-being of the victim. This consideration should also take priority over other institutional policing goals such as crime recording, complaint assessment and even the underlying detection of the alleged offender.

They clearly open themselves up to supporters and detractors. When you read some of the cases which they investigated, it is appalling to find that sometimes victims were held for long periods for various evidence gathering. There were other empty waiting periods for various bureaucratic events that occurred. This is all without any remedial assistance being given to the victim.

In one case, serious head wounds were present and were not dealt with until more than 24 hours after all of the various procedures. It is a callous situation when a doctor is engaged in taking various swabs for the presence of semen rather then assisting head wounds. The report does show real concern for improving police liaison and investigative ability in serious assault cases. In many police forces across

Canada, the following needs to be done. Training would include dealing with unwarranted police skepticism about sexual assault complaints. It should be directed towards creating understanding of the emotional consequences of rape and sexual assault for women. It is also important to get the complainant's cooperation for the success of the case. As is pointed out, complainants know more than they initially tell in such matters. This can be lost forever through investigative tactlessness. It can be recovered by empathy and general understanding.

Both the Toronto and Scottish studies drew attention to the terrible imbalance in male and female ratios in police work, particularly in detective work. Both of them call on the police to rethink their hiring strategies which are so heavily male- oriented. Both reject the idea of categorizing assaults on females or children or sexual assaults as only female work. They say we do not want to create yet another ghetto for women- only work.

It is less likely that a victim will decline to testify if she has been the recipient of some care and understanding during the process. If she has been kept notified of what is happening in the case, if some care and consideration of her feelings at all stages are constantly taken into account, she will be more likely to testify.

Secondly, if you have an integrated response to such assaults in which the police, the Crown and the referral workers are working together as a team, then crown council as a first response will not think so quickly about sending them to prison for contempt of court when they decline to testify. Obviously, there must be cases in which the judges have to use the contempt power, but my suggestion is that it is seldom a very practical solution to the problem.

One could argue that the high political profile given to police investigation, often prosecutorial pursuing of these violence cases, might lead to the assertion that if it can be done for domestic violence, why cannot similar political exhortation raise the consciousness in respect to all investigation and prosecution of violence.

This raises many more difficult problems. If we try to draw some strands together from the 1986 research in Manitoba, the 1984 research in Toronto and the 1983 research in Scotland, we can see that the coordinating theme is the idea of working with the victim, empathizing with the victim, working as a team with the referral services and the police and the police with the Crown. Through this recognition and understanding of the problems of the victim, there is likely to be a better outcome.

What we may be looking at is one of those things where the ethical high road becomes the practical low road. The very empathy towards the victim which the ethical high road requires will produce the practical low road of a victim more willing, more able, more cooperative to deal with the problems of pursuing these matters through to conviction. I think there is some evidence in the research that effective prosecution does have preventive spin-offs.

The second area I will touch on is the use of technology to improve the police capability in investigating a violent crime and to deter police violence in the investigation of crime. Canada is currently in the forefront in evaluating the use of audio visual taping of police interviews with suspects and accused persons. The audio visual technology records the crimes, records an identification parade and records certain statements of some victims and some witnesses.

When the Halton police in Ontario commenced using video technology at their Burlington station on July 1, 1985, they not only used it for supervising or monitoring the interviewing of suspects and accused persons, but they also used it to record 31 victim statements and 57 statements from witnesses. Let me explain some of the circumstances in which they are using this technology and what the perceived advantages are. They are recording the statements of children who have been allegedly sexually abused.

The advantages are that instead of the child being constantly made to repeat events to different people and professionals, you have a competent and complete investigative interview. The police, the Crown attorney, the defence council and various other referrals have the tape. There is no longer a need for the child to go over the very details which may be more traumatic than the events themselves. This technology is available to better record injuries to people than a set of still photographs could ever do.

Within this interviewing process, the tapes are useful in that police officers would not have to write down what the accused was saying and then spend hours in the witness box defending whether he was wearing a gun, whether another policeman was there, how big the room was, if they gave refreshments or not, whether threats were used, inducements were used or various atmospheres of oppression were created.

The Burlington police officer simply has a video cassette which becomes his electronic notebook. He pops it in the machine, presses the button, walks into the room and says, "I am Constable Smith and I am investigating an arson that occurred last night at Burlington shopping mall. You are not obliged to say anything unless you wish to do so." He goes right through the whole thing from there. This has been running for a year now, and in that year there have not been any allegations that the Burlington police were using violent, threatening or other improper means in their interrogation procedures.

What we are looking at is advanced technology making a contribution first to the detection of crime, often violent crime, and making another contribution to the eradicating of violence as a police response to the investigation. We will have to wait for the study to be completed in 1987.